British Pullman Trains

British Pullman Trains

A tribute to all Britain's steam, diesel and electric Pullman services

Charles Fryer

Silver Link Publishing Ltd

First published in August 1992
Reprinted September 1999

British Library Cataloguing in Publication Data
Fryer, Charles
British Pullman Trains: A Tribute to All Britain's Steam, Diesel and Electric Pullman Services
I. Title
625.2

ISBN 0 947971 78 5

Silver Link Publishing Ltd
The Trundle
Ringstead Road
Great Addington
Kettering
Northants
NN14 4BW

Tel/Fax: 01536 330588
email: sales@slinkp-p.demon.co.uk

Printed and bound in Great Britain

Contents

Bibliography

Books and other sources consulted:

Allen, Cecil J. *The Coronation and Other Famous LNER Trains*
Salute to the Southern
Titled Trains of Great Britain
Allen, G. Freeman *Luxury Trains of the World*
Behrend, G. *History of Trains de Luxe*
Pullman of Europe
Ellis, C. Hamilton *Railway Carriages in the British Isles*
The Trains We Loved
The London Brighton & South Coast Railway
Haresnape, B. *Pullman, Travelling in Style*
Hasenson, A. *The Golden Arrow*
Kidner, R.W. *Pullman Cars on the Southern Railway*
Morel, J. *Pullman*
Nelson, R.I. *Locomotive Performance: A Footplate Survey*
Nock, O.S. *The South Eastern & Chatham Railway*
Great Northern 4-4-2 Atlantics
Southern Steam
Rodgers, H.C.B. *Bulleid Pacifics at Work*
Winkworth, D.W. *Bulleid's Pacifics*
Southern Titled Trains
Bradshaw's Railway Guide: various copies from April 1910 onwards
GWR, LNER & SR Timetables: various, between 1923 and 1947
LB&SCR Timetable: June-September 1912
BR Timetables to May 1992
GWR Magazine: August 1929
The Locomotive: 14 January 1933
Modern Railways: July 1987
Railway Gazette: 15 April 1966
Railway Magazine: various copies
SE&CR Specification for 2 Pullman Parlour and 3 Pullman Buffet Cars: 26 July 1913

Acknowledgements

I am grateful to all who have given me permission to quote from books and magazines, or who have supplied me with photographs for illustrations - among the latter, more particularly Hugh Ballantyne, Colin Marsden, Thomas Middlemass and Brian Morrison. I wish to express special thanks to Mr Nicholson of the Science and Technology Department at the Mitchell Library, Glasgow, for help given at various times when I went there to research.

This book is dedicated to the doctors, nurses and ancillary staff of the National Health Service, who helped me to recover from a heart attack and provided me with Pullman-type comforts in Stirling and Glasgow Royal Infirmaries.

Pullman style - a table laid for lunch in the preserved VSOE Pullman Car *Vera*.
Brian Morrison

Prologue

For a year-and-a-half during my youth I was a junior clerk in an insurance company earning £50 a year. I worked in the city, my home was in Harrow, and I travelled from and to that place on the Metropolitan Railway. Each evening the train which I caught to go home in, always crowded with returning commuters so that one seldom had a seat, followed the evening businessmen's train to Aylesbury, non-stop from Baker Street to Rickmansworth, then stopping at all stations after exchanging its named electric locomotive for a steam one. This train had a Pullman car in its formation, and I would station myself on the platform at Liverpool Street Underground where I knew I could look through its windows and inspect its interior. It was usually the same car; I forget whether it was *Mayflower* or *Galatea.* I felt then like a pre-1789 French peasant peering in to the chateau of some wealthy French noble.

To me it seemed the very acme of luxury travel, utterly beyond my means, only possible to the wealthy directors and managers, the chairmen of many committees, the top brass of the business world, whom I saw boarding the cars and settling into their armchairs. Back some minutes later in the cramped six-a-side accommodation of a Metropolitan compartment coach, wedged on a seat between other passengers if I were lucky, or strap-hanging if I were not, I would daydream about what it might be like to belong to the higher echelons where one could afford to live and travel like a lord.

There they sat, the weary tycoons, each in his *Louis Quinze* chair at his own table, fingering the wine-list. Softly across the carpeted floor the attendant approached them, one by one. What would Monsieur like to drink? A gin and tonic, perhaps, after the labours of the day? By the time King's Cross was reached, each having been supplied with his own expensive beverage, their portly frames relaxed as they scanned the *Times* or *Telegraph*. Isolated from the common herd, from the junior clerks and girl typists who thronged the platforms or squeezed into the crowded compartments in front or behind, they could just stare out from plate glass windows like goldfish from bowls and just ignore the lesser bourgeoisie, much as French seigneurs before the Revolution stared at and ignored the *canaille*, the rabble, outside their chateaux.

From Baker Street onwards there would be no stop for half an hour, and during this time they would most likely nod off. Then a slight jar would awaken

British Pullman train routes
Numbers refer to the relevant chapters

them, as a handsome 4-4-4 tank engine backed on to their train, from which the electric locomotive had just been uncoupled; then away into the heart of Metroland, halting at Chorley Wood, Chalfont, Amersham, Great Missenden, Wendover, Stoke Mandeville and Aylesbury. At each of these a tycoon or two would ease himself from his seat, retrieve his briefcase and umbrella, have the door opened for him by the attendant, step out on to the platform and walk a few yards to the waiting limousine, thence to be chauffeur-driven to his mock-Tudor mansion among the beechwoods. To be one of *them* now, instead of just a scrubby junior clerk! But I knew very well that I would never experience such moneyed bliss unless I applied myself more to my clerkly duties and simulated an interest in them which I did not feel. My employers apparently agreed with me, for in September 1932 they dispensed with my services.

Such were a 17-year-old's imaginings, born largely from envy and frustration. Those of us who have experienced Pullman travel in somewhat later days can still get sentimental and misty-eyed when indulging their memories. A journey in a Pullman car, especially a First Class one, was something to be remembered. If one wants to know now what such travel was like, at a price well beyond most persons' abilities, one can do so, for the Venice-Simplon-Orient Express operators run excursions in their renovated cars, out-and-back journeys from Victoria on circular tours through Kent or to such destinations as Salisbury or Bath. In fact, if one so indulges oneself one will get a rather smoother ride than the original car would have provided, since all the cars now running have been re-bogied, and in any case run largely over continuous-welded rail.

Were I asked which of the former trains I would wish to travel on, if journeys backwards in time were a possibility, I think I should opt for the short-lived Devon Belle, for the variety of lineside scenery and for occasional speed thrills; it would also recapture memories of holidays spent on the North Devon coast. However, as with some other former Pullman journeys, even the rails the train ran on have now been removed, the line having been largely singled west of Salisbury and entirely lifted north of Barnstaple Junction. Failing the Devon Belle, I think I should go back to pre-war days and indulge myself with a weekly season ticket on the Eastern Belle, repeating five times over my previous experience going to Cromer.

Of course one cannot do such things in actuality; it is a pity that no novelist or poet, so far as I know, has made it possible by proxy. John Betjeman could have made a wonderful job of it, if he could have dragged himself away from Victorian churches for a while. But, as Cecil J. Allen would have remarked (in Latin, of course), the fugitive years slip away, and soon there will be no one to remember or praise this vanished phenomenon. Poor substitute though it be, a book such as this has to suffice.

1

Introduction

This book deals with a special manifestation of a particular phenomenon, a sort of *crème de la crème*. A railway traveller's basic requirements, once he has paid his fare, are safety, sufficient speed, adequate comfort and reasonable punctuality. In the earliest days the Third Class passenger, exposed to the elements and debarred from using the fastest trains, certainly never enjoyed the second and third requirements, and possibly not the first; he travelled on sufferance. By degrees he received more consideration; his money, after all, was as good as that of the more affluent, and there were more of his kind to buy tickets as the habit of travel increased. So his basic needs were accorded a more or less grudging recognition by the railway companies.

On the other hand, right up to the end of the 19th century and beyond the sentiment persisted among the more well-to-do that some classes of society were below recognition-level. In its earliest days the editorial staff of *The Railway Magazine* were thoroughly scornful of the notion of workmen being allowed to pay very low fares for travelling to work early in the morning. Let the worker live in a hovel adjacent to his place of labour and not begrime the upholstery of the compartments which more well-paid and later-rising clerks would have to use after him. In those days class levels and distinctions were largely taken for granted.

By the end of the 19th century broad social divisions were recognised and reflected in the types of accommodation offered in trains, and carriage upholstery gave in return for increasing fare levels the opportunity to rest, relax or wallow as the case might be. However, even higher reaches of physical comfort were obtainable, as the next chapter shows, in the United States, where people were ready to pay to travel in *de luxe* conditions in numbers sufficient to make it worthwhile building special carriages for them. Eventually the practice extended to Europe.

Thus arose the *crème* of railway travel. It showed itself in Great Britain first of all in the single First Class Pullman car marshalled in a train of ordinary First, Second and Third Class carriages. In America, where the distances between the chief population centres were considerable, long journeys meant night journeys, and the Pullman vehicle provided seats which could be turned into beds if necessary, while other beds could be let down from the roof. In

Great Britain only one railway company, the Midland, for a while provided this style of accommodation. It imported Pullman cars from the United States to run in its night expresses to the North, in co-operation with the North British Railway and Glasgow & South Western Railway, so that if one booked a First Class fare and paid a Pullman car supplement, one could recumbently doze one's way from St Pancras to Edinburgh, Glasgow or Stranraer, or vice versa. Distances, however, were shorter here than on the other side of the Atlantic, and passengers tended to travel either by day or by night, and did not require adaptable accommodation. Hence the day-saloon-cum-sleeping vehicle never caught on in this country, and towards the end of the 19th century special sleeping carriages with a bed in each compartment, First Class only, began to appear on long-distance night trains, and the MR then phased out its Pullmans.

In his book *The Trains We Loved*, C. Hamilton Ellis gives an imaginative account of a journey from St Pancras to Edinburgh in 1876, in which he describes one of these earliest Pullman cars and its customers, and waxes lyrical about the manner in which it muted the rigours of a long overnight rail journey:

> There in St Pancras stands the superb line of carriages: a twelve-wheel composite, some six-wheelers - even these very superior of their kind - and a Pullman sleeping car for Edinburgh. What a Pullman at that! The full exuberance of American decorative art of the President Grant era blossoms inside and out.

An early Pullman car, *St Denis*, built in 1883, rebuilt with bogies in 1885 and sold to the Midland Railway in 1888. It was used on the St Pancras to Stranraer overnight service for a number of years to provide sleeping accommodation. Note the central side door and florid decoration, more to the taste of the Victorians than their successors.

The name, *Castalia*, glitters in an oval-framed scroll on either side, amid a welter of panels gorgeous in gold leaf on a dark brown base.

Tragic *Castalia*, fated soon to be transferred by the Pullman Company to the Continent; eight years hence, on an Italian November night, she will be burnt down to the axles. But on this summer evening of 1876, terribly new and unblemished, she furnishes sleeping accommodation for the *best people*. She scintillates with silverplate and gilding, her handsome bronze kerosene lamps gleam in a coloured clerestory, shedding a warm radiance over rich panels and sleek plush. There in a little while stately gentlemen will be cautiously extracting themselves from broadcloth and starch, fine ladies and lovely girls will be shedding stiff linen and whalebone as delicately as possible within the uneasy privacy of their green-curtained berths - save for the plutocrats who have booked the single private compartment at the end. Here we see the dignity, the elegance, the last word in travelling comfort to be spoken in the mid-Seventies.

The marshalling of Pullman cars into a single train, to provide a sequence of drawing-rooms-on-wheels, began more modestly in short journeys from London to resorts on the South Coast. The London Brighton & South Coast Railway

Pullman evolution.
Below **The Southern Belle shortly before the outbreak of the First World War; six 12-wheeled cars with vans at the rear headed by superheated 'I.3' 4-4-2T No 25.** ***LCGB, Ken Nunn Collection Above right*** **One of the Midland Pullman units during testing on the single-line branch between Bedford and Hitchin shortly before introduction in 1960.** ***Colin J. Marsden Collection Below right*** **The end of an era - the last morning up service of the electrically-hauled Manchester Pullman on 10 May 1985, behind No 86101.** ***Hugh Ballantyne***

MIDLAND PULLMAN

showed the way, the South Eastern Railway followed suit, and after the First World War other companies took up the idea. In the case of the Great Western it was only a brief flirtation, for the Torquay Pullman had but a short life. The London & North Eastern became more seriously involved, the short-lived Sheffield Pullman being followed by others to the West and East Ridings of Yorkshire, with the Queen of Scots, the most prestigious of them all, plying from King's Cross to Edinburgh and Glasgow. As an unusual variant, the same company also for some years ran a Pullman train on each day of the week except Saturday to different resorts around the East Anglian coast from Clacton-on-Sea to Skegness, on which train special cheap all-in fares were charged.

Meanwhile the Southern Railway added other such trains to its collection, culminating in the daily Bournemouth Belle, and also worked its principal boat train service to Paris with an all-Pullman rake of cars which was eventually christened the Golden Arrow to match the connecting train that took its passengers on to Paris, *La Flèche d'Or*. The London Midland and Scottish Railway never operated any all-Pullman trains, though it did continue for a while the Caledonian Railway's practice of using Pullman vehicles as refreshment cars in trains which ran north of the Border.

It was not of course absolutely necessary to employ Pullman cars in order to provide luxury travel. In the later 'thirties the LNER built special rakes of carriages for trains which combined higher speed with additional comfort; such were the Silver Jubilee, between Newcastle-on-Tyne and King's Cross, the Coronation, between King's Cross and Edinburgh, and the West Riding, between King's Cross and Leeds; for travel on these a supplement was charged. They did not, however, replace the existing all-Pullman trains, which continued to attract passengers. Then came the outbreak of the Second World War which for a time brought to an end all luxury travelling, and Pullman cars were stored for the duration.

With the return of peace they crept out again into the sun, and many former all-Pullman services were resumed, together with some new ones. Among the latter was an interesting part-week summer-only addition, the Devon Belle, running from Waterloo to Ilfracombe and Plymouth; this, like the Coronation, included an Observation Car. These re-introduced or newly introduced services survived the change of ownership in 1948.

Later British Railways took over the Pullman Car Company of Great Britain, and Pullman external liveries then began to alter, the familiar umber-and-cream gradually disappearing. A new idea now came to the fore - that of the fixed-formation multiple-unit Pullman train with a motor coach at either end.

The pre-Second World War Brighton Belle, with its electrified motor coaches, had foreshadowed this development, but the new trains, which made their first appearance in 1960, were angled at business rather than holiday travel, and in the case of the Midland Pullman, from Manchester to London and back, were First Class only. These diesel-engined Pullmans were different from their predecessors both within and without. The 'de luxe' atmosphere was unostentatious, evocative rather of the boardroom than the parlour. However, they did not last very long as their riding qualities left much to be desired. With the advent of electrification on the West Coast Main Line a new and locomotive-hauled Manchester Pullman, running twice daily between that city and London in both directions, replaced the diesel train and continued for almost 20 years, while Pullman cars disappeared from all trains elsewhere.

During the 'eighties a new concept took the place of the old one, that of special Pullman-quality service being provided in the First Class coaches of certain designated trains, the business traveller being particularly considered. This is now the position. Ordinary First Class stock is used, but specially-trained attendants are there to provide extra service and convenience to make the journey more pleasant. Except on one train no extra charge is levied, and the train itself is generally a specially fast one. The Standard Class traveller is now debarred from Pullman travel altogether, though with the increase in comfort in Inter-City Standard Class accommodation this deprivation is probably not much felt. Indeed, so far as the quality of the ride is concerned, travel in a present-day Super-Sprinter is as comfortable as travel in a Third Class Pullman car was during the 'thirties; this I can assert, having had experience of both.

Such, in brief outline, is the story of the all-Pullman train in Great Britain; the chapters that follow will add flesh to the bones. It may be doubted whether anything like it will ever be reintroduced, for it has had its day. Ultra-luxury has left the railway and moved on to the road or into the air. The all-Pullman train has gone the way of the great passenger liner. What it offered can now only be seen in preserved vehicles - unless, of course, one can afford a trip in one of the refurbished coaches of the Venice-Simplon-Orient Express and indulge in some very expensive nostalgia.

2

The luxury-makers

Though others had done so before him in a small way, the first person successfully to undertake the construction of luxurious railway carriages on a large scale for the purpose of hiring them to companies or individuals was a citizen of the United States, George Mortimer Pullman. Born in March 1831, the son of a New York engineer, he became a typical American self-made man. Obliged to leave school at the age of 14, he worked for his living first as a store assistant and later as a sales representative for his older brother, who was a cabinet-maker. In this capacity, travelling from one state to another, he came to realise how uncomfortable railway travelling in ordinary coaches could be, especially by night, and this awareness was, so to speak, the grit in the oyster which gave rise to the pearl of Pullman luxury travel.

From commercial travelling he moved on during his twenties to set up a business of his own in Chicago. Here he undertook the removal of whole buildings bodily by jacking them up, attaching wheels and then rolling them to the desired position. Almost incredibly he succeeded, among other achievements, in shifting a four-storey hotel in this manner, damaging neither it nor its contents in the process - a peculiar foreshadowing of his later business of building 'hotels on wheels' for rail travel. Gaining fame locally, and amassing a certain amount of capital, he then decided to launch out in a completely new direction.

Going into partnership with an old friend, B. C. Field, who contributed some additional capital, he persuaded the Chicago, Alton & St Louis Railroad Company to provide him with two of its 44-foot open-ended passenger coaches, and converted their interiors so that they had extra-comfortable seats that could be turned into bunks for night journeys. These, the first Pullman coaches, were put into service in 1859. They had luxurious plush upholstery and each had its own uniformed conductor to attend to passengers' needs. They ran between Chicago and Bloomington, a distance of 100 miles, and each passenger paid Pullman an additional 50 cents over and above his rail fare.

So far, so good - but then came a setback. In April 1861 the American Civil War broke out, and the whole of the Chicago, Alton & St Louis Railroad's rolling-stock was commandeered for the duration. Pullman shrugged his shoulders and took himself off to Colorado, where a gold rush was currently in

George Mortimer Pullman. ***Mitchell Library, Glasgow***

progress. Here he displayed his entrepreneurial abilities by selling the necessaries of life to miners at inflated prices, making more money than most of them did. Towards the end of the war he returned to Chicago with a capital of $20,000, and along with Field resumed his luxury travel project, using a little more than the whole of that sum to build and equip a single car, expending on it five times as much as the cost of construction of an ordinary rail coach.

It seems surprising that so hard-headed a person should not have taken sufficient account of the requirements of the railway's loading gauge, but in fact he made the vehicle too high and too wide. The consequence was that as soon as it was put on the rails it began to foul such things as platform edges. Pullman's masterpiece had become Pullman's Folly; the car was put into store, and it looked as if he had thrown his entire fortune away.

A national tragedy then became his salvation. In April 1865 President Lincoln, then at the height of his fame and popularity after (from the point of view of the North) bringing the Civil War to a successful conclusion, was assassinated. It seemed right that the train assembled to make the funeral journey should include, for the conveyance of visiting dignitaries, the most splendid vehicle which the country could offer. The Chicago, Alton and St Louis Railroad at once made rapid and appropriate modifications to its lineside structures between Chicago and Springfield so that Pullman's massive carriage could be used. Within it the chief mourners at the funeral accompanied the dead President's body to its last resting-place. Enormous numbers of people lined the route, so that Pullman received a huge publicity boost.

His future was now secure and he began to build cars again. A year later he had constructed as many as 48, all for daytime use but convertible at night into sleeping carriages.

The Maximum of Luxury at the Minimum of Cost.

"PULLMAN" and "PERFECTION"

are synonyms when they refer to Car Building, in which art the Pullman Car Company leads the world. In elaborate design, substantial construction, and luxurious finish, Pullman Cars represent the highest standard of excellence.

Ingenuity and skill are constantly being applied to the improvement of details with a view to adding to the comfort of travel. Every Car is in charge of an experienced well-trained Conductor, whose services are always at hand from start to finish of a journey, and invalids and ladies with children can always rely upon ready attention to their comfort and convenience.

Cleanliness is also a special feature, coupled with perfect ventilation and good lighting, thus making travelling a real luxury.

Pullman Drawing Room, Buffet, Dining, and Observation Cars are in operation on the following important lines :—

Southern Railway :

L. B. & S. C. Section: Victoria and London Bridge to Brighton, Hove, Worthing, Eastbourne, Bognor, Newhaven, Portsmouth, &c.

S. E. & C. Section: Victoria and Charing Cross to Dover and Folkestone in all the Continental Services. Also Deal, Ramsgate, Margate, and Kent Coast Towns.

London and North Eastern Railway :

Gt. Eastern Section: Buffet Cars (First and Third Class) between Liverpool Street and principal stations, also First Class on Continental Trains.

Interior of Car "Rosemary"
London (King's Cross), Harrogate and Newcastle Train.

Gt. Northern and North-Eastern Section: King's Cross to Leeds, Harrogate, Ripon, Darlington and Newcastle.

London Midland and Scottish Railway :

Caledonian Section Glasgow & Edinburgh to Aberdeen, Oban, Perth, Stirling, Gleneagles, Dumblane, Forfar, Callander, Lockerbie, Loch Awe, Carstairs, Beattock, Carlisle, &c.

Highland Section: Blair Atholl, Newtonmore, Kingussie, Kincraig, Aviemore, &c.

Metropolitan Railway :

Buffet Cars are run between Aldgate, Liverpool Street, Baker Street, Aylesbury, Chesham, and Verney Junction.

HARROGATE BY THE PULLMAN IN 4 HOURS.

"The Southern Belle."

The most Luxurious Train in the World.

Daily (including Sundays). Pullman Train de Luxe. Running between LONDON AND BRIGHTON.

THIRD CLASS "PULLMAN" CARS between LONDON, BRIGHTON, EASTBOURNE, PORTSMOUTH, &c.

"The Clacton Pullman."

LONDON (Liverpool Street) and CLACTON-ON-SEA.

Refreshments. Breakfasts, Luncheons, Teas, Suppers, and other refreshments can be obtained on the Cars.

Reservations. Reservations can be effected through the Station Superintendent at the various termini, either by letter, telegram, or telephone.

Special Facilities. Cars for private parties can be specially reserved, under certain conditions, upon application to the various Railway Companies.

The Pullman Car Company, Limited.

Chief London Office—

VICTORIA STATION (S. E. & C. R.), PIMLICO, S.W. 1.

Telegraphic Address—"Pullman, Phone, London." Telephone No.—Victoria 9978 (2 lines).

Branch Office—CENTRAL STATION (Caledonian Section, L.M.S. Railway), GLASGOW.

Telephone No.—Central 7473.

From then onwards there was no halting his progress; he was carried forward on the crest of the tidal wave he had created. He built for the wealthy and the wealthy responded. Not only did he hire his coaches to railroad companies, but individual tycoons also purchased their own. At first his factory was sited at Detroit, but in 1881 he established a large new one to the south of Chicago, and built around it a model town for his employees.

Pullman died in 1897 at the age of 66 after a heart attack which was due in part to the business and industrial pressures under which he lived, and in part to exasperation at a strike brought about through his inflexible attitude to those who worked for him. By this time his operations had extended to Europe, and a number of his cars were running in Great Britain.

Pullman was not without his emulators, either in his own country (where he bought most of them out) or in Europe. In 1868 a young Belgian, Georges Nagelmackers, the son of a wealthy banker, became involved in an amorous entanglement from which his parents extricated him by packing him off to America. Here he came into contact with Pullman and was infected with his ideas. He noted in particular that the latter's luxury coaches operated without hindrance over the whole of the United States, and reflected that the same was possible in Europe, apart from Russia, Spain and Portugal, in which countries the rail gauge was wider then the standard 4 ft $8^1/_2$ in gauge of the other European states, so that through running across *their* frontiers was not feasible; elsewhere, however, there would be no difficulties.

Nagelmackers determined to follow Pullman's example in Europe, and returned to Belgium in 1870, believing he could rely on backing from his family, to whom he set out his plans for a European Sleeping Car Company. His family, however, gave him only a grudging and limited support. Moreover, as in Pullman's case, a conflict upset his calculations. The Franco-Prussian war broke out, and not until it was over could he begin to persuade railway companies that his plan was worth adopting. Even then, the best he could do at first was to persuade some of them to make short-term contracts with him.

Unlike Pullman's large and lengthy cars, Nagelmackers's first luxury coaches were only four-wheelers, inside which he fitted seats that could be converted into berths, with extra berths being lowered from the ceiling; he also managed to find room in each car for two toilet compartments, one of which contained a wash-hand basin. With these he organised a service from Ostend to Cologne, which was later extended to Berlin. Unfortunately, European railway companies in general proved unenthusiastic, and when the German government insisted that no sleeping cars used on its railways should have fewer than six wheels, Nagelmackers's family refused to give him any further backing. It looked as though the enterprise would founder.

Salvation then came from an unexpected quarter. A retired American military engineer, Colonel W. D'Alton Mann, who had made a pile of money by

***Left* The spread of the Pullman empire in Britain - a Company advertisement from *The Railway Magazine*.**

devising for army use pieces of engineering equipment whose employment he was in a position to ensure, and all of which he had been careful to patent, had also seen a future for luxury railway carriages. However, he reckoned that Pullman had too great a start on him in the United States and preferred not to compete with him after his own variation on the Pullman car, in which closed compartments replaced the open interior, failed to attract the American public. Instead he came to Europe and joined forces with Nagelmackers to form the Railway Sleeping Carriage Company, with headquarters in London.

Mann provided the money, Nagelmackers the business expertise. A number of railway companies now agreed to make contracts with them (though still only short-term ones) and Mann was able to use a little discreet influence in high places to ensure that a journey by a highly-placed personage brought welcome publicity. The Prince of Wales, later King Edward VII, was to visit Russia to be present at the wedding of his brother Alfred to a daughter of the Tsar in 1874, and he was persuaded to use one of Mann's and Nagelmackers's luxury sleeping cars as far as the Russian border, *en route* for St Petersburg.

The aversion at first manifested by European railway companies, and in particular by those in France, to the luxury seating-plus-sleeping concept now began to erode, and Nagelmackers managed to achieve an ambition he had cherished for some time - the inclusion of one of his company's vehicles in a through train between the two cultural capitals of Europe, Paris and Vienna. The success of this service led later to a lengthier and far more famous one, by which Paris was linked with the Near East by a train composed entirely of dining and sleeping car carriages. This was the Orient Express, which first began running in 1883, though its extension to Constantinople was not achieved for some years after that.

By this time Nagelmackers had made enough money to buy out Mann. After doing this he moved his headquarters to Belgium and changed the company's name to *Compagnie Internationale des Wagons Lits et des Grands Express Européens*, which words were inscribed beneath the edges of its coach roofs and became well known to all continental travellers who used its prestige vehicles. It provided special coaches for the Trans-Siberian Railway after the latter's completion in 1903. One of its later specialities was the provision of sleeping cars constructed to fit within the British loading gauge, which were used on the Night Ferry between Victoria and Paris during 1936-80.

The picture by 1880 was of two giant companies, together with a few smaller ones, in the United States and Belgium, which supplied the means of *de luxe* long-distance rail travel for the wealthy in two continents. Great Britain, meanwhile, stood geographically well away from the Pullman sphere of influence, and slightly apart, being an island state, from that of Nagelmackers and his successors. It might have been expected that any specially-built luxury coaches for use in Great Britain, if purchased from abroad, would have come from Belgium rather than America, and in fact it *was* the Belgian company which made the first advances in the early 'seventies.

Mann was still then a partner in the firm and it was still being operated from

London, when one of his sleeping cars was given an experimental period of running on the GNR between King's Cross and Leeds. At the same time a special luxury saloon, built for the Wagon Lits company at Longhedge Works on the London Chatham & Dover Railway, was experimentally running on Continental trains between Victoria and Dover.

Nevertheless, in neither instance was a firm contract made to run for a period of years. Pullman, however, was already from America trying to muscle in on the English market and, in the same year that Mann disappeared from the European railway scene, some Pullman 'Parlour cars' were shipped across the Atlantic to be used on the London Brighton & South Coast Railway, beginning an association with that company which lasted to the end of its separate existence and beyond, and which, as described below in a subsequent chapter, gave rise to Great Britain's first luxury train. In the previous year he had also done a deal with the Midland Railway, hiring out to this line a number of vehicles, one of which was alluded to in the previous chapter. Thus began the long association of the Pullman Car Company with several British lines, which was to endure for some 80 years.

3

London to Brighton

1881-1908

The LB&SCR was the first company in the United Kingdom to put an all-Pullman train into service, though not the first to include Pullman cars among other carriages in ordinary service trains. As already noticed, the MR was using such cars, imported from the Pullman Works in the United States in parts and assembled at Derby, on a number of its trains - particularly, from 1874 onwards, on night expresses to Scotland to provide First Class sleeping accommodation. The GNR, too, experimented with one, a parlour-kitchen car *Prince of Wales*, on its London to Leeds service for a short while, to provide dining facilities for First Class passengers. The LC&DR had also toyed with the idea, borrowing the Derby-assembled car *Jupiter* for use on its London-Dover trains for a few years, before passing it on to the LB&SCR.

But these were experiments rather than permanent arrangements, and eventually both the MR and GNR began to build their own restaurant and sleeping cars. The Brighton line, however, though first using Pullman cars in a tentative manner, continued to employ them, and eventually introduced an all-Pullman express on the London to Brighton service which was to continue, with changes of title, until 1972, the continuity being broken only during the two World Wars.

The Pullman services on the Brighton line were of a quite different kind from those on the MR and GNR, which were for purposes similar to those for which American Pullman cars in their own country were intended - refreshment and dormitory facilities for long-distance travellers. The LB&SCR's luxury provision was chiefly confined to the direct route between the capital and Brighton, which was only just over 50 miles long, and the aim was to offer an upper class drawing-room atmosphere in which passengers could relax in restful surroundings, not all that different from the parlours in their own homes, and less cramped and more decorative than ordinary First Class compartments, with toilet and refreshment facilities handy and uniformed servants in attendance. Large side windows would enable them to enjoy views of the Surrey and Sussex landscape, which was much more pleasant and unspoiled a century ago than at the present day, once one was clear of the London suburbs, which did not then extend beyond East Croydon. If one were having a day's outing at the seaside - and Brighton was then a fashionable watering place for the upper classes as well as a resort for those of lesser means - one could, for an extra payment of one shilling and sixpence, make the outward or return journey a part of the day's experience.

In 1875 the LB&SCR tested the temperature of the water by hiring a single Pullman car - one that had been assembled at Derby and contained upper berths for night use, which of course were not needed on the Brighton line - for use on the Victoria-Brighton run. It was marshalled between ordinary coaches, six-wheelers with shallow-arc roofs, and with its great length, bogie wheelbases and clerestory roof must have stood out prominently, a palace on wheels between cramped apartments fore and aft. It ran for a short while, but experience showed that the time was not yet ripe; customers did not present themselves in adequate numbers. In 1883 it was passed back to the Pullman Car Company, who transferred it to an Italian railway.

In 1881 another experiment was tried, of including a number of Pullman cars in the same rake of coaches, together with First, Second and Third Class carriages of the ordinary kind. Again ex-MR vehicles were obtained, four in all, to which new names were given: *Victoria* (formerly *Adonis*), *Maud* (formerly *Ceres*), *Beatrice* (formerly *Globe*) and *Louise* (formerly *Ariel*). The whole train was entitled The Pullman Limited Express and ran between Victoria and Brighton, taking 1¼ hours. (The schedule, which would now seem very slow, was in part dictated by the congestion of the line between London and Redhill, and in part by signalling difficulties.) At first it was hauled by one of William Stroudley's handsome single-wheelers; later their places were taken by the newer 0-4-2 'Gladstones'. However, this should still be regarded as an intermediate stage in the progress towards an all-Pullman train, for it did not yet run on its own, but was associated with a rag, tag and bobtail assortment on ordinary carriages.

The Pullman Limited Express was at first only a qualified success. The difference between the quality of the accommodation it offered and that of an ordinary First Class carriage was not sufficiently marked. It was otherwise in the United States, where there were no distinctions of class, and where the additional comfort of the Pullman seating and facilities for getting a night's rest on a long journey were appreciated. But Victorian Englishmen and Englishwomen valued privacy more than did their American cousins, and this was more likely to be had in an ordinary First Class compartment than in an open Parlour car. The supplement of 18 pence (equivalent to about £4 by today's prices if one uses the cost of a postage stamp as an index) seemed a great deal to pay for the difference between reasonable comfort with privacy and superior comfort without it over a 50-mile journey. True, toilets and wash-basins were at hand, but contemporary prudishness made people reluctant to advertise their physical needs in front of strangers; one had learned how to wait.

On the credit side, in cold weather there was the warmth of the Pullman car's interior, thanks to the stove which made the acquirement of footwarmers unnecessary, and a polite attendant would bring you tea and freshly-prepared sandwiches on request. But the idea of travelling by Pullman caught on only slowly. It had its attraction for the young couple going on their honeymoon to Brighton, and young gentlemen could impress their lady friends by taking them for a day at the seaside in this manner - the equivalent of today going in a flash car, perhaps.

Custom picked up slowly, but sufficiently to keep the cars running. At first they ran seven days a week, but Victorian reluctance to travel on a Sunday caused patronage to decline on that day, when respectable people attended either church or chapel during the forenoon, so after a while the Sunday service was withdrawn.

Meanwhile William Stroudley, the Brighton company's Locomotive, Carriage and Wagon Superintendent, was experimenting with electric lighting; interior illumination was important even in summer on a system where so much of the main line was in tunnel. The first Pullmans had relied on kerosene lamps, which were a great improvement on the primitive oil lamps let down through the roofs in ordinary coaches, but they were nevertheless a fire risk. With a short journey lasting an hour and a quarter it was feasible to organise electric lighting from batteries stored beneath the coach, which could be recharged from steam-driven dynamos at Victoria when the train had returned there - though if it were badly delayed the current might begin to fail and the lights start to flicker and wane.

However, the notion that a moving train might generate its own electricity was an obvious one, and Stroudley eventually devised a system in which a specially-modified guard's van held a dynamo operated by a band passing round a

A contemporary postcard of the Sunday Pullman Limited made up of six cars, a rear luggage van and the 'Pullman Pup' behind the engine, a Billinton 'B.2' 4-4-0. The cars are in the bronze livery favoured at the time. *Author's Collection*

pulley wheel on one of the axles below. The current thus generated activated the lights throughout the train, so that recourse to batteries was only necessary during stops. The holes in the van's floor made the interior draughty and chilly in cold weather, but the guards were the only sufferers and were not expected to complain. When in 1888 a new set of Pullman cars was provided for the Brighton service, a special guard's van with a dynamo, painted to match the other cars, was attached to it. It was colloquially known as the 'Pullman Pup'.

This set of coaches, three in number, was imported in parts direct from the Pullman Works in America and assembled at the LB&SCR workshops in Brighton. They were given names associated with Royalty: *Prince* had a pantry that supplied light refreshments; *Princess* was reserved for ladies; *Albert Victor* was for smokers (which in those days meant men, for respectable women never smoked). The cars were permanently coupled by buckeye couplings in the American manner, ordinary buffers and drawgear being fitted only at the extreme ends of the rake, so that the dynamo van could be attached to one end and ordinary coaches at the other. An innovation was the vestibule connection that joined one car to another. All the vehicles had swivelling seats beside windows which, though deep, were not yet as wide as in later Pullman cars. Seven years later three more cars were obtained, similar in structure and furnishings; they were named *Her Majesty*, *Duchess of York* and *Princess of Wales*. Two sets of three, each with its dynamo van, were thus now available. They were given a bronze livery, lined out in gold and with rose-painted roofs, while the bogie-frames were painted brown and lined out in yellow.

Patronage of these cars was at first disappointing, but custom gradually increased. Society, moving on from the staid and respectable 'eighties to the 'Naughty 'Nineties', from the age of Tennyson to that of Oscar Wilde, began somewhat to unbutton, and travel on the Sabbath Day was winked at. In 1898 a 'Sunday Pullman Limited' was introduced - four Pullman Parlour cars with a matching dynamo van, which after 1900 made the journey from Victoria to Brighton and vice versa in the even hour, thanks to track-widening between Croydon and Redhill, where there had previously been a two-tracks-only bottleneck.

This was now the LB&SCR's fastest train. The railway journalist Charles Rous-Marten made several journeys to Brighton and back on it and was impressed by its comfort and punctuality. By this time the 'Gladstones' which had previously hauled the Pullman trains had been replaced by 4-4-0s of R. J. Billinton's design, the later ones of which proved to have quite a turn of speed.

In July 1903, in order to give public proof that even a 50-minute timing between London and Brighton was a possibility, Billinton organised a special demonstration run in which one of his latest engines, No 70 *Holyrood*, set up a record in both directions. Rous-Marten was an invited guest and reported the event fully in the columns of *The Railway Magazine*. The intention was to show that steam could do as well as electricity. A Bill had been presented to Parliament seeking powers to construct an electric railway between London and Brighton which would make possible a journey time of 50 minutes. The

LB&SCR sought to discredit the proposal in advance by this demonstration that if necessary it could provide an equally fast passage on its own line.

The train used was one of the two earlier rakes of Pullmans with a dynamo van at either end, weighing in all 130 tons. On the day chosen the weather was unpropitious, heavy rain having made the rails slippery, but *Holyrood* climbed vigorously up the initial 1 in 64 to Grosvenor Bridge, passed Clapham Junction at 60 mph, maintained between 62½ and 64¼ between Croydon and Merstham tunnel, with a minimum at the summit of just under 60, reached 80½ in the Horley dip, fell to 66½ up Balcombe bank, accelerated to 90 beyond Hayward's Heath, did not go below 70 at Clayton tunnel and arrived at Brighton, with a very slow finish, in just under 48¾ minutes. The return journey was a little slower since a strong side wind and permanent way operations hampered progress; the maximum speed attained was 85 on the descent from Balcombe tunnel.

Over the years since the train was first introduced there was some replacement of older cars by newer ones. In 1899 two splendid vehicles appeared which ran on six-wheel bogies and had wide end-vestibules; they were named *The Arundel* and *The Chichester*. Each had 24 seats beside windows that were long as well as deep, and a third of the way along each there was a buffet bar and a toilet compartment. These cars were unusually lengthy, each measuring 65 ft 8 ins between buffer faces. Three similar ones soon followed in 1906, *Duchess of Norfolk*, *Princess Ena* and *Princess Patricia*; the original pair were then given other names to prevent passengers from supposing that they were actually going to the places they were named after. All were included, with some of the older vehicles, in the existing Brighton Pullman Limited, as the Sunday Pullman train had now been re-named. According to C. Hamilton Ellis, in his book *The London Brighton and South Coast Railway*:

> Their furniture and decoration were grandiosely drawing-roomy; green and gold was the later colour scheme, with red leather and oak in the smokers. Their steadiness and gentleness at speed were very marked. The 'Empire' clerestory, ie that containing a false arch and coves to the decklight transoms, was the form used. These three cars also initiated a new style of external finish - umber below the waist and cream above - which has survived since then, save that from about 1930 the upper quarters have also been painted in umber... To a great admirer of

Above right **The Arundel*, a 12-wheeled car built in 1899 for use on the Sunday Pullman Limited. A larger and smaller saloon, holding 16 and eight seats respectively, were separated by a section containing a buffet and toilet compartment. For its time it was an unusually long vehicle, 65 ft 8 in between buffer faces. It was later renamed *Majestic* and converted to a Kitchen car. The photograph shows it in its original bronze livery, lettered and lined out in gold. *Burtt Collection, NRM, York***

Right **Interior of *The Arundel* as first constructed. Note especially the elaborate clerestory with semi-elliptical side-lights and electric lamps, the lace antimacassars and the tasselled seats and arm rests. The picture is taken in the large saloon, looking through to the smaller one. *Burtt Collection, NRM, York***

THE ARUNDEL

First Class car *Duchess of Norfolk*, built in 1906 for the Sunday Pullman Limited, and similar externally and internally to *The Arundel*, but in the later umber and white livery. *Lens of Sutton*

> the classic American Pullman car they were lovely carriages; one still regrets the obsolescence.

By 1907 the former reluctance to travelling by Pullman car had dissolved, and custom had built up to the extent that each set had been augmented to comprise six or seven cars. Each rake posed quite a tough task for the Billinton 4-4-0s on the 60- minute schedule if the weather were bad. The train had now very definitely become the LB&SCR's prestige train, and many postcard reproductions were made.

When D. E. Marsh succeeded Billinton in the Locomotive Department he faced the need to provide even more powerful engines to haul the Pullman and built five 'Atlantic' type 4-4-2 tender engines modelled on the GNR 'Atlantics' built at Doncaster where he had previously been H. A. Ivatt's assistant. Meanwhile, the LB&SCR and the Pullman Car Company of Great Britain, an offshoot of the American company now established at Preston Park near Brighton under the chairmanship of Mr Davison Dalziel (later Lord Dalziel of Wooler), were preparing a new train to replace the existing one, and in 1908 it came into service. Its fortunes are described in the next chapter but one.

4

Pullman-type trains on the South Eastern Railway

Strictly speaking, this chapter is not about train services employing Pullman cars, but about Pullman-type services which differed from the genuine article in name only and offered the same sort of travelling experience. As it turned out, many of the vehicles mentioned were later reconstructed by the Pullman Car Company and continued their existences bearing the Pullman name, so perhaps the illogicality will be excused.

It was not unusual during the 19th century for bitter antagonisms to develop between the controlling personalities on competing railways, so that mutual abhorrence got the better of good judgement. The most prominent example of this in the century's later years was the rivalry between the two Chairmen of the Boards of the South Eastern and the London Chatham & Dover Railways, Sir Edward Watkin and James Staats Forbes. In 1875 the latter began experimenting with the inclusion of a single Pullman car in some of his company's London to Dover trains, as mentioned in the previous chapter, but after a while the attempt to attract First Class passenger custom in this way was given up. Forbes bided his time, and in 1889 made a similar attempt in a rather bigger way. It was the year of the Paris Exhibition, at which the rival South Eastern line exhibited one of James Stirling's 4-4-0 express engines, No 240, which gained a gold medal. Not to be outshone, Forbes determined that visitors to the Exhibition travelling from London should at least be taken there in a specially luxurious train. In collaboration with the Chemin de Fer du Nord he put on a special Paris Limited Mail from Victoria to Dover, which connected with a similar train running from Calais to Paris, each comprising four saloon carriages specially built by the Wagons Lits company, which were vestibuled together and connected to a *fourgon fumoir*, a baggage van of which part was adapted to provide accommodation for smokers. The whole ensemble, so far as the English element was concerned, bore some resemblance to the Brighton Pullman Limited of the LB&SCR, except that there was no dynamo car. This train ran for five years but, prestigious though it was, and brilliant in its bright green livery, it did not pay its way.

Sir Edward Watkin in his turn, also determined not to be outdone, contacted the Wagon Lits company, and later in the same year put on a similar train that ran from Charing Cross to Dover and back, to connect with the same boat service. Forbes had not given his train any distinguishing title, but Watkin called his service a Continental Club Train. The public thereupon began to refer to both trains as 'Club Trains', but did not notably favour the one rather than the other. The confusion was natural since both rakes of coaches on this side of the Channel were painted in the same colour.

C. Hamilton Ellis, in his book *Railway Carriages in the British Isles*, tells a good story in connection with them. Both trains had guards named Snow, who happened to be brothers. On one occasion, when the cross-Channel boat from Calais had just berthed, the only passenger for London was a Mr Davison Dalziel, who was later to become the Chairman of the Pullman Car Company of Great Britain. Despite being brothers, the two guards argued fiercely about whose train should have the privilege of carrying the solitary passenger to London, and eventually came to blows on the quayside. It is not related which of them was successful, or whether the distinguished passenger watched the fray, but the event made it more than obvious that neither service was a viable proposition, so Forbes and Watkin agreed that both should be discontinued.

Meanwhile Watkin had found another adversary. The LB&SCR was already offering Pullman travel to Hastings over its own metals in single cars included in through trains from Victoria by way of Lewes. The route was more circuitous than that of the SER's short cut by way of Sevenoaks, Tonbridge and Battle, but the added luxury was an attraction, and there was a risk that First Class custom might be lost to the LB&SCR. Watkin therefore determined to go one better, and not merely to offer a single luxury coach over the shorter route, but a whole train of them. He would not have anything to do with the Pullman Car Company, but there were other firms in the United States which the latter had not yet absorbed and which still competed with it, notably the Gilbert Car Manufacturing Company of Troy, New York State. In 1891 he bought six coaches from them, which were shipped in sections across the Atlantic and assembled at Ashford Works, being there given standard SER wood-centred wheels and British buffing gear. Since the Pullman Car Company held the patent for vestibule connections, these were not included, entry being by an open platform at either end. The cars were somewhat short, being only 51¼ feet long and less than 8½ feet wide, but this was necessary since between Tonbridge and Hastings there were narrow tunnels which carriages of a larger dimension might have fouled. The interior decoration, according to Hamilton Ellis, was

> ...in a rather frenchified style quite different from the massive plushery of contemporary Pullmans. Four had swivelling armchair seats arranged singly on either side of the central gangway; a fifth, with similar seating, had in addition a pantry with an oil cooking stove and (an innovation, this) a refrigerator. The sixth car was at first used only for baggage, but was later given seating similar to that in the other five. Each car had a larger non-smoking compartment with a men's toilet adjacent. Batteries beneath the car supplied current to electric light bulbs mounted in the clerestories. Brake vans were attached at either end and painted to match the maroon livery of the cars themselves.

A postcard reproduction of a painting of the interior of a First Class Pullman-type Saloon car built for the SER at the end of the last century for use on London-Folkestone trains. Compare this with the interior of *The Arundel* on page 29. Surprisingly, no supplementary fare was charged for travelling in such luxury. *Author's Collection*

The effect was magnificent, but modifications were soon found necessary. Corridor endings with 'concertina' coverings to the sides of and above the walkways between the coaches were already being used in Great Britain on the through East Coast and West Coast trains to Scotland, and the SER rebuilt its own cars accordingly in 1896, doing away with the end platforms; no doubt this was done discreetly since the Pullman Company in America never raised any objection. Battery lighting was replaced by Stone's system, in which each car had its own dynamo beneath the frame, driven from one axle of one bogie by a long flexible band. Three of the cars were converted for use by Third Class passengers and one for Second Class passengers. The train seems to have been successful in attracting custom since it ran for many years.

The SER decided to obtain some more. In 1897 one was ordered from Messrs Jackson Sharpe of Wilmington, Delaware, the Gilbert Company having now gone out of business. Eight more were built by the Metropolitan Carriage & Wagon Company of Great Britain. These later cars were rather longer and a trifle wider than the Gilbert cars, and were not intended for the Hastings line but for the main route by way of Ashford to Folkestone and Dover. They constituted a complete set, joined by vestibules and American-style couplings, and had a combined Brake Third Class coach at each end with a very unusual appearance, in that the clerestory roof did not extend over the guard's compartment. The vestibules were unusually wide, a full 7 feet, and had small glass windows with bevelled edges. Internally the arrangements were similar to those in the Gilbert cars.

A postcard reproduction of the interior of one of them shows a most luxurious vehicle indeed. Large windows, laterally oblong, display views of the Kentish countryside framed by pale violet curtains draped on either side and above. Beneath each window a ledge some 6 inches wide served to hold cups of tea or plates of sandwiches. Armchairs, shown facing inwards but presumably able to swivel, had seats and seat-backs covered in flowered cloth and red velvet arm-rests with yellow piping along the seams; the lower edges were tasselled to conceal the supports below and reached almost to the patterned red carpeting. Each chair-back was crowned by a lace antimacassar arranged triangularly so that the top looked rather like the handle of a rat-tailed teaspoon. Luggage racks, elaborately decorated, ran lengthwise along the edges of the ceiling. The latter was coloured a delicate shade of green and made up of lincrusta panels divided by ornate gold-painted ribs. Centrally there ran a rose-tinted clerestory from which depended brass lamp-fittings alternating with brass ventilator openings, the former holding electric light bulbs ensconced in glass shades shaped like bells with crinkled edges. At the far end curtains masked the outer wall of the toilet compartment, the end-lobby being reached through a side door. A journey to Folkestone in one of these First Class saloons must have been an experience indeed, and one can only sigh for such vanished glories.

The whole set ran as a complete train with the unusual title of The Folkestone Vestibuled Limited. Most unusually, no additional charge was made for travelling in it. The cars continued in use right up to 1914, and are mentioned in the introduction to the SE&CR section of *Bradshaw's Railway Guide* for 1910, as follows:

AMERICAN SALOON CAR TRAINS
1st, 2nd & 3rd class, warmed (IN WINTER) with
Hot-water pipes and lighted by electricity,
run between LONDON, HASTINGS, FOLKESTONE and
DOVER every weekday.

The timetable, however, gives no indication as to which trains had the benefit of these luxurious vehicles. One may guess, so far as the Folkestone and Dover service was concerned, that at any rate in 1910 they were the morning up and evening down business expresses, since these were the only ones which did not also run beyond Dover along the coast to Deal.

During the First World War the cars were stored, and after hostilities had ended the Pullman Car Company of Great Britain took them over and rebuilt them between 1919 and 1920. They were all transformed into First Class cars, given names, and considerably altered inside, the swivelling chairs being replaced by the more usual types in Pullman vehicles which could be moved but did not swivel. After reconstruction they were run singly on important expresses along with the other Pullman cars which the SER had now begun to

An evocative representation of Charing Cross prior to December 1905 (when the arched roof collapsed and had to be rebuilt), with the 'Folkestone Vestibuled Limited' waiting to leave. Note the Edwardian costume, the gas lamps and the clerestoried coach roofs over the passenger accommodation but not over the guard's van.

employ. They received the standard maroon livery, which they retained to the end of their days, their working lives being, with one exception, extended for a further decade.

The exception was *Carmen*, which was involved in the Sevenoaks accident of 24 August 1927, when the 'River' Class 2-6-4 tank engine hauling the 5 pm business express from Cannon Street to Ashford, Folkestone and Dover left the rails just before passing through Sevenoaks station as the train was going under a road bridge. *Carmen* was one of the two coaches which received the greatest damage when they struck a bridge abutment. Hamilton Ellis mentions a sequel to this event:

> Someone on The Street (Fleet Street) informed his Editor's shocked readers that nearly all the fatalities in this accident *occurred in the Pullman Car*, a statement which brought forth an indignant denial from the Pullman Car Company, pointing out that nobody was badly hurt in the much-abused *Carmen* and that the car's lights remained on for a long time after the accident. Looking back... the writer believes that the American style of construction, with the underframe and body in one piece, saved the situation. His old friend and senior colleague, W.A. Willox, on whose division the accident happened, pointed out that nevertheless there was not much shock resistance left in the old thing after such a battering. Both ends had come to violent concussion with implacable masonry and the body was split along the cant-rail. When the breakdown van tried to move it away, first the vestibules fell off, and then the body folded up and tumbled to pieces. All the same, makers and owners came out of this deplorable business with credit.

The remaining American cars were all withdrawn between 1928 and 1930. By this time the SE&CR had been merged into the Southern Railway, which latter had begun to run what was perhaps the most celebrated of all British Pullman trains, the Golden Arrow, described in a later chapter.

5

The Southern Belle

1908-32

Until 1908, as already related, the Brighton Pullman Limited had been a train that ran only on Sundays with, at first, only a modest clientèle. However, upper class affluence was now beginning slowly to percolate downwards through society, and an increasing number of Londoners were prepared to expend surplus money in luxury travel, though only with the really well-to-do did this go as far as purchasing a motor-car. (In this regard, an interesting footnote appears on many of the pages of the LB&SCR timetable for 1912: 'A. Horses and carriages are not conveyed by these trains'. On some services there existed the equine equivalent of the present-day Motorail, though the facility cannot surely have been widely used since it would have entailed the addition of a special van to the train.) Leisure travel over any considerable distance still meant travelling by rail, and the increased demand for it between London and Brighton was recognised in the addition of extra cars to the Brighton Pullman so that by 1908 its maximum complement had become seven vehicles, plus the indispensable dynamo van.

Through the Edwardian period one could make a day return journey on this train for an inclusive fare of 12 shillings. This may seem an exceedingly low figure for 100 miles of First Class Pullman travel, but it was well beyond the means of the ordinary working class or lower middle class person in the days when an agricultural worker's weekly wage was only half as much again. There was not much risk of any inconvenient and mutually embarrassing mixing of the classes.

Patronage increased steadily and in 1908 the LB&SCR decided to make the service a daily one. A new rake of cars was obtained, built for the Pullman Car Company, now established in its headquarters at Preston Park, Brighton, by the Metropolitan Railway Carriage & Wagon Company. They differed considerably from the older ones. In the first place they were larger, with more seats. Secondly, they were mounted on six-wheeled bogies to achieve better riding. (This was a feature that did not long endure in Pullman vehicles, since in fact the extra four wheels made little real difference to the quality of the ride; the wheel-knocks as each pair passed over rail-joints were hardly less emphatic when a sequence of two threes replaced one of two twos, though perhaps they were a little more muffled.) Thirdly, the hitherto universal clerestory roof was

144

BRIGHTON.

PULLMAN DRAWING ROOM CARS

ARE RUN IN THE UNDERMENTIONED TRAINS: -

WEEK DAYS.

DOWN.				SO	SO													
	a.m.	a.m.	a.m.	p.m.	p.m.	p.m.	p.m.	p.m.	p.m.	p.m.	p.m.	p.m.	p.m.	p.m.	p.m.	p.m.	mid.	
VICTORIA ... dep.	10 5	11 0	11 40	1 0	H	1 55	3 10	3 40	...	4 30	...	5 35	...	6 35	7 15	9 50	12 5	...
LONDON BG. ,,	...	B	...	...	1 20	...	B	...	4 0	...	5 0	...	6 0	...	...	...	T	...
BRIGHTON... arr.	11 24	12 0	12 50	2 15	2 30	3 0	4 10	4 45	5 12	5 35	6 0	6 40	7 15	7 35	8 45	11 20	1 10	...

UP.													SO	
	a.m.	a.m.	a.m.	a.m.	a.m.	p.m.	p.m.	p.m.	p.m.	p.m.	p.m.	p.m.	p.m.	p.m.
BRIGHTON ... ... dep.	8 45	9 20	9 45	9 55	11 0	12 20	1 20	3 50	4 55	5 45	6 5	7 30	8 30	10 0
LONDON BRIDGE arr.	9 55	10 31	...	11 6	...	B	...	...	...	B	...	...	...	...
VICTORIA ... ... ,,	10 0	...	10 55	...	12 15	1 20	2 20	4 55	6 17	6 45	7 30	8 57	9 53	11 11

SUNDAYS.

DOWN.						
	a.m.	a.m.	p.m.	p.m.	p.m.	p.m.
VICTORIA ... ... dep.	11 0	11 5	12 15	1 10	6 30	9 25
	B				B	
BRIGHTON ... arr.	12 0	12 20	1 34	2 25	7 30	10 35

UP.					
	p.m.	p.m.	p.m.	p.m.	p.m.
BRIGHTON ... dep.	5 0	5 5	6 30	9 30	9 35
	B			B	
VICTORIA ... ,,	6 0	6 5	8 8	10 30	10 54

B—"The Southern Belle," consisting of Pullman Cars only—see Notice below. SO—Saturdays only.
H—Cold Luncheons can be served in the Pullman Cars, 2/6 per person. T—Cold Suppers can be served in the Pullman Cars, 2/6 per person.

☛ On Bank Holiday, Monday, August 5th, certain Trains shewn in this Time Table will not be run. ***For particulars see special bills.***

Passengers holding First Class Tickets can avail themselves of the Pullman Car by payment at the Booking Office or to the Conductor in charge, of Sixpence extra for any distance not exceeding 26 miles, and One Shilling beyond for each seat occupied.

HOT MEALS are served in the Pullman Cars, running in certain Trains between London and Brighton, on Week-days.

NEW PULLMAN CAR LIMITED TRAIN

VICTORIA AND BRIGHTON,

"The Southern Belle."

The New luxuriously appointed Pullman Car Train "The Southern Belle," will run as under:—

WEEK-DAYS.

	E	G		J	K
	a.m.	p.m.		p.m.	p.m.
Victoria ... dep.	11 0	3 10	Brighton ... dep.	12 20	5 45
Brighton ... arr.	12 0	4 10	Victoria ... arr.	1 20	6 45

SUNDAYS.

	E				
	a.m.	p.m.		p.m.	p.m.
Victoria ... dep.	11 0	6 30	Brighton ... dep.	5 0	9 30
Brighton ... arr.	12 0	7 30	Victoria ... arr.	6 0	10.30

E—Return fare, including Pullman Car, **12s.,** available to return by **the 5.45 p.m. Week-days, 5.0 and 9.30 p.m. Sundays, or any other Train on the day** of issue only.

Passengers reserving seats in "The Southern Belle" at 11.0 a.m. and 3.10 p.m. from Victoria by Telephone, Telegram or Letter, are requested to be at the Station not later than 10.55 ~~a.m. and 3.5 p.m.~~ to claim them.

G—Return Fare, including Pullman Car, **12s.,** available to return by any Train on the day of issue only.

J—Every week-day Cheap Day Tickets are issued from Brighton to Victoria by "The Southern Belle" leaving Brighton at 12.20 p.m. Return Fare **12s.**

K—Every Wednesday, Thursday and Saturday, Cheap Day Return Tickets are issued from Brighton to Victoria by "The Southern Belle," leaving Brighton at 5.45 p.m. Return Fare **12s.**

Passengers who desire seats reserved for them in the Return "Southern Belle" Train at 5.45 p.m. on Week-days and the 5.0 p.m. or 9.30 p.m. on Sundays, must give notice to the Conductor on the Down journey, or at the Brighton Station before 4.30 p.m. on Week-days and 4.0 p.m. (for 5.0 p.m.) and 8.0 p.m. (for 9.30 p.m.) on Sundays.

Passengers holding First Class Season Tickets, or ordinary First Class Tickets, requiring to travel by "The Southern Belle," must obtain their Pullman Car Tickets at the Booking Office, as they are not issued in the Cars by the Conductors. Pullman Car Tickets must be presented at the Platform Barrier giving admission to the Train.

Passengers holding First Class Tickets can avail themselves of the Pullman Car by payment at the Booking Office of One Shilling for each seat occupied.

Tickets for "The SOUTHERN BELLE," leaving Victoria at 11.0 a.m. on Week-days can be obtained at the undermentioned Agencies:—

MESSRS. THOS. COOK & SONS, Ludgate Circus.
Do. do. 13, Cockspur Street.
Do. do. 38 & 39, Piccadilly.
MESSRS. PICKFORD'S OFFICE, 156, Brompton Road.
ARMY & NAVY STORES, LTD., Victoria St., Westminster.
CIVIL SERVICE SUPPLY STORES, Bedford Street, Strand.
Do. do. 136, Queen Victoria Street, E.C.
REGENT STREET OFFICE, 28, Regent Street.

MESSRS. DEAN & DAWSON, 285, Oxford Street, W.
CIVIL SERVICE CO-OPERATIVE STORES, 28, Haymarket.
HARROD'S STORES, Brompton Road.
HAY'S OFFICE, Cornhill.
GROSVENOR HOTEL.
HOTEL METROPOLE.
HOTEL VICTORIA.
CARLTON HOTEL.
LANGHAM HOTEL.

Intending Passengers requiring any particular seat reserved must arrange this through the Station Superintendent at Victoria.

HOT and COLD LUNCHEONS, TEAS and other REFRESHMENTS are obtainable at all times on this Train.

A page from a 1912 LB&SCR timetable.

replaced by one with an oval contour. The clerestory was never a satisfactory way of obtaining additional daylight, and it made the work of carriage cleaners more difficult. Fourthly, the dynamo vans were discarded, electricity for lighting being provided by a dynamo beneath each coach frame worked by a belt from one of the bogie axles, which not only lit the lamps but also kept batteries of accumulators under the car floor charged for use when the train was stationary. Fifthly, food was now cooked on the train; it was no longer necessary for it to be cooked beforehand and kept warm until it was served. Finally, the new Pullman livery of cream and umber proclaimed the company's new flagship-train in a distinctive and eye-catching manner.

The seven new vehicles comprised the following: two end-saloon Brakes, *Verona* and *Alberta*, with baggage compartments; a Kitchen Parlour car, *Grosvenor*; four Parlour cars, *Belgravia*, *Cleopatra*, *Desborough* and *Princess Helen*. (The practice, it will be noted, of naming the cars after Royal personages was beginning to disappear.) Each was 63 ft 10 ins in length, 8 ft 8¼ ins wide, 13 ft 2 ins high from rail to roof-top, and 8 ft 6 ins high inside. The bodies, as before, were built entirely of timber and the roofs had domed ends. The armchairs were movable. A contemporary brochure put out by the Pullman Car Company in 1910 described the interior of one of the cars:

> Upon entering the Southern Belle we leave London behind ... we have come into a place of enchantment, of beauty and exquisite comfort. The spirit of a cultured man or woman is uplifted at once by this palace of elegance and refinement. Watch some pretty, well-dressed woman making her choice of seat for this short journey. She gives a little cry of delight upon entering the first carriage ... her eyes are filled with admiration as she looks at the beautiful mahogany panelling inlaid with satin wood, at the delicate molding[1] of the frieze and cornices, at the fluted pillars[2], at the carpet with its soft shade of green with its *fleur de lys* pattern, at the damask silk blinds and at the cosy chairs and settees in a restful shade of green morocco.

And so on, for many laudatory paragraphs. All this could be the First Class passenger's for an extra shilling on top of the First Class fare!

The complete train accommodated 219 passengers, but the demand to travel in it soon became so great that in 1911 two more cars were added to match the

[1] The spelling, as in other parts not quoted here, betrays the hand of a transatlantic panegyrist.

[2] Presumably pilasters is meant. No British saloon carriage ever needed free-standing pillars to support its roof.

Above right **The interior of the Parlour car *Belgravia*, one of the Southern Belle cars, from a contemporary painting intended to show that the train offered all the amenities of an upper class Edwardian drawing-room. *NRM, York***
Right **The interior of *Grosvenor*, built in 1908 for the Southern Belle. Note the bar counter, in the cupboard behind which boxes of cigars figure prominently, the leather-seated chairs and the ashtrays on the floor. *NRM, York***

rest, the 28-seat *Vivienne* and the 23-seat buffet car *Myrtle*, which brought the tonnage up to 360 when all the cars were in use, though on days when the traffic was light their number might be reduced to five or six. Meanwhile the number of daily journeys increased. When the train was first introduced in November 1908 it made a morning down and evening up journey every day. Four weeks later it ran two double trips on Sundays, and after a further six months this was extended to weekdays also. In every case the 60-minute non-stop schedule was adhered to, and it continued to be the fastest train on the whole LB&SCR system. In 1912 the Southern Belle was running as follows:

Down:		Up:	
Victoria	Brighton	Brighton	Victoria
Weekdays			
11.00	12.00	12.20	13.20
15.10	16.10	17.45	18.45
Sundays			
11.00	12.00	17.00	18.00
18.30	19.30	21.30	22.30

During the pre-First World War years, apart from the Cornish Riviera Express on the GWR, the Irish Mail on the LNWR and the Grampian and Granite City on the Caledonian, the Southern Belle was the only named express train, and uniquely the only luxury train in the whole country. It was very much a prestige service, and looked the part. Many postcard representations of it were published, in colour or black and white, usually showing it in full cry somewhere between Coulsdon and Clayton tunnel. No such splendid sight had ever before graced British rails than this sumptuous train of cream and umber cars headed by an umber-liveried Marsh 'Atlantic' 4-4-2 or 4-6-2 tank locomotive. One may surmise that it produced invisible earnings for the company in the form of pennies spent on platform tickets bought at Victoria, Brighton or intermediate stations by boys of all ages carrying notebooks or cameras to secure records of its departure, arrival or passage at full speed. It also started a fashion of naming luxury trains as 'Belles' of one sort or another, as will be seen. In its heyday it was a unique British institution.

From 1913 onwards, however, its history became confused and subject to many changes. These are perhaps most conveniently shown as in the accompanying table, extending until the time when the LB&SCR finally merged into the Southern Railway system.

The background to all these alterations, cancellations and reinstatements was the European War and its aftermath, together with the determination of the company to secure more passengers. The latter first showed itself in the addition of ordinary Third Class coaches to the main train, which spoiled its appearance but offered the poorer traveller the speed and convenience of the service, though not its luxury. Then came the shock of the outbreak of the war, which turned the would-be excursionist's mind away from jaunts to the seaside;

Changes in the Southern Belle service between 1913 and 1922

NB: 'N/c' = no change from the arrangement previously obtaining.

Period	**Weekday trains**				**Sunday trains**			
	1st down	**1st up**	**2nd down**	**2nd up**	**1st down**	**1st up**	**2nd down**	**2nd up**
1/13-8/14	N/c	3rd cl ordinary carriages added to Pullman cars		N/c	N/c	3rd cl ordinary carriages added to Pullman cars		N/c
8/14-9/14	Service suspended altogether on outbreak of First World War							
10/14-3/15	Train reinstated as during 1/13-8/14							
3/15-10/15	Third Class coaches added to Pullman cars in all trains							
10/15-12.15	N/c	N/c	N/c	N/c	Third class carriages not included in the train on Sundays			
1/16-2/16	N/c	N/c	N/c	N/c	N/c	N/c	Train canc'ed	Train canc'ed
3/16-9/17	Whole service suspended							
10/17-2/18	N/c	N/c	N/c	N/c	All-Pullman train reinstated, unnamed, on 65 min schedule	N/c	N/c	
3/19-5/19	N/c	N/c	N/c	N/c	Train re-named Southern Belle on 68 min (down) and 70 min (up) schedules		N/c	N/c
5/19-2/20	Reinstated with additional 3rd cl carriages, on 69 min (down) and 70 min (up) schedules	N/c	N/c	N/c	N/c	N/c	N/c	
3/20-11/20	N/c	N/c	N/c	N/c	N/c	N/c	Train re-instated, on 78 min schedule in both directions	
1/20-3/21	Trains speeded up to 60 min schedules		Services resumed on 60 min schedules		N/c	N/c	Trains speeded up to 60 min schedules	
4/21-11/21	Whole service suspended due to national coal strike							
12/21-7/24	Whole service reinstated as during 12/20-3/21 on 60 min schedule							
Train service from 14/7/24 all on 60 min schedules	Dep Vic 11.05am	Dep B'ton 1.35pm	Dep Vic 3.05pm	Dep B'ton 5.35pm	Dep Vic 11.00am	Dep B'ton 5.00pm	Dep Vic 6.30pm	Dep B'ton 9.30pm

Shortly before the outbreak of the First World War, the Southern Belle has arrived at Victoria in the early evening, comprising a train of 12-wheeled vehicles behind Marsh 'Atlantic' No 41. ***NRM, York***

hence the wholesale cancellation of the service for the first two months.

People, however, soon adjusted to the war situation and were willing to look for an escape from its daily horrors. The LB&SCR's lines, too, were not so much needed for military traffic as were those of the adjoining SE&CR and LSWR. So the status quo was resumed the following spring. Then followed a really significant change in railway and Pullman policy. For the first time, by adaptation from existing First Class cars, Third Class Pullman cars were produced which offered luxury at a lesser level in return for a lower supplement for passengers holding Third Class tickets. A 2 + 1 seating arrangement took the place of the former 1 + 1; antimacassars on seat-backs were dispensed with; the seats were made a little narrower and were fixed instead of being movable. The improvement over ordinary Third Class accommodation was considerable. Both the LB&SCR and the Pullman Car Company were beginning to realise that their bread could be buttered on both sides. The use of Third Class cars was later to spread to other lines, and all the special all-Pullman trains of the future, until the introduction of the Midland Pullman in 1960, had more, sometimes many more, Third Class seats available than First Class.

By the spring of 1916 the exigencies of the war caused the train again to be suspended for a while. At the end of 1917 the military prospects began to brighten and the Southern Belle, though not yet flaunting its title on its head-boards as before, crept into view in the timetable, running only on Sundays and on a slower schedule that reflected track dilapidations owing to necessarily inadequate maintenance. With the end of the war, still operating only on Sundays, it resumed its title and re-commenced weekday running, at first only once each way daily.

After that came what appeared to be a complete recovery, the double journey being done to a 60-minute timing twice each day. A national coal strike caused a final interruption, but the last year of the LB&SCR's separate existence saw the service's full resumption. Thus it continued until the Southern Railway took control, when it became one of the only two named trains on this system, the other being the Thanet Pullman Limited, dealt with in a later chapter.

The Southern Belle of 1922 was not what it had been ten years earlier. Many of the original 12-wheeled cars had gone to be used elsewhere, and eight-wheeled cars predominated. The train was now an assortment rather than a unity. The weight varied according to the season, but could reach ten cars, in which case there were problems for the locomotive department. In the train's earliest days, when the load did not exceed seven cars, a Marsh 'Atlantic' or 'I.3' 4-4-2 tank engine could manage it, but as the load increased six-coupled engines became necessary. Just before his retirement Marsh built an express 4-6-2 tank engine, with the haulage of the Belle particularly in his mind, and another was added later. His successor, L. Billinton, felt even more power was desirable, and in 1914 produced his 4-6-4 express tank locomotive No 327 *Charles C. Macrae*, which was followed a year later by a second. The war delayed their further manufacture but once peace had returned five more were

A post-First World War postcard of the Southern Belle showing a seven-car train hauled by 4-6-4T No 332. ***Author's Collection***

constructed, and they proved able to keep time on the Belle in all seasons and weathers, being fitted with extra large cylinders to enable rapid hill-climbing and acceleration from stops and slacks. Some examples of their performance on the Southern Belle are given later.

Once established as one of the SR's principal express trains, the Southern Belle's history was comparatively uneventful until its eventual replacement by electric Pullman units in 1933. During this period it was made up of quite an assortment of Pullman cars, some being older American-built vehicles of pre-1908 vintage reconstructed to take Third Class passengers and given numbers instead of names. After 1925 new eight-wheeled cars replaced such of the 12-wheelers as still remained. The only high spots in the even tenor of its way were an anniversary celebration and the occasion of its final run.

On 1 November 1929 it celebrated its 21st birthday, and the 11 am departure from Victoria, behind a 'King Arthur' No 793 *Sir Ontzlake*, carried a commemorative headboard and flags above the buffer beam. It was driven by driver W. Coughtray, who had been the fireman on the inaugural run on 1 November 1908 when the engine had been one of Marsh's 4-4-2 tanks. The rejoicings were somewhat muted, however, since only a little earlier the SR had announced publicly that the line to Brighton was soon to be electrified - and in fact the train did not last long enough to have a Silver Jubilee. On 31 December 1932, the last day when it ran steam-hauled, an attempt was made to recall history; the two 12-wheeled cars *Vivienne* and *Myrtle* were brought back to convey the First Class passengers, but the other coaches were a heterogeneous assemblage of Third Class cars, some rebuilt from former First Class vehicles and still having clerestory roofs. The locomotive selected was the aptly-named 4-6-4 War Memorial engine No 333 *Remembrance*. Time was easily kept with 1¼ minutes to spare despite signal delays. The run is described below.

The SR's locomotive provision for the Belle between 1923 and 1932 was at first one or other of the batch of 4-6-4 tanks which had been inherited from the LB&SCR; later on the choice became more varied. In 1925 the Chief Mechanical Engineer, R. E. L. Maunsell, put some of his newly-built 'River' Class 2-6-4 express tank locomotives on to Central Section metals, and these showed they were able to perform as well as the 4-6-4s; though slightly smaller they had a higher boiler pressure and more sophisticated front-end arrangements. In 1926 some 'King Arthur' 4-6-0s were brought in, and these gradually displaced the tank engines. Occasionally, at times of heavy traffic when the usual engines were needed elsewhere, one of Maunsell's 'U' Class mixed traffic 2-6-0s took a turn on the Pullman train. In effect this was a reversion to the use of 2-6-4 tanks, since all the latter were rebuilt as 2-6-0 tender engines after one of them had come off the rails at Sevenoaks in August 1927 at the head of a Kent Coast express, causing considerable loss of life.

More, probably, than any other all-Pullman train in Great Britain, the Southern Belle attracted the notice of railway enthusiasts who were addicted to train-timing. The shortness of the run meant that one could do the return journey with a day return ticket quite cheaply, and the glass-topped table in front of

A 'King Arthur' on the Southern Belle, a lightly-loaded train whose haulage would have presented little difficulty to No E797 *Sir Blamor de Ganis*. 'King Arthurs' were the usual engines on the train after 1926, and No E797 is one of the so-called 'Scotchmen' built by the North British Locomotive Co in that year, and given a six-wheel tender. *Steamchest*

one's seat made a convenient resting place for stopwatch and notebook. It seems worth while, therefore, to give a sample collection of timed runs in the accompanying tables, which should be considered with reference to the gradient profile of the route, which included three distinct summits at Merstham, Balcombe and Clayton tunnel entrances. The ruling gradient from Merstham southwards was 1 in 264 in both directions. Performances by each of the locomotive types mentioned above are included.

In the first run in Table 1 a superheated Marsh 'Atlantic', somewhat heavily loaded, stalled on Grosvenor Road bank after starting and had to be given rear-end banking assistance; in consequence it was 11 minutes late passing Clapham Junction. No time was recovered until the first summit had been surmounted at Merstham, but 4 minutes were then regained through a vigorous and fortunately unchecked effort, with unusually high maximum speeds at Horley and Wivelsfield and good climbs to Balcombe and Clayton summits. The second run illustrates the abilities of one of L. Billinton's 4-6-4 tanks on the final run of the steam-hauled Belle mentioned above. A very fast start was made to Croydon, a high minimum was achieved at Merstham tunnel entrance and an even more surprisingly high one on the rise to Balcombe runnel. Signal checks prevented further fast running but Brighton was reached well before time.

Table 1

Run No	**1**			**2**			**3**			**4**		
Locomotive No	421 (4-4-2)			333 (4-6-4T)			805 (4-6-0)			792 (2-6-4T)		
Gross load in tons	325			310			440			280		
Miles	min	sec	speed	min	sec	speed	min	sec	speed	min	sec	speed
0.0	00	00		00	00		00	00			00	00
	delay - see text											
0.6 Grosvenor Rd Box	11	34		02	35		01	58				
2.7 Clapham Junc	16	23		05	35	47	05	24	46	05	35	
4.7 Balham	19	09		08	05	44½	08	03	42	08	25	
7.5 Norbury	22	43		11	24	58	11	34	53½			
10.5 East Croydon	26	18		14	41	54	15	08	49	15	53	
13.5 Purley	29	51		18	00		18	45				
15.0 Coulsdon North	31	34	54	19	39	55	20	26	53	21	20	48
17.5 Mp 17¼ (summit)	34	54	43	22	28	50	23	33	48			
21.9 Earlswood	39	14		26	45		27	58		29	30	62
26.0 Horley	42	34	80½	30	11	77	31	33	74	33	12	73
29.5 Three Bridges	45	50		33	16		34	59				
							eased					
32.0 Mp 31¾ (summit)	48	22	54	35	42	60	38	11	44	39	01	54
										p.w. slack		
34.1 Balcombe	50	24		37	42		40	41				
				sigs								
37.9 Haywards Heath	53	40		42	07		44	26		46	25	
41.1 Keymer Junc	56	14	79	45	05	68	47	17	69	49	16	68
				sigs								
46.2 Mp 46 (summit)	61	21	55				52	25	53½			49
49.6 Preston Park	64	32	66	55	54		55	57	60	58	08	
				sigs			sigs			sigs		
50.9 Brighton	67	02		58	41		59	14		60	49	

On the third run tabulated a 'King Arthur' had a very heavy load and made what as far as Three Bridges was the best run in the table. The start from Victoria up the 1 in 64 to Grosvenor Road Box was unusually vigorous. After Three Bridges the engine was eased considerably, but in spite of a concluding signal check time was kept with ¾ minute to spare. In run No 4 a 'River' tank with a fairly light load gave a competent performance without any striking displays of speed, which would have been quite adequate for timekeeping had it

Table 2

Run No	1			2			3		
Locomotive No	24 (4-4-2T)			325 (4-6-2T)			1632 (2-6-0)		
Gross load in tons	290			295			340		
Miles	min	sec	speed	min	sec	speed	min	sec	speed
0.0 Brighton	00	00		00	00		00	00	
1.3 Preston Park	03	27		03	22		03	35	
4.7 Mp 46 (summit)	08	14	48	07	53	52½	08	36	45
7.1 Hassocks	10	47		10	20		11	15	
9.8 Keymer Junction	13	09		12	47		13	45	
13.0 Haywards Heath	15	55	74	15	27	71½	16	45	68
16.8 Balcombe	sigs			19	40	50	21	25	48
18.9 Mp 31¾ (summit)	sigs stop			22	16		p. w. slack		
21.4 Three Bridges	31	31		24	44		27	10	
24.0 Horley	34	34	75	27	48	74	30	25	68
29.0 Earlswood	38	18		eased 31	46		34	45	
32.1 Quarry Box (summit)	41	39	50	35	25		38	25	45
37.4 Purley	47	03	75	40	55		44	10	69
40.4 East Croydon	49	38		sigs 43	47		47	00	
43.4 Norbury	52	46		47	33		50	05	
46.2 Balham	55	18		50	29		sigs 53	10	
48.2 Clapham Junction	57	08		52	34		55	40	
50.3 Grosvenor Rd Box	59	40		55	49		sigs		
50.9 Victoria	61	13		58	38		61	58	

not been for the concluding signal delay. (In regard to this run the restraint shown by the engine may well have been due to uneasiness on the part of the locomotive crew; the 'Rivers' were not popular with Central Section drivers because of the tendency to roll unexpectedly if they passed over a patch of imperfectly-maintained track.)

In the opposite direction the first log in Table 2 shows the performance of a 4-4-2 'I.3' tank hauling the original seven-car Belle soon after its institution.

The train was badly checked in the region of Balcombe tunnel, and momentarily brought to a stand. The driver then set about time-recovery, making an excellent climb to Quarry Box, accelerating to an unusually high speed before Croydon and, after the service slack there, finishing very vigorously to bring the train into Victoria only 1¼ minutes late. In the second run the first of Marsh's 4-6-2 tanks performed well enough with a moderate load of seven 12-wheelers, with fast climbs to Clayton and Balcombe tunnels; after Horley the engine was eased, but the arrival at Victoria was over 2 minutes early despite the concluding signal check. A 'U' Class two-cylinder 2-6-0, with only 6-foot driving wheels and a sizeable load, kept time to Clapham Junction despite a permanent way slowing through Balcombe tunnel which prevented a high maximum at Horley, and a signal check after Norbury, but a second signal delay made the train 2 minutes late into Victoria.

Performance recorders could therefore expect good locomotive running if they travelled on the Southern Belle during its first seven and final ten years of operation, and many must have made the journey with chronometers at the ready, maybe with a cup of the Pullman Company's tea at their elbow, or possibly with a nip of something stronger. The writer regrets not having been among them; his own train-timing days came a little later, and he was too young and impecunious to indulge in such pleasures while the Belle was still steam-hauled.

6

The Eastbourne Sunday Pullman

1908-1957

Although both were seaside resorts within easy reach of London and on the fringe of the South Downs, Eastbourne and Brighton were as different as chalk from cheese in their general atmosphere and in the type of people they attracted as holidaymakers. Brighton during the present century has become less a place for the fashionable visitor, more a resort for the ordinary person and a dormitory town for those working in the capital. Eastbourne has changed less and remains dignified, exclusive and (to use that delightful Victorian term) 'genteel'. The splendid vulgarity of the Prince Regent's many-domed Pavilion is foreign to Eastbourne's character. It was always been a refined place where people from the upper levels of society could take apartments for a few weeks and stroll along its promenades or perambulate its pier without ever being greeted by the odour of fish and chips being eaten from a newspaper. Retired persons with comfortably large pensions come here to end their days, as at Bath, Torquay or Harrogate. It was and is a deeply respectable place, which distrusts the day tripper.

However, this is a free country, and the tripper cannot be excluded from any part of it (except by the Ministry of Defence) if he or she wishes to come. When the LB&SCR replaced its Sundays-only Pullman train to Brighton with the seven-days-a-week Southern Belle it had spare First Class Pullman cars to use elsewhere than on its direct main line, and Eastbourne suggested itself as a destination to which they could be dispatched instead. Eastbourne had been favoured by special trains before; there could be no objection to easy access for the right people, who were prepared to stay for a while and patronise the shops and amenities. But what the railway company was now proposing was a train for day visitors, a special facility with an all-in day return fare.

Four weeks after the Southern Belle began to ply to and from Brighton, four of the former American-built cars, refurbished and re-attired in the now standard umber and cream livery, together with a dynamo van and a six-wheeled luggage van, commenced to run every Sunday non-stop to Eastbourne, leaving Victoria at 10.15 am and arriving at 11.45; the return was at 17.15, Victoria being reached at 18.45. It was at first advertised in the LB&SCR timetable, but was billed in a 'Train Alteration Notice' as a new all-Pullman service to and from Eastbourne, available for an inclusive day return fare of 12 shillings and

EASTBOURNE.

PULLMAN DRAWING ROOM CARS

ARE RUN IN THE UNDERMENTIONED TRAINS:—

DOWN.	WEEK-DAYS.				SUNDAYS.	
	a.m.	p.m. Sats. only.	p.m.	p.m. Not on Sats.	a.m. *	a.m.
VICTORIA ... ...dep.	11 15		3 20		10 45	11 15
LONDON BRIDGE ,,	...	2 3	...	5 5	...	...
EASTBOURNE .. arr.	12 45	4 2	4 55	6 35	12 15	1 7

UP.	WEEK-DAYS.			SUNDAYS.	
	a.m.	a.m.	p.m.	p.m. *	p.m.
EASTBOURNE ... dep.	8 30	9 30	2 26	5 15	5 55
LONDON BRIDGE arr.	10 0	...	...	...	...
VICTORIA ... ... ,,	...	11 0	4 17	6 45	7 40

Passengers holding First Class Tickets can avail themselves of the Pullman Car by payment at the Booking Office, or to the Conductor in charge, of Sixpence extra for any distance not exceeding 26 miles, and One Shilling beyond for each seat occupied.

* For the Sunday Pullman Limited Train between Victoria and Eastbourne, an extra charge of One Shilling and Sixpence for the Single Journey, or Two Shillings and Sixpence Return, in addition to the First Class Fare.

HOT MEALS are served in the Pullman Car running in the 8.30 a.m. Train from Eastbourne on Week Days.

TO EASTBOURNE. EVERY SUNDAY.

EASTBOURNE PULLMAN LIMITED. (Pullman Cars only).		FROM	By Train leaving at	Return Fare (including Pullman Car).	TRAINS FOR RETURN.
Victoria ... dep. 10 45 a.m. Eastbourne arr 12 15 p.m Eastbourne dep. 5 15 p.m. Victoria ... arr. 6 45 p.m.	Return Fare (from Victoria) 12/6	VICTORIA ... ... Clapham Junction ... East Croydon	a.m. 11 15 11 22 11 38	12/-	Returning from EASTBOURNE by any Ordinary Train same day. A Pullman Car is run in the 5.55 p.m. Train from EASTBOURNE.

The Eastbourne Sunday Pullman advertised in a LB&SCR timetable of 1912.

sixpence - only sixpence more than was being asked for a similar service to Brighton, though the journey was 14 miles further, and in either direction one's occupation of a Pullman armchair seat lasted half an hour longer.

At first Eastbourne took little account of the new train, though its inhabitants may have reflected that the supplement-paying day tourists were bound to be of a superior type, that they would arrive when the hours of divine service in churches and chapels were almost over, and that in any case not many more than one hundred could arrive at once. What the Eastbourners were really wanting was a convenient Sunday train service in the opposite direction; as things were, all they had on a Sunday were one fast train in the morning (if one could call a journey time of 1¾ hours 'fast') and one in the evening. However, the new train slipped quietly into service a little before Christmas, eventually appeared in the pages of *Bradshaw's Guide*, and was somewhat later billed in the railway's timetable, where it was designated as the Eastbourne Pullman Limited. Despite its discreet inauguration it was destined actually to outlast, as a steam-hauled train, its more famous sister by 2½ years, continuing until the line from Keymer Junction to Eastbourne and Hastings was electrified in 1935.

Like the Southern Belle it was a prestigious service; nevertheless, it did not at first enjoy haulage by one of the company's latest locomotives. In 1908 many veteran engines were still going strong, and during the autumn, winter and spring months it was usual to provide a 'Gladstone' 0-4-2 for the double journey. The schedule was certainly not a demanding one, even for a 25-year-old locomotive of antique design; 90 minutes for the 66 miles was an easier task than 60 minutes for the 51 miles covered each way by the Belle, which had three considerable summits to surmount *en route* instead of only two. On the other hand the Eastbourne trains had to make service slacks at Keymer Junction, Lewes and Polegate. No doubt it was fairly easy work for a 'Gladstone' in good condition.

However, it cannot have been quite so easy for the engine detailed to work the train during the summer periods of 1910-12. This was the 30-year-old Stroudley single wheeler No 329 *Stephenson*, which was reserved for the train and kept specially maintained for the purpose. Never before or since has a single-wheeler worked an all-Pullman train, and one would like to know how well *Stephenson* managed, but no logs of performance by it are extant and probably none was ever made.

As with the Southern Belle, the years 1913-21 saw this service altered again and again, in a not dissimilar pattern. First came the addition, from 1 January 1913, of ordinary Third Class carriages to the Pullman rake, the train's title being at the same time modified to The Eastbourne Sunday Limited (the word 'Pullman' being presumably omitted so that a would-be Third Class traveller would not suppose that the train was not for him). In June 1914 a West Worthing portion was added to the rear of the train and slipped at Haywards Heath to serve all stations beyond. The train as it left Victoria was now in effect three trains, the front Pullman portion being specifically First Class with its own 12s 6d day return fare. The former 0-4-2 and 2-2-2 haulage now gave place to the more powerful 4-4-2 tanks of Marsh's design, the superheated 'I.3s' whose prowess had previously been displayed on the Southern Belle before that train became too heavy for them.

When the First World War broke out in August 1914 there was an immediate but short-lived cancellation of this train, just as had happened with the Belle, but it was back in service at the beginning of October. A year later (as also with the Belle) came the introduction of Third Class Pullman cars, rebuilds from previous First Class vehicles, and the ordinary Third Class carriages were taken from the train in consequence; the slip portion for Worthing was nevertheless retained. This altered service continued until the end of the following year and was then completely withdrawn.

In October 1917 the train reappeared, unnamed and with both the Third Class cars and the Worthing portion omitted; it reverted to its former departure time at Victoria and, as before, ran on a 90-minute timing. The return departure was fixed for the very late hour of 9.10 pm, and a stop to set down was made at East Croydon. It is not clear why this alteration was made. D. W. Winkworth, in his book *Southern Titled Trains* speculates rather light-heartedly that there might have been some famous preachers in Eastbourne at that time and that the railway company was giving opportunity for visitors to sample their pulpit oratory. It is a delightful thought which one discounts with regret; one feels that it is more likely that servicemen on leave were being given a little more time for their money. Whatever the reason for the change, the earlier departure time was resumed two months later.

Matters remained thus for the next four years, departure and arrival times remaining much the same, but with changes in the train's composition, the First and Third Class Pullman vehicles being sometimes removed, either or both, but with Third Class ordinary coaches always present to take some passengers. In the up direction the East Croydon stop was always made. No distinctive title was yet restored.

At the beginning of December 1921 the name Eastbourne Sunday Limited was given back, and it ran once more as a train of Pullman cars only, for both classes. Then followed a 12-year period without change, so far as the vehicles were concerned. The former rake of American-built cars which had composed it in the earlier days had disappeared by 1924, later British-built cars taking their places. In this year the schedule was quickened to a non-stop run of 85 minutes in both directions; the load varied according to seasonal needs, from five to nine cars.

In regard to locomotive provision, during the war years 'I.3' 4-4-2 tank engines were first employed; these were succeeded by rebuilt 'B.4' Billinton 4-4-0s. At this period, however, Pullman cars were all being constructed or reconstructed to operate with vacuum brakes, so orders were given by the Chief Mechanical Engineer, R. E. L. Maunsell, that either 'King Arthur' 4-6-0s or rebuilt ex-LSWR 'L.12' 4-4-0s were to replace the Westinghouse air-braked ex-Brighton line engines. During 1925 a 'River' tank was occasionally seen on this train; a year later most of them were taken away to be used on the Eastern Section, and after the Sevenoaks derailment in August 1927 they were all converted to 2-6-0s. Maunsell's 'U' and 'U.1' two-cylinder and three-cylinder 2-6-0s also took turns on this duty.

The Eastbourne Sunday Pullman on its morning down run in the 1920s near Merstham. Four of the five Pullman cars are ex-Southern Belle vehicles of Edwardian vintage. The front car is something of a puzzle - it looks like a converted and repainted Pullman. Three Third Class coaches bring up the rear. The locomotive is ex-LSWR 4-4-0 No E433, built by Drummond and rebuilt by Urie. *R. W. Airy, The Railway Magazine*

As already mentioned, the last 2½ years of the steam-hauled Eastbourne Sunday Pullman's existence were a period when it was the only locomotive-headed all-Pullman train on the Central Section; this was its time of autumnal glory. Not only were cars from the defunct Belle transferred to it, but there was a further speed-up to an 80-minute journey each way, so that it became the Central Section's fastest steam-operated train, comparable now in difficulty of haulage with the former 60-minute steam schedule from Victoria to Brighton. A great variety of locomotives now took turns in hauling it. Since on this Section steam was on the way out, many engines had little to do, especially on a Sunday. At first Drummond 'T.9s', as superheated by Urie between 1912 and 1922, were entrusted with it. Then for a brief while 'King Arthurs' were used. Then the old Marsh 'Atlantics', now vacuum-braked, took a turn. Now and then a Billinton 4-6-4 appeared. Finally members of the 'Schools' Class of 4-4-0s were drafted in after damage to a bridge near Lewes caused a weight restriction to be imposed at this point. The last 2½ years were therefore a period of great variety so far as engine provision was concerned.

On 6 July 1935 the Eastbourne Sunday Pullman made its final run; the following day the current was switched on between Keymer Junction, Eastbourne and Hastings, and regular steam operations ended. Thenceforward for nearly 13 years the only Pullman cars to be seen east of Keymer Junction were the composite ones included in the electric multiple unit trains which now served East Sussex from Victoria and London Bridge. The all-Pullman train, it seemed, had gone for good. But after the absorption of the SR into British Railways the train was given a fresh lease of life, though its former name was not restored. One of the three five-car Brighton Belle all-Pullman units was used on Sundays, at first with the same departure and arrival times as before and on the former 80-minute schedule, and Eastbourne, which did not now particularly mind having them, received up to 200 excursionists and entertained them for five hours.

In 1954 the departure from Victoria was fixed at 10.12 and the train was slowed by 6 minutes in either direction. It was now definitely a train for day tourists, charging less than £1 for a Third Class seat in both directions. (Seat prices had doubled in 40 years - an indication of how low inflation then was, despite the interposition of two World Wars.) This service lasted till 1957 and was then discontinued. Another citadel had fallen to the advancing army of the private car.

7

British Pullman cars in the early 20th century

At this point it seems opportune to halt the narrative for a while and look at the construction and interior arrangements of those Pullman cars which were built and used in Great Britain during the 50 years or so which followed the inauguration of the Southern Belle. All were built by one or another railway carriage building firm in Britain and delivered to the Pullman Car Company's headquarters, whence they were transferred to run on routes of railway companies that had entered into contracts to hire them. The latter received the fares paid for travel; the Pullman Company levied the supplementary charges in return for which the traveller had a reserved seat at which he or she was served with refreshments or a meal as desired. In this way both parties profited from satisfactory levels of patronage.

A Pullman Car was readily distinguishable both externally and internally

from an ordinary vestibuled passenger coach. From without its livery proclaimed what it was, even if one saw it at a distance; only the GWR painted its own coaches in a colour scheme anything like the Pullman cream and umber. A closer view showed the name or number of the vehicle (only first class or composite cars were named) inscribed in gilt lettering across the centre of the lower umber-coloured panels beneath the windows on either side, with the word PULLMAN spread out in the narrow space between the eaves of the roof and the upper edges of the windows. (Until 1930 this was against a white background, but subsequently appeared along a narrow umber band.) The end doors at each side opened inwards - in this respect Pullman vehicles were unique, so far as passenger entrances were concerned - and had long glass lights reaching below waist-level, usually oval in shape; on either side were vertical brass grab-rails. The car windows were large, laterally elongated and with sliding ventilators above.

At one or both ends of the car toilet compartments betrayed their presence

Left ***Bertha,*** **preserved at Sheffield Park on the Bluebell Railway, Sussex, shows the ornate style in which Pullman vehicles were named. This was one of the composite cars built to be included in six-vehicle units when the main lines of the Central Section of the Southern Railway were electrified in 1933. The arrows on the roof are misleading - it was never used outside the Central section.** ***Author***

Right **A closer view of one of** ***Bertha's*** **inward-opening end doors and end wall, showing the characteristic Pullman elliptical windows.** ***Author***

Third Class car No 64, also preserved at Sheffield Park, showing the details of lining out and the Pullman coat-of-arms as it was in the 'thirties. ***Author***

by small oval windows with translucent leaded panes, the centre pane always being diamond-shaped. The ends of the cars were slightly curved on either side of the wide vestibule connection, and had narrow windows. In cars which had a brake compartment the umber livery extended from bottom to top along the car sides in this region. In each car the Pullman coat of arms was applied on either side of the cartouche which carried the name or number.

Internally, the Pullman car differed from almost all contemporary passenger vehicles except restaurant cars in being a saloon, or series of saloons; a coupé compartment might be included, usually at one end, as a concession to the English passion for privacy, but in general it was assumed that people who could afford to pay the extra supplement would find the company of fellow-supplement-payers, if not congenial, at least unobjectionable. From Edwardian times onwards this was increasingly the case, so that even before the Second World War some railway companies were building open saloon coaches, and at the present time it is hard to find a compartmented side corridor coach except on a few standard gauge preserved steam railways where they appear as slightly scruffy reminders of the past.

Pullman cars of this period were very solidly built of timber. Wooden coach construction was usual until the inter-war years, when steel outer panelling gradually became the rule; the all-steel coach came later. To build a coach entirely with wood, except for the bogies, did not necessarily make for a flimsy vehicle. One may recall the wooden battleships of the past, which were expected to withstand a pounding by heavy cannon balls from enemy guns. As already noted in chapter 4, an ancient wooden Pullman car could withstand sudden impact remarkably well. What caused the eventual disappearance of wooden railway coaches was the risk from fire occurring after an accident, especially when they were gas-lit.

A specification sent to the manufacturers in 1913, when Pullman cars were ordered for use on the South Eastern and Chatham Railway, gives some indication of the Company's requirements. One cannot do more than quote a few relevant passages:

> BODY FRAMING: The body framing is generally to be of pitch pine, excepting the vertical side light and intermediate pillars, which are to be of Ash and Mahogany respectively, well jointed and braced, secured by strong knees, tie rods, etc. Above the bogies the sides to be further stiffened by a steel truss extending for some distance on either side of the bogie centres, and connected together by means of a steel angle secured to each side pillar.
>
> The body end also to be stiffened by steel bracings and pressed steel knees, with a steel flitch plate attached to the body side, passing over the vestibule side door and attached to the framing by wood screws.
>
> The body sides at the cantrails to be connected by channel section carlines bent to the shape of the outside roof and filled in with ash [*wood, not cinders!*] for the fixing of the inside roof boards.
>
> Above each partition a 3" by 1½" ash roof stick to be placed, and at each cross partition the cantrails will be connected by a flat iron brace built into the partition. All corner pillars to be stiffened by angle irons running their entire length, the archrails being flitched in a similar way.
>
> The outside matchboarding and panelling to be of Mahogany, all spaces behind same being filled with ⅜" Red Deal blocking and the side pillars rabbeted to receive the same. The whole to be glued together solid.
>
> ROOFS AND ROOF COVERING: The inside and outside roof boards to be of Red Deal with the exception of the vestibule roof boards which will be of Rock Elm, laid in narrow widths. The roofs to be covered with prepared canvas properly bedded in white lead, the vestibule end portion being further protected by copper sheathing. Water rails in one length over the whole length of the cars to be fitted.
>
> FLOORS: Floor boards to be in two thicknesses laid diagonally of ¾" Red Deal and separated by ¼" felt; a layer of this is also placed between the lower floor boards and side sills.
>
> Brackets and frames for notices of standard design to be provided for all corner pillars, but fixed by the Pullman Co Ltd.

Following details of the interior furnishings and fittings, comes the specification for the

> UNDERFRAME: The underframe to be of timber well jointed and secured by

strong tie bolts and knees, consisting of two pitch pine soleboards 7" x 5" and four pitch pine longitudinals $5\frac{1}{4}$" x 4" running the whole length of the body, four main crossbars of teak $6\frac{1}{2}$" x 5" passing from two solebars 8" by $4\frac{1}{8}$" flitched by $\frac{3}{8}$" plates on either side, two headstocks of $\frac{5}{16}$" pressed steel plates, two crossbars of 8" x 4" flitched by $\frac{3}{8}$" plates on either side and four longitudes 6" x 3" properly secured together with knees and tie bolts.

A bolster consisting of three teak beams 10" x $4\frac{7}{8}$" and flitched by $\frac{3}{8}$" steel plates securely bolted together is mounted on elliptical springs which are bedded on to a spring plank of teak 1'$4\frac{1}{2}$" x 3" carried by adjustable suspension links with I.R. shock absorbers which transmit the weight at the crossbars through brackets secured to same, the load being transmitted from thence by coil springs to equalising beams which transfer the weight again to the journal through the medium of the axlebox. A rubber pad 9" x 4" x 1" to be fixed to solebars opposite ends of bolsters.

The axleguards are made of cast steel, bolted to the solebars, a wrought iron stretcher connecting them together and to the headstocks. These stretchers to be arranged to take two cross ties holding them together.

AXLEBOXES: The axleboxes to be of cast iron modelled on the S.E. & C. Rly. standard type fitted with bearings of Stone's bronze and lined with Stone's Railway White Metal, also spring lubricating pads. The centre pivots and bottom side friction blocks of cast steel to be provided.

WHEELS: The wheels and axle to be of standard wood centre type 3'6" diameter on tread and 9" x $4\frac{1}{2}$" diameter journals.

STEPS: To obtain the proper clearance going round curves, the lower step boards will be fitted to the bogie.

From the above, the care taken to obtain a strong and sturdy vehicle will be appreciated. One turns now to passenger comfort.

INTERIOR: The interior of the cars to be of specially approved designs and furnished in the following selected woods:

One parlour car in Almond
" " " " Satinwood
One Buffet Car in Curled Mahogany
" " " " " "
" " " " Amboyna

The Lavatories, Vestibules, and lavatory and kitchen portions of corridor to be finished in solid mahogany panelling.

CEILINGS: The ceilings of the passenger compartments to be of 3 ply veneer, $\frac{3}{16}$" thick, covered with 'Tynecastle' and suitably decorated with carved wood mouldings, with the exception of the kitchen and larder which will be red deal, the former being covered with alluminium [sic] sheets. The whole of the 3 ply ceilings to be backed with $\frac{3}{8}$" red deal sheeting.

FLOOR COVERINGS: The floors of the passenger compartments and the portion of the corridor adjacent to same to be covered with carpet of approved colour and make, each carpet for one compartment being woven in one piece and secured with tacks. Underfelt for carpet, also canvas runners 18" wide to lay down when cleaning are to be provided.

Above Wall marquetry in a First Class Pullman car. The effect was gained by carefully cutting veneers from different kinds of wood and fitting them together like pieces of a jigsaw puzzle. *Author*
Below The Pullman coat-of-arms woven into the carpet in the entrance vestibule of *Barbara*, preserved on the Kent & East Sussex Railway at Tenterden. *Author*

The floors of the vestibules, lavatories and lavatory and kitchen portion of corridor to be covered with India Rubber Tiling, black and white interlocking pattern, $^3/_8$" thick.

The following fitments are required in all the passenger compartments:

(1) Removable tables with glass tops, metal fixing brackets and floor bolts and sockets, also small tables for one passenger where required. Each table to be provided with a thick green cover to prevent heat attacking the polish on the woodwork. All tables for three or more passengers to be of an approved extending type.

(2) Arm chairs finished and upholstered to match interior decoration of compartments, with head covers and dust covers for same: hassocks to match carpet and strips covered with carpet to prevent chairs coming in contact with panelling.

(3) Parcel racks, hat and coat hooks, electric bell pushes, seat numbers, electric ceiling and wall-bracket lights, and standard table lamps with silk shades, all to be of standard designs.

(4) Carpet covered foot rests over heater pipes.

A pair of Third Class seats in a preserved Pullman car. Note that the seat next to the gangway tips up to allow access to the seat by the window - something that the single table-leg also facilitates. *Author*

Top The polished brass bag-and-umbrella rack above the window of a First Class car. *Author*
Above The rather simpler style of baggage rack above the window of a Third Class car. Note that the curtains do not pull right across to meet each other, as in a First Class vehicle. *Author*
Right A roof lamp mounted in a brass imitation torch socket. Note that the frieze also bears marquetry. *Author*

(5) Damask silk blinds for each side and corridor partition window, of standard quality and design.

(6) Clock in each Buffet Car from H. Hughes & Son.

The whole of the metallic furniture in the passenger compartments to be of mercurial gilt finish, the remainder of the fittings to be of polished brass. In the Buffet cars a cabinet with mirror back and shelves to be fitted into the cross-partition adjacent to the larder. Shelves to be covered in plush to match furniture.

LAVATORIES: The lavatories will be fitted with white porcelain W.C. with push valve and flushing cistern and wash basic complete with Hot and Cold Water Supply, both supplied by Messrs Twyfords Limited. Cupboards for soiled and clean towels, hat and coat hooks, bell pushes, grab handles and mirrors, suitably disposed. The Cold Water Supply to be contained in an overhead copper tank, to be made to take up and down. All lavatory doors to lock.

KITCHEN: The kitchen to be fitted with one gas-cooking suite, with combustion chamber and plate warmer, and gas pressure gauge, one large sink, and drain board, the sink to be zink [sic] lined throughout, one chopping board and all necessary cupboards, shelving, etc. Hot and Cold Water to be laid on to the sinks and the Cold Water Supply to be from an overhead copper tank. The cooking suite to be supplied by Messrs Fletcher, Russell & Co Ltd of Warrington, and the supply of gas to same to be contained in reservoirs carried under the underframe. Adjustable side ventilators to be fitted in the top portion of the kitchen lights, together with all necessary 'Torpedo' ventilators. The lining of the kitchen throughout, including ceiling, to be of alluminium [sic] sheets not painted.

In the corridor partition a sliding hatchway to be provided for serving purposes.

A Larder complete with all necessary shelves, cupboards. Removable serving table and a large sink is to be provided adjacent to the kitchen and easily accessible through the corridor by means of a sliding door. The floor of the kitchen and larder to be of 'Decolite'. All shelves throughout Car to have ledges to prevent falling of utensiles [sic].

All kitchen utensils, glass, cutlery, napery, etc, etc, to be provided by the Pullman Co Ltd.

There is much else in the specification, which goes into further details about the compartmentation of cupboards and the provision of detachable fittings, which it would be wearisome to include. Enough has been quoted to show the thoroughness with which a new Pullman car was planned. *Topaz*, one of the cars being referred to, is illustrated.

For nearly half a century the pattern did not much alter; a Pullman car was recognisably similar in the early 'fifties to what it had been just before the First World War, except that there was a tendency for them to be made a few feet longer than the ones referred to in the specification, which were 59 ft 8 ins in length between buffer faces.

The best way of getting a satisfactory impression of what these vehicles were like to travel in is to see one for oneself. Quite a few are to be found on preserved railways, such as the Bluebell Line at Sheffield Park or the Kent & East

Above *Topaz*, a First Class Parlour car built for the SE&CR in 1914 and shown here in the maroon livery that company favoured. *NRM, York*
Below *Topaz* as repainted in post-1930 umber and white Pullman livery and seen from the opposite side. Note the addition of holders for roof-boards. *NRM, York*

The Pullman look: *Top Juno,* built in 1923, was one of the cars used in the 'White Pullman'/Golden Arrow between 1924 and 1939. It was later converted to a Third Class car and used on the Devon Belle. *Above Minerva,* built in 1927 for use on the LNER, and rebuilt in 1951 with oblong toilet windows for use on the post-Second World War Golden Arrow. *Top right* Third Class brake No 81, built in 1930 and used in LNER pullman trains. *Right* Third Class Car No 34, used on the Golden Arrow between 1951 and 1962. *all Lens of Sutton*

Sussex Railway at Tenterden - or if one is willing to part with a very considerable sum of money one can take an excursion in the rake of restored Pullman cars used by the Venice-Simplon-Orient Express Company for the Victoria-Folkestone part of their route to Venice, which fill up their waiting time by going on trips to selected destinations such as Bath, Salisbury or the Kent Coast. Failing personal experience one has to make do with photographs, and I

The interior of First Class car *Irene*, built in 1923 and used on the Queen of Scots. The tables are laid for luncheon. Note the ornate cover of the roof ventilator and the marquetry-surrounded mirrors on the partitions. *NRM, York*

have endeavoured to provide a selection of interior shots.

In some respects the Pullmans were unlike any other contemporary coaches (though in the late 'twenties the GWR attempted to build saloon carriages for use on the long-distance trains to the West of England which were obviously modelled on the traditional Pullman - even to the extent of being given names). One recalls the inward-opening doors, which were always operated by the attendant and *never* opened unless the train was at a standstill at a station platform. One's memory dwells on the sumptuous interior furnishings, especially the marquetry on the walls. One appreciated the large windows, through which from one's seat one could look not only out, up and around, but also down towards the permanent way, since the glass-topped tables were several inches above the level of the window-ledges. This was very helpful if one were trying to time a train; it was much easier to sight a milepost from a Pullman window if one were on the track adjacent to the lineside than from the much smaller and higher-placed window of a compartment-coach.

One remembers the Pullman attendants in their dark blue trousers and short white monkey-jackets with light blue lapels. My memory may be behaving selectively, but I remember them as having sleek dark hair cut short, and somewhat saturnine expressions. One remembers the toilet interiors, somewhat larger than customary in a railway carriage, with much polished metalwork and polished rubber-tiled floors; thus, one felt, it must be in places like Buckingham Palace. Most of all one remembers the table lamps with their pink shades.

Some variations in detail showed themselves as time passed, notably the increasing use of steel in the bodywork. There were of course considerable modifications needed when a Third Class car was built, or rebuilt from a former First Class one. A Third Class Pullman car was comfortable enough - certainly much more so than the usual Third Class compartment provided on most lines where, if there were three-a-side seating, only one seat would be beside a window, and in which the dividing arm rests were mere cloth-covered bars that could be pushed back into the upholstery and were expected to be pushed back if the train were crowded, so that people could sit four-a-side. The Third Class Pullman traveller had head rests and sizeable arm rests, as well as the convenience of a table. However, there had to be *some* lessening of the luxury which a First Class passenger enjoyed; the ambience within the saloon interior was not quite so reminiscent of upper-class gracious living, nor were the marquetry patterns and brass fittings quite so artistically fashioned. In regard to such things as these, however, one was to notice, in cars built after the Second World War, some simplification of decoration in line with changing public taste, as can be seen by comparing like with like in some of the photographs in this book. Such changes will be mentioned in later chapters.

8

The Thanet Pullman

1921-28

The Isle of Thanet (so-called, for it has long ceased to be separated from the rest of Kent by a slowly-silting branch of the Stour) has three main seaside resorts and one or two lesser ones, which 70 years ago were separated by intervening countryside but now form almost a single conurbation from Westgate-on-Sea right round to Pegwell Bay. Nowadays Thanet sends thousands of commuters to the capital daily and receives them back in the evening; it has an hourly multiple unit express service over electrified track connecting it with Victoria, as well as special business expresses to Cannon Street.

Back in the 'twenties it was more remote. Margate, Broadstairs and Ramsgate attracted tourists on Bank Holidays and during the summer months, who perambulated their promenades and piers and refreshed themselves in their cafés; off-season, however, Thanet was nothing like as populous as it is now. A rural countryside lay behind the coastal resorts, where one could come across ancient churches and the remains of Roman fortresses, as well as a public house which unblushingly advertised 'Free Beer To-morrow' on a permanently painted sign.

Margate was the more popular resort, Broadstairs the more select, Ramsgate the terminus of the former London Chatham & Dover line, somewhere between the two in social grading. They had been important enough places to be the destinations of named trains in the past, such as the Granville and Cliftonville Expresses, but the SE&CR had not, until a year and a half before its absorption into the SER, thought to send any luxury vehicles in their direction. Who, the company's directors might well have asked, would want to go to Thanet of all places by First Class Pullman car, when its resorts were lower in the social desirability scale than any of the seaside towns on the South Coast?

However, the example set by the LB&SCR on the western side of Victoria Station evidently affected its neighbour on the eastern side. In July 1921 individual First Class Pullman cars, each flanked at either end by ordinary First and Third Class coaches, began to operate daily in trains between Victoria and Ramsgate, calling *en route* at the principal North Kent coast resorts from Whitstable onwards. These were not specially aimed at the day tourist, but in the same month a Sundays-only Thanet Pullman Limited, composed of six First Class cars, still in the maroon livery favoured by the SE&CR, together with a luggage van, set off from Victoria at 10.10 am with Margate as the first stop.

Accommodation was limited to a maximum of 124 passengers, for each of whom an inclusive return fare of £2 2s 0d was charged. Return was at 5.30 pm from Ramsgate. One could hardly suppose that such a train would be a money-spinner for the company, since it could not expect to fill to capacity every Sunday of the year, for the north-facing and east-facing Thanet resorts were not so attractive in winter time as to ensure heavy patronage. Was it perhaps put on purely for prestige reasons, to keep up with the LB&SCR Joneses?

What was really surprising about this train was its fast schedule. Only once before had a regular service been booked between London and Margate in as little as 90 minutes either way. At the time it was introduced the Thanet Pullman had one of the most demanding schedules in the British Isles, even though its average speed was not quite 50 mph. The route was hilly, with long banks as steep as 1 in 100 over the first part of the journey. The whole stretch from the Medway Bridge at Rochester to Gillingham through Chatham had to be negotiated with caution, and there was a slack at Faversham for the curve on to the North Kent line. In contrast with the 90 minutes taken by the Eastbourne Sunday Pullman between Victoria and its destination, over a route 10 miles shorter and with easier gradients, this was a tough task with a 200-ton train.

Fortunately a locomotive type of adequate power had just been produced. R.E.L. Maunsell and his design team at Ashford had faced up to the challenge of providing a new brand of passenger engine light enough to be able to travel over the former LC&DR main line (along which there were many weight restrictions over underline bridges which had not been built to support heavy axle-loads and which it would take many years to strengthen) yet forceful enough to tackle the Continental boat expresses from London to Folkestone and Dover. These latter trains were now using that line over the first 12 miles out of Victoria before diverging on to the old SE&CR route near Petts Wood. Maunsell's solution to the problem had been to rebuild some of Wainwright's existing 'E' Class 4-4-0s, which had been built some 15 years earlier, giving them more up-to-date front-end arrangements in the cylinders and valves to enable steam to be used more expansively and to ensure it got into and out of the cylinders more readily. At the same time much non-essential metal was cut away from the frames and other structures in order to lighten the load on the engines' axles.

These new 'E.1' Class engines came into service between February and July 1920, and showed that they could easily cope with Continental trains which had formerly needed to be double-headed. The six-car Thanet Pullman would be manageable, even on a 90-minute timing to Margate, by such a locomotive, and from the beginning the train was entrusted either to a single 'E.1' or a very similar rebuilt 'D.1' 4-4-0 re-fashioned from one of the slightly earlier 'D' Class during 1921.

As an all-Pullman train with First Class accommodation only, the Thanet Pullman Limited did not have a long life. It survived the winter of 1921-2, but at the end of the following summer it was combined with a rake of ordinary coaches, the number of First Class cars being reduced to correspond with the lessened custom. In regard to this alteration, the SE&CR was somewhat coy. It advertised the two elements as separate trains which left Victoria at the same time - whereas in fact they were combined and hauled by the same engine. An extra stop was added, at Westgate-on-Sea, and a portion was slipped at Faversham, so that the train took 10 minutes longer to reach Margate. This remained the arrangement during the autumn, winter and spring months, but with the coming of summer the two parts ran separately again, the all-Pullman portion reverting to its former 90-minute timing.

Arrival and departure times varied somewhat from year to year. When the SR absorbed the SE&CR it altered the return time at Ramsgate from 5.30 to 7.05 pm, but in 1925 it was put back by 5 minutes, and the following year by another 10 minutes. Departures from Victoria also varied between 10.00 and 10.15 am. In 1923 there was a surprising reduction in the all-in return fare, to £1 4s 0d - the cost of a First Class single ticket by any other train. These changes, made apparently to attract custom, applied only to the summer service.

The Thanet Pullman Limited eventually faded out. It made its final all-Pullman run on 30 September 1928. The following summer the combined train ran in its place, continuing until 28 June 1931, with a timetable note that 'Thanet Limited Cars (First Class)' were included in its formation. From 5 July onwards no mention was made of the title; there were one or more First Class cars in the train, and that was all. Thus the Thanet Pullman expired - to be resuscitated under another name nearly 17 years later, as will be described in a subsequent chapter.

9

The Clacton Sunday Pullman and Eastern Belle

1922-39

In 1914 the Great Eastern Railway acquired a new General Manager, Henry W. Thornton, an American by birth, all of whose railway experience had been gained in the United States. Among the new ideas he brought with him was the deployment of Pullman cars in selected trains. Hitherto, apart from the early experiments by the MR and GNR already alluded to, they had not been used north of the Thames, but Thornton evidently believed that on the GER they could prove a passenger attraction.

He had some justification for this belief; not only were they a familiar sight in the USA, where many railroad companies had contracts with the Pullman Car Company of Chicago, but in England the Brighton line had been using them profitably for some years, and there were similarities between it and the GER. Both reached out beyond intensively-used suburban networks to a coast-line sprinkled with holiday resorts, which in the case of the latter line were sited all around the East Anglian shore from Southend-on-Sea to Hunstanton. Both ran a well-patronised Continental service, that from Liverpool Street to Holland and Belgium by way of Harwich matching that of the LB&SCR from Victoria to Paris by way of Newhaven. Furthermore, just as wealthy patrons were accustomed to travel on race-meeting days to Epsom and Goodwood by special Pullman trains, so they might equally be persuaded to go to Newmarket in the same way. What was sauce for the Victoria goose might also be expected to suit the Liverpool Street gander.

It was Thornton's misfortune to have signed on with a company which, at the time of his appointment, had only eight years of independent life left, four of them in the hampering circumstances of the First World War (though he himself personally profited from them, obtaining a knighthood for his contribution to the national effort). The decision to amalgamate the several independent British railway companies into four larger ones, which came into force on 1 January 1923, caused the great man to shrug his shoulders and accept an offer to take up the post of President of the Canadian National Railways. Before he went, however, he had negotiated contracts between the GER and the Pullman Car Company of Great Britain, and the summer timetable for 1922 shows how the cars were used when they first entered service.

They ran singly or in pairs between London and the seaside resorts of

Above The Clacton Sunday Pullman on its morning down run from Liverpool Street, hauled by rebuilt superheated 'Claud Hamilton' 4-4-0 No 1818. W. J. *Kohning, The Railway Magazine*
Below An advertisement from *The Railway Magazine* of 1922.

G. E. R.

SUNDAYS BY THE SEA
THE CLACTON PULLMAN
NON-STOP EXPRESS.

Every Sunday.

Liverpool Street	dept.	10.0 a.m.	Clacton-on-Sea	arr.	11.37 a.m.
Clacton-on-Sea	dept.	5.10 p.m.	Liverpool Street	arr.	6.45 p.m.

DAY RETURN FARES
including Pullman Car supplementary charge

1st class 28/- 3rd class 14/-

Season Ticket and ordinary ticket holders can travel by this train upon payment of the Pullman Car supplementary charge of :—2/6 1st class and 1/9 3rd class in each direction.

MEALS AND LIGHT REFRESHMENTS
served on the train.

Seats can be booked in advance at the Liverpool Street Booking Office, or at the Company's West End Ticket and Information Bureau, 71, Regent Street, W. 1.

Cromer, Yarmouth and Clacton-on-Sea on weekdays - curiously, on some trains only Third Class Pullman accommodation was on offer - while the nightly Continental expresses to Harwich, connecting with the steamers to the Hook of Holland and Antwerp, each had a pair of First Class cars as well as a complete assemblage of non-Pullman coaches of both classes, including restaurant and kitchen cars. In the down direction the addition of two heavy First Class Pullman vehicles made the Hook of Holland Continental the hardest proposition that any GER express engine had to face, with its considerable weight and sharp 82-minute schedule from Liverpool Street to Parkeston Quay, Harwich, but it was a prestige train hauled by selected engines, and time was usually kept.

What did not appear in the timetable, but was separately billed, was the Clacton Sunday Pullman, composed entirely of Pullman cars of both classes. Like the Thanet Pullman and the Eastbourne Pullman it was aimed at the day tourist market, an all-in fare being charged (£1 8s 0d First Class and 14s 0d Third Class) for the out-and-home journey on the same day. Ordinary First and Third Class ticket holders were permitted to travel in it if there were seats available, and were charged an additional 2s 6d and 1s 9d respectively. Departure was at 10.00 am from Liverpool Street with a Clacton arrival at 11.37; the return was at 5.10 pm from Clacton, reaching London at 6.45. These were not rapid schedules - they could not compare with the 90-minute run of the Thanet Pullman from Victoria to Margate - but the route was not easy. The GER main line had originally been laid down as cheaply as possible, so that there were many short, sharp gradients as well as a number of moderate or severe slacks *en route*.

During its short life the train does not seem to have attracted the attention of timers, which is not surprising; a merely timekeeping run would no doubt have been a dull affair. In any event, the GER had never been noted for the speed of its trains, one or two prestige services excepted. The Pullman no doubt suited the sedate requirements of the average Sunday day tourist, who could drink a leisurely cup of coffee on the way down and, if he wished, enjoy a Pullman dinner on his return with plenty of time in which to do so.

As a Sundays-only train the Clacton Pullman lasted no longer than the 1922 summer season. Once the control of the main lines out of Liverpool Street had passed to the Board of the LNER the whole question of the deployment of Pullman cars came under review. It was decided that a better use could be found for them than dispatching them to the East Anglian coast in ordinary service trains, and some re-negotiations were entered into with the Pullman Car Company, resulting in a number being transferred to be used on the main line out of King's Cross - as will be described in the next three chapters. The cars on the Continental services were, however, retained.

Six years later the LNER decided to re-introduce the Clacton Sunday Pullman service. It ran successfully during the 1928 summer season, and the following year was brought back to run to a 90-minute schedule, out in the morning and back in the evening as before. This time, however, a more intensive use of the cars was decided upon, and a new name bestowed on the unique service in which they were engaged.

Whereas the Thanet Pullman had succumbed to adverse economic circumstances, the new Eastern Belle became the instrument of a more assertive policy. The cars during weekdays, excluding Saturday, were to be used for 'Excursions de Luxe' at very low fares, going to a different holiday resort each day; the changes were rung of Dovercourt, Felixstowe, Aldeburgh, Lowestoft, Yarmouth, Cromer, Sheringham, Hunstanton, and even Skegness, which was outside the ambit of the former GER. Fares of either 6s 6d or 7s 6d, Third Class, and half as much again First Class, were charged according to whether the journey was a shorter or a longer one.

Considering that the longest of the runs, the 145 miles from Liverpool Street to Skegness by way of Cambridge, Ely, March, Spalding and Boston, took about 3¼ hours each way, this indicated that the Third Class excursionist would be carried at less than a third of a penny a mile, or a penny for each 4½ minutes of seat-occupancy - and that in a Pullman car, not an ordinary coach.

There was nothing like this anywhere else in the country; it was far cheaper than ordinary Third Class travel. Furthermore, passengers were offered the use of the train throughout the whole of any week in return for buying a season ticket costing £1 5s 0d Third Class and £1 17s 6d first, during which time they could visit five different resorts. I never found myself able to make use of one of these tickets, but there must have been many impecunious junior clerks like myself who spent their week's annual holiday in this manner.

While at first the schedules of the Eastern Belle, to whichever destination it was bound, were not very fast, the general speed-up of train services on the LNER from 1933 onwards affected it, and from 1934 to 1939 it made faster times than before. Whenever it was booked through Ipswich it was allowed only 79 minutes for the 68¾ miles. If it were going to Cromer or Sheringham it had to pass Trowse Junction, just outside Norwich, in 128 minutes for the 114 miles from Liverpool Street, which was 6 minutes faster than the pre-war booking of the famous Norfolk Coast Express, the GER's flagship service. The time allowed to Felixstowe, 84½ miles, which required very slow running through and beyond Ipswich, was only just over 2 hours. Going down to Aldeburgh, a non-stop run of 78 minutes to passing Ipswich was the fastest time ever booked over that section. On the Skegness journeys no fireworks were possible because of the many slacks which had to be observed, but 107 minutes non-stop from Liverpool Street to March was the quickest timing known so far.

The train began to operate each year at or around the end of May, and ran during a full four months of the year. With such schedules locomotives of adequate power were needed, and a 4-6-0 was generally provided, at first one of the ex-GER inside-cylindered type, either in its original state or as rebuilt by Gresley, but later on the newer three-cylinder 'Sandringhams' were used.

I have a personal memory of travel on the Eastern Belle, in 1937. For some reason I had a day off work, possibly to celebrate the King's birthday; the Civil Service was very decent on such occasions then, and either gave you a day off or paid you more for working. I chose an occasion when the train was going to

Above A 'Sandringham' on the Eastern Belle; No 2800 *Sandringham* itself has just arrived at Clacton-on-Sea in June 1929. *LCGB, Ken Nunn Collection*
Below The Eastern Belle on one of its weekday excursions, hauled by ex-GER 'B.12' 4-6-0 No 8509. The ungainly-looking device behind the chimney is part of the experimentally-fitted Worthington feed-water heating apparatus. *Steamchest*

Cromer. It left in mid-morning, and I managed to get a single Third Class seat on the left-hand side of the train, from which I could easily sight the mileposts. I took a log of the journey, which (like the Norfolk Coast Express) was non-stop to North Walsham, and I remember that we kept time with our seven-car load, the engine being a rebuilt 4-6-0. At Cromer the station was high above the town, and a strong cold north wind was blowing straight off the sea. With four or five hours to put in, I did not feel any inclination to go sight-seeing. I had not come suitably clad to avoid wind-chill, so I made for a fish-and-chip shop and stayed there as long as I decently could, carefully transcribing the rough log of the down journey into the ledger in which I kept my fair copies of train-performance records. (It was lined out for cash transactions, but made a most useful repository for logs, with mileages going where dates were intended, station names etc in the information space, and minutes, seconds and speeds in the £sd columns.)

Eventually I strolled round the shops, bought a few souvenirs, and made my way back up the hill to the station and rejoined the train. I cannot remember much about the return journey, since the strong sea air and the fish-and-chips had made me drowsy; I began timing the train, but dozed off, missed some timing points and gave up. On my return home my mother inquired where I had been, and after I had told her she thought I was crazy. However, it had only cost me eight and sixpence, and on the whole I had enjoyed it.

10

The Sheffield Pullman Limited

1924-25

Most of the 'de luxe' trains so far dealt with or alluded to in this book were introduced to cater for leisure traffic to well-patronised holiday resorts. However, when the newly-formed London & North Eastern Railway put on a special all-Pullman train to Sheffield in 1924, holiday traffic was clearly not what its Board of Directors had principally in mind. No one goes to Sheffield to relax or recuperate; it is one of Britain's largest industrial cities, specialising particularly in steel products and famous for its cutlery. It would seem that the LNER wished to provide a businessman's train.

Even a Third Class Pullman car offered better facilities to a business executive than a compartment in an ordinary coach. Apart from the comfort of the seating and the excellent lighting from the large windows, there was the glass-topped table, complete with shaded lamp, on which papers could be spread out, so that one might conveniently do a certain amount of work during the journey - and if one needed occasionally to refresh one's jaded faculties (and what businessman does not?) one had only to press a button and the attendant would come and take one's order.

The former GNR, now absorbed into the LNER, had had a tradition of running a specially fast service to Sheffield from King's Cross, which had been stimulated originally by competition with the Midland Railway operating from St Pancras and the Great Central from Marylebone. In the later years of the previous century it was running expresses, very lightly loaded though of extremely comfortable stock, between King's Cross and Sheffield which took only a few minutes over 3 hours either way to or from the capital, and at the head of these trains Patrick Stirling's famous single wheelers had done some of their best running. Then, with the extension to London of the GCR, which had signalled its entry to the Metropolis by inaugurating a non-stop service that at first took only 2 hours and 50 minutes to and from Sheffield (though this timing was too optimistic and had later to be eased), the GNR was again stirred first to compete and later to co-operate with its rival. In 1910 it was running a 'Special Through Dining Car Express' which reached Sheffield in exactly 3 hours, a stop being made at Grantham to change engines; here a GCR locomotive took over from the usually provided Ivatt 'Atlantic' and hauled the train over the second half of its journey, continuing beyond Sheffield across the

Pennines by the Woodhead tunnel route to Manchester, which was reached in a fraction over 4 hours - almost as fast a service as the MR could offer from St Pancras by its shorter route through Derby. However, the outbreak of the First World War put an end to all this enterprise.

Once the amalgamations of 1923 had been accomplished, the newly formed LNER was minded to renew the former tradition. It had suitable locomotive power for hauling a fast light train, for many of the Ivatt large-boilered 'Atlantics' had now been superheated and their performance had greatly improved in consequence. It also had Pullman cars available, inherited from the former GER, which could be given a more extensive use on the main line to the North. Sheffield seemed the obvious place to aim at.

The train assembled for the new service was a five-car rake of Pullmans, of which only one was a First Class car; this meant that six times as many Third Class as First Class passengers could be carried - a much higher proportion than was customary in the case of leisure traffic. (The practice of business executives going First Class, and justifying this by claiming that the efficient performance of any work they did *en route* required such accommodation, was still in the future. Class of travel then depended on position in society. I recall that in HM Customs and Excise, in which during the later 'thirties I was a very junior official, one had to go very high up the promotional ladder before First Class rail journeys were a permitted expense which could be refunded if one were travelling on duty.) Supplements for the whole journey were 6s 0d each way to

The speed of the down Sheffield Pullman defeats the camera as it runs between New Barnet and Hadley Wood on 2 June 1925, hauled by Ivatt 'Atlantic' No 3284, *en route* for Sheffield and Manchester via Retford. *LCGB, Ken Nunn Collection*

Sheffield First Class and 3s 6d Third Class.

The route, too, was unusual. The GNR had built a branch from Grantham to Nottingham which ran by way of Bottesford Junction to link with the former GCR route south of Arkwright Street station, thus enabling through running into Nottingham (Victoria), and thence by the GCR route through Hucknall and Staveley to Sheffield (Victoria). The Grantham-Nottingham line required a severe slack beyond Grantham station, and was not otherwise well suited to express running, so speeds along it had to be moderate; beyond Nottingham, too, the line was very steeply graded, and also to some extent affected by colliery subsidences which made reductions in speed necessary. A 3-hour timing to Sheffield by this route was therefore not possible, but the fact that the new train would also serve Nottingham promised to offer additional custom, since in the down direction it was 10 minutes quicker than the mid-morning express to that city from St Pancras, and its corresponding competitor in the up direction in the early evening was slower still.

The new train entered service on 2 June 1924. It was fast as far as Grantham (where it did not stop) but afterwards distinctly on the slow side. Similar timings prevailed on the return journey. Unlike the special express of 1910 it left London in the morning and returned in the evening. The schedules were:

Down:		Up:	
King's Cross	dep 11.05	Sheffield	dep 16.45
Peterborough	(pass) 12.26	Nottingham	arr 17.34
Grantham	(pass) 13.00		dep 17.38
Nottingham	arr 13.28	Grantham	(pass) 18.09
	dep 13.32	Peterborough	(pass) 18.39
Sheffield	arr 14.20	King's Cross	arr 20.00

There were some curiosities in the passing times. On the outward run, the Hatfield to Hitchin stretch, largely uphill, required an average of 61 mph, and from Hitchin to Huntingdon 67½ mph was expected, whereas there were no pass-to-pass averages as high as 60 mph required on the up journey, though between Grantham and London it was 4 minutes faster than in the opposite direction.

Within a month this service was completely altered in regard to the times of day when it ran, though the point-to-point timings were not altered. The expected customer out from and back to London did not sufficiently materialise, so the pattern was changed to reverse the morning and evening directions. Overnight stabling of the cars was transferred to Sheffield; the train ran up to London in the late morning and returned during the evening. It was now the Sheffield and Nottingham business communities whose interests were being considered, not those in London, though only 4 hours were available in the capital in which to do business if one were to use the Pullman both ways. The altered service continued till the following spring, the timings now being:

Up:		Down:	
Sheffield	dep 10.30	King's Cross	dep 18.05
Nottingham	arr 11.19	Nottingham	arr 20.28
	dep 11.23		dep 20.32
King's Cross	arr 13.45	Sheffield	arr 21.20

Intermediate passing times gave the same intervals as before.

Again, patronage turned out to be disappointing, especially where Nottingham was concerned, and the decision was taken to re-route the train north of Grantham and run it by way of Retford and the former Great Central line, first to Sheffield and then onwards to Manchester. This was the route taken by the 'flyers' of 1910. In this way it was hoped that the very slight amount of custom which Nottingham had generated would be more than replaced by a much greater use by the Manchester business community. There was also some acceleration between London and Sheffield, to a 177-minutes non-stop run in each direction.

Since over half an hour was needed to cover the slack-infested 23 miles from Sheffield to Retford, which ends with a curve on to the main line so sharp that it could not be taken at more than 10 mph, the journey between London and Retford was fast in both directions. The timings now were:

Up:		Down:	
Manchester	dep 09.50	King's Cross	dep 18.05
Sheffield	arr 11.00	Sheffield	arr 21.02
	dep 11.03		dep 21.05
King's Cross	arr 14.00	Manchester	arr 22.12

The train ran from and to Manchester Central station, not London Road, which added 6½ miles to the journey and something like 12 minutes in extra journey time, so that it could not compete with similar expresses running to Manchester from Euston and St Pancras at about the same hour in the evening. This may have affected the use made of it to that city. From Sheffield to London and back the Pullman did provide the fastest time on offer, but a mere 4 hours in London was scarcely long enough in which to transact much business. So once more the patronage was disappointing.

Quite a number of locomotive types were used on this train. At first Ivatt large-boilered 'Atlantics' were given the duty, and coped easily. Later ex-GCR engines were given the job. One of the 'Sir Sam Fay' Class of inside-cylindered 4-6-0s was sometimes used; a 4-4-0 'Director' was often chosen. There was no change of locomotive during the journey. How successful these engines were in keeping time with the Pullman is not known; I have not been able to discover any published logs. No doubt the 'Atlantics' and 'Directors' gave good accounts of themselves; one cannot feel so sure about the 'Sam Fays', which never fulfilled their designer's hopes, being somewhat sluggish through having firegrates whose rear ends easily got choked with ash.

At the Ordinary General Meeting of the Pullman Car Company in April 1925 Sir Davison Dalziel, its Chairman, informed shareholders that the Sheffield Pullman had 'met with considerable public support'. The phrase was perhaps deliberately vague, intending to pull the wool over his hearers' eyes. In fact, the train had been anything but successful, and at the time when he made the announcement the LNER was already considering the second change, to omit Nottingham and serve Manchester. This third pattern of use endured only over the summer months of 1925. In September the service was discontinued altogether and the Pullman cars were included in a train which served the West Riding of Yorkshire.

Thus for the time being the experiment of giving Sheffield its own Pullman train service ended. As will be seen later, however, this city did have a potential market for such a service, as also did Manchester. The first Sheffield Pullman was before its time and 35 years had to elapse before a second and successful attempt to run such a train was made.

11

Pullman trains to Harrogate and Scotland

1923-39

The acquisition of a stock of Pullman cars intended originally for service on the GER posed for the newly-formed LNER the question of where they could best be used. As already seen, one possible route was to prove unremunerative. However, even before the Sheffield Pullman began its short career another all-Pullman train from and to King's Cross had already been inaugurated, which was eventually to become the country's most celebrated long-distance luxury train.

Unlike the GWR, which served four important spa towns, and the LMS which served three, the LNER had only one of any size within its ambit, Harrogate, which shared with several South Coast resorts the distinction of attracting affluent retired people as residents. It was England's most northerly spa. Though it could not offer the amenities of a seaside resort, or the all-the-year-round mild climate of a south-country watering place, it had its own cultural life and was the gateway to some of the best scenery in the Yorkshire Dales. It also lay on a loop-route (part of which has now been dismantled) from King's Cross to the North, which diverged from the East Coast Main Line at Doncaster and took in the cities of Wakefield, Leeds and Ripon as well as the spa of Harrogate before re-joining the main line at Northallerton. Harrogate itself had one daily through service to London by way of Leeds, but no trains from the south went beyond it.

The initiative in regard to providing the Pullman service to Harrogate appears to have come from its Corporation, according to the LNER's General Manager, Mr (later Sir) Ralph Wedgwood, who at the celebratory dinner at the town's Majestic Hotel, where various LNER officials were being entertained on the Saturday evening before the introduction of the service, said in the course of a speech that '... the Harrogate Corporation came forward with their proposal for a Pullman train service which should combine the last thing in luxury with the best thing in speed, [and that] they had found the Railway in responsive mood.'

However, Harrogate was not to be only favoured town. The LNER did not lose the opportunity of serving Leeds also and continuing the train northwards so that it provided a link for both with Tees-side and Tyneside. The route was several miles longer than that via York, and more heavily graded over the loop section than over the main line, so the Corporation's wish to have 'the best thing in speed' could hardly be realised, but the town was certainly brought several minutes nearer both to King's Cross and Newcastle. It was hoped that the added luxury of Pullman accommodation would attract both residents in and visitors to Harrogate, and with an eye to this the train was entitled The Harrogate Pullman Limited. It began to operate in July 1923.

In regard to its timings, it was quicker than other main-line expresses as far as Doncaster, and faster than any previous service as far as Leeds, which was reached in 3 hours 25 minutes. At Leeds Central it was necessary to reverse, another locomotive being attached to the other end of the train to take it on to Newcastle. It then climbed to Bramhope tunnel, descended to cross the Wharfe, ascended steeply once more, rounded the sharp curve over Crimple viaduct and so reached Harrogate. Over this short 18-mile stretch there were not only severe gradients but several permanent service slacks, so that a half-hour timing was not really excessive. Beyond Harrogate the line went steeply downhill to cross the Nidd, after which there was a halt at Ripon. The gradients then levelled out, the main East Coast route was re-joined at Northallerton, and the train proceeded to Newcastle, stopping only at Darlington. Routing it by way of Leeds added some 40 minutes to the journey, the extra distance being 12½ miles. The 1923 schedule, including principal passing times, was as follows:

Down:		Up:	
King's Cross	dep 11.15	Newcastle	dep 09.20
Hatfield	(pass) 11.38	Darlington	arr 10.00
Hitchin	(pass) 11.52		dep 10.14
Huntingdon	(pass) 12.17	Ripon	arr 10.46
Peterborough	(pass) 12.35		dep 10.47
Grantham	(pass) 13.08	Harrogate	arr 11.08
Newark	(pass) 13.23		dep 11.15
Retford	(pass) 13.42	Leeds	arr 11.45
Doncaster	(pass) 14.02		dep 11.50
Wakefield	(pass) 14.24	Wakefield	(pass) 12.07
Leeds	arr 14.40	Doncaster	(pass) 12.30
	dep 14.45	Retford	(pass) 12.48
Harrogate	arr 15.15	Newark	(pass) 13.08
	dep 15.20	Grantham	(pass) 13.24
Ripon	arr 15.34	Peterborough	(pass) 13.54
	dep 15.35	Huntingdon	(pass) 14.13
Darlington	arr 16.10	Hitchin	(pass) 14.40
	dep 16.13	Hatfield	(pass) 14.55
Newcastle	arr 17.00	King's Cross	arr 15.15

The train attracted more custom than the Sheffield Pullman was to do the following year, and between its inception and wartime cancellation in 1939 increased in popularity, so that the original pair of six-car rakes were increased to seven-car ones. In one of the latter each car had a kitchen section so placed that it adjoined a paired car; in the other, one First Class car had no kitchen section and four more seats than its neighbours. In either rake the Third Class cars each held 33 passengers except for one which, having no kitchen, held 39. Curiously those cars which ran on six-wheel bogies were all Third Class cars, whereas all the First Class vehicles had four-wheel bogies; the former were rebuilds from First Class cars of an older design, and were built entirely of timber, whereas the newer ones had steel underframes. Each Third Class car had two saloons, a pantry and a lavatory compartment. Each First Class car had a four-seat coupé at one end.

In the autumn of 1925 a change was made in the timetable. The stop at Leeds was omitted, since the vehicles of the discontinued Sheffield Pullman were being used to give Leeds and Bradford a Pullman train of their own, which left King's Cross in the northbound direction a little ahead of the Harrogate train, and in the other direction arrived in London an hour and a half earlier. (This train is dealt with in the next chapter.) The Harrogate Pullman accordingly took a different and somewhat unusual route in either direction beyond Doncaster, by way of Shaftholme Junction, Knottingley, Ferrybridge, Church Fenton and Tadcaster; part of this diversion was over LMS metals. The mileage was actually shorter than that through Leeds, and entailed no reversal, so Harrogate was reached in 5 minutes less time, and Darlington 10 minutes earlier. The train was also extended to serve Edinburgh. From September 1925 the timings were as follows:

Down:		Up:	
King's Cross	dep 11.20	Edinburgh	dep 08.30
Harrogate	arr 15.03	Berwick	arr 09.43
	dep 15.08		dep 09.45
Ripon	arr 15.22	Newcastle	arr 11.05
	dep 15.23		dep 11.12
Darlington	arr 15.59	Darlington	arr 12.01
	dep 16.01		dep 12.04
Newcastle	arr 16.50	Ripon	arr 12.42
	dep 16.57		dep 12.43
Berwick	arr 18.17	Harrogate	arr 12.59
	dep 18.20		dep 13.03
Edinburgh	arr 19.35	King's Cross	arr 16.45

Both down and up trains took the same time between the two capitals. Despite the detour and the five intermediate stops the Pullman took no longer over the whole distance than did the Flying Scotsman, which had only four stops; the latter's leisurely schedule was the consequence of an agreement still being maintained by both the East and West Coast route companies to keep the minimum time between London and Edinburgh at 8¼ hours.

PULLMANS TO THE NORTH

WEST RIDING PULLMAN

		A.M.			A.M.
KING'S CROSS	dep.	11.10	HARROGATE	dep.	11.15
WAKEFIELD (Westgate)	arr.	P.M. 2a18	HALIFAX (Old)	,,	11. 8
LEEDS (Central)	,,	2.40	HALIFAX (North Bridge)	,,	11.11
BRADFORD (Exchange)	,,	2.55	BRADFORD (Exchange)	,,	11.35
HALIFAX (North Bridge)	,,	3.21	LEEDS (Central)	,,	11.50
HALIFAX (Old)	,,	3.24	WAKEFIELD (Westgate)	,,	P.M. 12b13
			KING'S CROSS	arr.	3.20

HARROGATE-EDINBURGH PULLMAN

		A.M.			A.M.
KING'S CROSS	dep.	11.20	EDINBURGH (Waverley)	dep.	8.30
		P.M.			
HARROGATE	arr.	3. 3	NORTH BERWICK	,,	8c38
RIPON	,,	3.25	DREM	,,	8.56
DARLINGTON	,,	3.59	BERWICK	,,	9.47
NEWCASTLE	,,	4.50	NEWCASTLE	,,	11.14
BERWICK	,,	6.17			P.M.
DREM	,,	7c 8	DARLINGTON	,,	12. 5
NORTH BERWICK	,,	7.21	RIPON	,,	12.38
EDINBURGH			HARROGATE	,,	1. 5
(Waverley)	,,	7.35	KING'S CROSS	arr.	4.45

NEW WEEK-END PULLMAN

SATURDAYS ONLY. (Commences 16th July.)		P.M.	SUNDAYS ONLY. (Commences 17th July.)		P.M.
KING'S CROSS	dep.	4.50	HARROGATE	dep.	3.15
LEEDS (Central)	arr.	8.15	LEEDS (Central)	,,	3.50
HARROGATE	,,	8.50	KING'S CROSS	arr.	7·15

All First and Third Class
Usual Pullman Charges

a—Connecting trains arrive Dewsbury 2.47 and Batley 2.52 p.m.
b—Connecting trains leave Batley 10.39 and Dewsbury 10.45 a.m.
c—Passengers to and from North Berwick change at Drem.

QUICKEST AND MOST LUXURIOUS ROUTE

An advertisement for East Coast Pullman services in a 1927 issue of *The Railway Magazine*.

An account of a journey on the Harrogate-Edinburgh Pullman soon after it was re-routed appeared in *The Railway Magazine* for January 1926. The article is unsigned but appears to have been the work of the Editor, J. F. Gairns, and looks like a space-filling exercise since it is well padded out with irrelevant material. Gairns was evidently impressed by the standard of comfort and the service provided, and some details emerge from the verbiage. Only one First Class car was now included in the formation. The six-coach train, weight 255 tons tare and headed by Ivatt 'Atlantic' No 3274, reached Harrogate 3 minutes early; a somewhat slow start to Finsbury Park was followed by fast running between Hitchin and Peterborough and a good climb to Stoke summit, so that despite a cautious approach Doncaster was passed ahead of time. At Harrogate a newly-built Gresley 'Pacific' took over the train, and lost time through delays between Northallerton and Darlington, none of which it was able to recover.

At Newcastle an ex-NER 'Z' Class 'Atlantic' replaced the 4-6-2 and made a time-keeping run to Berwick, but on the last stage to Edinburgh it ran a little too easily and arrived half a minute late.

In May 1928 the service was altered again. The rather prosaic title previously given was replaced by the more attractive appellation of the Queen of Scots, by which it continued to be known through the rest of its existence. The train was once more routed by way of Leeds, since the other Pullman train serving that city had been given an evening path in the northbound direction and no longer ran just ahead of the train to Edinburgh. The up Queen of Scots also received a later path, leaving Edinburgh at 11.15, so that it became the mirror-image of the down train. The Berwick stop was omitted, but a halt at Drem in both directions, which had been introduced during 1926 for the benefit of passengers going to or from North Berwick, a 'quality' dormitory town for Edinburgh and seaside resort on the southern shore of the Firth of Forth, continued to be made. Finally the train was extended beyond Edinburgh to serve Glasgow (Queen Street). This lengthened the total journey to about 440 miles. No doubt few passengers made the trip end-to-end; the extension was for the convenience of Glaswegians going to or from Tyneside, Tees-side and Leeds.

The 1928 schedule remained in force until May 1932. In that month a general progressive acceleration began to affect all the chief expresses of the LMS and LNER companies. The agreement to keep the minimum time between London and Edinburgh to not less than 8¼ hours was terminated by mutual consent, and along with other trains the Queen of Scots was given quicker timings, first of 8 hours between the two cities, then (from May 1933) 7 hours 55 minutes, then (1936) 7¾ hours, the same intermediate stops being made with the exception of Ripon, to or from which an insufficient number of people appeared to want to travel. The schedules were now as follows:

Down:		Up:	
King's Cross	dep 11.20	Glasgow	dep 10.20
Leeds	arr 14.31	Edinburgh	arr 11.15
	dep 14.35		dep 11.20
Harrogate	arr 15.04	Drem	dep 11.43
	dep 15.07	Newcastle	arr 13.40
Darlington	arr 15.51		dep 13.45
	dep 15.52	Darlington	arr 14.33
Newcastle	arr 16.37		dep 14.34
	dep 16.41	Harrogate	arr 15.20
Drem	arr 18.40		dep 15.23
Edinburgh	arr 19.05	Leeds	arr 15.51
	dep 19.10		dep 15.55
Glasgow	arr 20.13	King's Cross	arr 19.05

The regular loading of the train was now two first and five Third Class cars.

Locomotives were now changed three times in each direction, at Leeds,

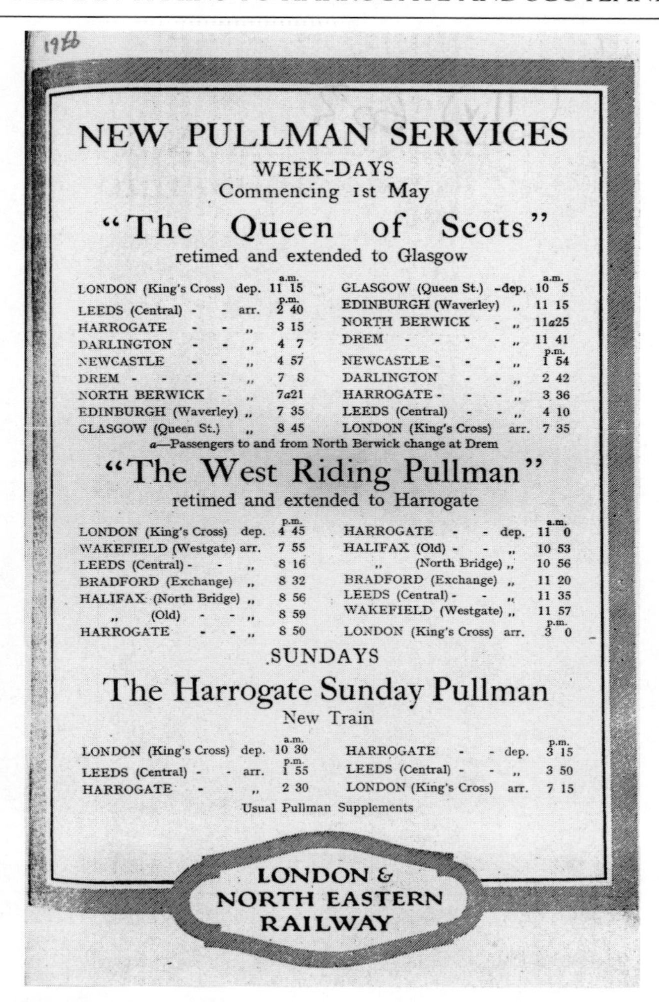

A May 1928 LNER advertisement from *The Railway Magazine*.

Newcastle and Edinburgh. North of Leeds the usual haulage during the 'thirties was by a Gresley 'Pacific', and onwards from Edinburgh, over the flat and easily-timed stretch to Glasgow, by a 4-4-0 'Director' of the batch built by Gresley for service in Scotland. South of Leeds the Ivatt 'Atlantics' continued to be used. Since the southern part of the run was the fastest, it may seem surprising that engines which in some instances were 25 years old should be employed on this section. This was due to the exigencies of locomotive supply, and in fact the older engines proved well able to keep or regain time. The Pullman link was a prestige duty reserved for well-maintained locomotives and experienced crews. In the trains's earlier days GCR four-cylinder 4-6-0s and two-cylinder 'Director' 4-4-0s were at times used in place of 'Atlantics', but the former were

A variety of motive power on the Queen of Scots. *Above left* Ivatt 'Atlantic' No 4419 nears London with the up train. The locomotive as rebuilt by Gresley is fitted with 'booster' cylinders on the trailing truck. Note the external piping taking steam to the boosters under the footplate; the boosters were only employed when the train was starting, recovering from a slack or climbing a heavy gradient. A. C. *Cawston Collection, NRM, York* *Left* In 1930 the Pullman ascends Cowlairs incline behind 'Director 4-4-0 No 6401 *James Fitzjames*. *LCGB, Ken Nunn Collection* *Above* 'A1' (later 'A3') 'Pacific' No 2571 *Sunstar* at Low Fell, south of Newcastle, in 1935. *LCGB, Ken Nunn Collection*

always running short of steam, while the 'Directors' could only just cope with the long non-stop run and had little in reserve, so in the end only large-boilered superheated ex-GNR 'Atlantics' were used.

The Queen of Scots did not much attract the attentions of train timers north of Leeds, where the schedules posed no problems for the 'Pacifics', but south of Leeds it was much noticed by the railway cognoscenti, and Cecil J. Allen in his *Railway Magazine* articles frequently included logs of its running sent in by correspondents. After the accelerations of 1935 some of the 'Atlantic' performances were very fine indeed. It would require too much space to include a number of these logs here, but one may mention three and give brief details.

In the up direction, working to the 1932 schedule of 195 minutes, with 'Atlantic' No 3284 and a 325-ton train, Driver Payne recouped nearly 4 minutes of a late start in spite of as many as six signal checks and a permanent way slack, achieving a net time of 181$^{1}/_{4}$ minutes, with maximum speeds of 85 mph near Carlton-on-Trent and 88 at Essendine, and minima of 60 at Markham, 48 at Stoke and almost 50 at Stevenage - the latter would have been higher had it not been for a 40 mph check at Sandy. On the 1935 schedule with No 4456 and a train one coach lighter, despite encountering three signal checks, a permanent way slack and a special stop at Peterborough to take water (as Werrington troughs were temporarily out of action) Driver Worboys managed to keep time with half a minute to spare. He set out to gain as much time as possible before having to stop at Peterborough, and topped Stoke summit at 55 mph, after which he averaged 90 for 2 miles on the subsequent descent. After refilling his tender tank he continued to King's Cross in one minute less, start to stop, than the pass-to-stop schedule laid down, with minima of 57 up Abbots Ripton bank, 53½ at Stevenage and 69 at Potters Bar, the maxima at Huntingdon and near Hatfield being 79 and 82 respectively. The net time on this run was only 176 minutes.

In the opposite direction, on the 191-minute schedule, with No 4423 and a load of 290 tons, Driver Rogers lost only half a minute despite three signal checks, two of them severe, and a permanent way slack. Maximum speeds were 90 mph beyond Hitchin and 83½ near Claypole; minima were 55½ beyond Huntingdon, 48½ at Stoke and 56 at Markham; net time was 183¼ minutes. These were typical runs, so speed recorders were likely to enjoy some thrills on this train south of Leeds; on the northern sections, with similar loads but more powerful engines running to easier timings, performances did not need to be so energetic.

I have a personal memory of a run on the up train, made in 1937, when we gained a couple of minutes behind an 'Atlantic' with the usual seven-coach load, despite a couple of slacks; we attained 85 on the descent from Stoke. I have unfortunately lost the log I made of the entire journey, but I recall that when I approached the driver's cab to congratulate the crew and ask for their names I was unable to get near them, since several bowler-hatted business men had got there first and were expressing their appreciation. The drivers on these Pullman trains were among the élite locomotive men of the LNER and included such notable characters as Sparshatt, the first one to reach 100 mph with an unrebuilt Gresley 'Pacific', and Duddington of 126 mph *Mallard* fame. More than any other Pullman train in Britain the Queen of Scots offered train-timing excitements as well as journeying comforts.

The advent of the streamliners between 1935 and 1937 put the Queen of Scots Pullman somewhat in the shade, but did not lessen its popularity or the patronage it enjoyed. It ran right up to the outbreak of the Second World War, and them, like its historical namesake at Fotheringhay Castle in 1586, was axed, the cars being put into store for the duration.

12

Pullman trains to West and East Yorkshire

1925-39

The LNER's decision to introduce a second all-Pullman train to serve the chief towns and cities of the West Riding of Yorkshire was made after two years' experience with the Pullman train to Harrogate and Newcastle had shown it to be a profitable venture, whereas the experiment with a similar service to Nottingham, Sheffield and Manchester had proved to be a loss-maker. Discontinuing the latter had set free a sufficient number of Pullman cars to make a second such service possible. Like the Queen of Scots (except during the two years of the latter's divergence through Ferrybridge and Church Fenton) it was to run to Leeds Central and reverse there; part of the train was then to proceed to Bradford and Halifax, while the other part went on empty to Harrogate. (Why *empty* is explained below.) There was also to be a stop at Wakefield before reaching Leeds. In this way the four principal centres of population and industry in the West Riding would have their own Pullman link with London and would, it was hoped, generate enough traffic to make the service a paying proposition.

The northbound service was timed to leave King's Cross 10 minutes ahead of the Edinburgh train, and take 5 minutes longer to Leeds to allow for the stop at Wakefield. The southbound train was more or less a mirror image of its fellow. Both began to operate in September 1925. The timings were as follows:

Down:		Up:	
King's Cross	dep 11.10	Halifax	dep 11.08
Wakefield	arr 14.18	Bradford	dep 11.35
Leeds	arr 14.40	Harrogate	dep 11.15
Bradford	arr 14.55	Leeds	dep 11.50
Halifax	arr 15.24	Wakefield	dep 12.13
		King's Cross	arr 15.20

It will be noted that passengers were conveyed *from* Harrogate in the up direction but that there was no corresponding down service. The latter was not needed since the Harrogate-Edinburgh Pullman catered for travellers to that town from London. On the return journey, however, the two Pullman trains ran in paths an hour and a half apart, so that the one service did not duplicate the other.

This arrangement continued until May 1928, when there was some re-casting of timetables. The train, now named the West Riding Pullman, had its northbound departure from London delayed until the late afternoon, so that a single rake of cars could operate the service in both directions. This had the advantage not only of economising in the use of stock, but also giving businessmen in West Yorkshire the opportunity of a convenient and comfortable journey home after a day's work in the capital. The schedule now became:

Halifax	dep 10.53	King's Cross	dep 16.45
Bradford	dep 11.20	Wakefield	arr 19.55
Harrogate	dep 11.00	Leeds	arr 20.16
Leeds	dep 11.35	Bradford	arr 20.32
Wakefield	dep 11.57	Harrogate	arr 20.50
King's Cross	arr 15.00	Halifax	arr 20.59

This, it will be observed, restored the northbound service to Harrogate, there being now no reason to avoid duplicating a facility since the service by the Queen of Scots was almost 6 hours earlier. With two Pullman services from London each way daily, the Yorkshire spa was now as well favoured as Brighton. A slight acceleration of the train in the northbound direction will also be noticed.

The up West Riding Pullman near Potters Bar in April 1933, hauled by Ivatt 'Atlantic' No 4459. *Steamchest*

In the summer of 1929 the Harrogate portion of the train was extended to Darlington and Newcastle, in timings similar to those of the Queen of Scots, the latter city being left in the morning at 9.10 and reached again in the evening at 10.25 pm, so that for a short while both these places also enjoyed two all-Pullman links with London each day.

This remained the pattern for the next six years, until in the autumn of 1935 the first of the LNER's non-Pullman streamlined extra-fare trains, the Silver Jubilee, was introduced. Its timetable slot, both northbound and southbound, closely paralleled that of the West Riding Pullman so far as Newcastle and Darlington were concerned. Consequently the latter train reverted to serving the West Riding towns only and went no further north than Harrogate. It also included a Hull portion, a stop being made at Doncaster in either direction to attach or detach it. It was now re-named The Yorkshire Pullman. From September 1935 the service ran as follows:

Up:		Down:	
Halifax	dep 10.32	King's Cross	dep 16.45
Bradford	dep 10.59	Doncaster	arr 19.22
Harrogate	dep 10.40	Hull	arr 20.15
Leeds	dep 11.14	Wakefield	arr 19.52
Wakefield	dep 11.36	Leeds	arr 20.13
Hull	dep 11.10	Harrogate	arr 20.45
Doncaster	dep 12.04	Bradford	arr 20.30
King's Cross	arr 14.40	Halifax	arr 20.57

This, apart from a one-minute quickening of the times between Doncaster and London either way a year later, which brought both runs into the mile-a-minute category, remained the pattern for the next four years until the whole-sale cancellations of September 1939.

With the added cars for Hull, one First Class and one Third Class, the Yorkshire Pullman had now become quite a heavy train, with a load of up to 11 coaches, and the 'Atlantic' haulage which had at first been sufficient now gave place to that by Gresley 'Pacifics', which proved well able to keep time. My own personal recollections of travelling on this train include a complete end-to-end journey in the Hull portion when I was travelling back from my home to my place of work in the port. The train was well filled, and the only seat I could secure was in a Third Class coupé compartment right at the rear of the train; it was not next to a window, and darkness had already fallen when we left King's Cross, so I was not able to make a log of the journey, which was extremely comfortable and entirely uneventful; we were on time both at Doncaster and Hull.

The following summer I also made five trips on the Hull portion between Doncaster and that city using a 'Runabout' ticket which covered that stretch of line, 40½ miles, over which the two Pullmans were allowed 45 minutes non-stop - a timing only recently equalled by HST services going to or from London with a stop at Brough. This midget of a train, weighing several tons less than the GNR 'Atlantic' which always hauled it, could be relied on, I hoped, to provide some interesting performances if for any reason the train from London were late in reaching Doncaster and there was time to be made up. The route was level but had a number of service slacks at junctions and across the bridge over the Humber near Goole, so brisk running would be needed and I anticipated some spurts exceeding 80 mph. However, there were no late arrivals of the main train to stimulate such efforts. Being young and brash, I made a point of contacting the driver each time, to say I would be timing the train, to which on four out of five occasions they good-humouredly responded by giving me a time-keeping run. On the fifth, however, a grumpy driver read me a lecture on the inadvisability of running faster than necessary merely to gratify a young recorder's whim, and was careful to teach me a lesson by losing a quarter of a minute on the journey.

The pre-Second World War West Riding Pullman and Yorkshire Pullman did not attract much attention from train performance recorders, particularly after 'Pacifics' replaced 'Atlantics' at their heads. There were other and faster trains now to engage the attentions of the stopwatch brigade, notably the Silver Jubilee, Coronation and West Riding streamliners. However, the solid values of comfort and service which the Pullmans provided ensured that it was they, rather than the new flyers, which returned when the war had ended, and which ran eventually, after the introduction of the legendary 'Deltic' diesels, on timings faster than ever before.

The Pullman trains to Scotland and the West Riding were weekday services, but Pullman travel on Sundays was an established thing on the Central and Eastern Sections of the SR. The old prejudice against journeying on the Sabbath had now largely died out, and, quite apart from the day tourist, people wishing to take a longer holiday often found it a convenient day on which to go or come back - especially since it was usual then to work on a Saturday morning. Harrogate, moreover, had a considerable population of retired well-to-do persons - natural 'Pullman fodder', if the term be permitted, who might well prefer to go on holiday or return home on a day when trains were unlikely to be filled with people going on business. In 1927 the LNER decided to employ some of its available Pullman cars in a 'New Week-end Pullman' to Harrogate, calling at Leeds in both directions. During its first season it left King's Cross late on Saturday afternoon, returning the following day; the timings were as follows:

Down: (Saturday)		Up: (Sunday)	
King's Cross	dep 16.50	Harrogate	dep 15.15
Leeds	arr 20.15	Leeds	dep 15.50
Harrogate	arr 20.50	King's Cross	arr 19.15

At the end of the summer season the train was discontinued, but re-introduced the following May. A change was now made; it ran on Sundays in both direc-

"THE YORKSHIRE PULLMAN"

Hull & London in 3½ hours

Every Weekday

		a.m.			p.m.
Halifax (Old) -	dep.	10 32	King's Cross -	dep.	4 45
Bradford (Exch.)	,,	10 59	Doncaster -	- arr.	7 22
Harrogate - -	,,	10 40	Hull - - -	,,	8 15
Leeds (Central) -	,,	11 14	Wakefield (Westgate) -	,,	7 52
Wakefield (Westgate) -	,,	11 36	Leeds (Central) -	,,	8 13
Hull - - -	,,	11 10	Harrogate - -	,,	8 45
		p.m.			
Doncaster - -	,,	12 4	Bradford (Exch.) -	,,	8 30
King's Cross -	arr.	2 40	Halifax (Old) -	,,	8 57

OTHER PULLMAN LIMITED TRAINS

"The Queen of Scots" Weekdays: King's Cross, Leeds, Harrogate, Darlington, Newcastle, Drem, Edinburgh (Waverley) and Glasgow (Queen Street).

"The Harrogate Sunday Pullman" King's Cross, Leeds, Bradford and Harrogate.

LONDON & NORTH EASTERN RAILWAY

The Harrogate Sunday Pullman makes an appearance in an East Coast Pullman advertisement in the November 1935 *Railway Magazine*.

tions, leaving King's Cross at 10.30 and taking 4 hours to Harrogate as before. It was now entitled The Harrogate Sunday Pullman. The 205-minute allowance to Leeds, on a day when extensive track-possession for maintenance was quite common, would not exactly have conduced to time-keeping; in the opposite direction it would not have mattered so much, as during the latter part of the run track possession would have ended.

The train became well-established and popular, so it was continued during the winter months and became an all-the-year-round service. In the summer of 1930 a Bradford portion was added. In September 1931 the departure time from King's Cross was made half an hour earlier, probably in the interests of time-keeping (since the turn-round time at Harrogate was only three-quarters of an hour and late arrivals on the down train would be apt to delay the return departure). The up train, however, kept its previous times. The service remained in this pattern until it ended abruptly when the Second World War broke out.

Records of the running of this train are naturally somewhat scarce, since after 1931 its northbound schedule was too leisurely to invite attention, while coming south, while the timing between Leeds and London was originally as fast as that of the Queen of Scots on weekdays, it was never accelerated and remained at 205 minutes for the 185½ miles. On the up train meritorious runs were occasionally made in the interests of time recovery. In his book *Great Northern 4-4-2 Atlantics* O. S. Nock cites a run of good quality on a day when high winds hampered progress, and when permanent way checks and signal delays experienced all the way to Grantham put the train 10 minutes behind time at this point. The engine, No 3251, the first large-boilered 'Atlantic' to be built on the GNR and now 30 years old, with an eight-car train weighing 325 tons full, then regained 6¾ minutes, running as if on the regular Queen of Scots schedule. The finest work was done from Peterborough onwards, with notable minima of 51½ mph at Stevenage and 59 at Potters Bar, 80 being almost attained on the descent beyond. A year later, with a load lighter by a single vehicle, No 3280 ran even faster from Peterborough to Hitchin and achieved a net time between Leeds and London of 186½ minutes, 3½ minutes less than the schedule then in force with the Queen of Scots. Fast Sunday running was then not at all usual, and credit must be given to the keenness of the footplate men who were so expert at handling these old Ivatt 'Atlantics' and enduring without complaint the very rough rides their footplates provided.

The down Harrogate Sunday Pullman near Potters Bar in August 1930, headed by Ivatt 'Atlantic' No 4461. ***LCGB, Ken Nunn Collection***

13

The first Golden Arrow

1924-39

Most of the all-Pullman trains already referred to ran mainly to cater for excursionists or holidaymakers within England, who preferred to travel in style and were ready to pay more in order to do so. With the ending of the First World War another luxury market appeared. It became fashionable once more to visit Paris. Although one had to cross the Channel to do so, which meant that a single de luxe train would not suffice, co-operation between the railways in England and France, the Southern Railway and the Chemin de Fer du Nord, could provide a linking pair of them so long as there was a suitable boat service to ply between the Channel ports. London was still the principal centre for business and commerce in Europe, and Paris was the cultural capital, attractive to the visitor at all times and especially in the spring. It had recently been the gathering place for famous persons from all over the world, attending the Versailles Peace Conference that settled the affairs of Europe following the war. It was also the gateway to the south of France, the Riviera and Italy. A daily luxury train between the two cities promised, therefore, to be a paying proposition.

Chief among the supporters of such a venture was Sir Davison Dalziel, soon to be ennobled as Lord Dalziel of Wooler, whose unusual experience at the Dover quayside when he was a young man has already been narrated. He was now eminent in the business world and had influence on the Continent, being Chairman of the Pullman Car Company of Great Britain and also of the *Compagnie Internationale des Wagons Lits*. He could therefore effectively promote his schemes on both sides of the Channel. It was, however, necessary first to await the amalgamation of the British railway companies into four groups. After that came the reorganisation of the SR's Continental services over the former SE&CR's main line, with departures and arrivals concentrated on Victoria and a pattern of seven daily services to one or other of the Channel ports, the mid-morning departure from London and the corresponding noon departure from Paris being the principal ones which attracted the wealthier style of passenger.

In November 1924 pressure from Dalziel persuaded the SR authorities to introduce on this service a train of First Class Pullman cars which, together with an ordinary First Class brake coach to provide accommodation for the

The up 'White Pullman', later to be named the Golden Arrow, headed by 'King Arthur' 4-6-0 No E773 *Sir Lavaine*.

guard, two vans and two flat-topped trucks to take the sealed containers for registered luggage, made up a maximum tare weight of some 450 tons when traffic was at its heaviest. When the demand was less some of the Pullmans were withdrawn and the weight could then fall to rather over 300 tons. At first the de luxe element in the service obtained merely between Victoria and Dover, only ordinary First Class accommodation being provided on the French side. But Dalziel was busy exerting his influence, and a year later two more trains of British-built Pullman cars were put into service between Paris and Calais to connect with the boat, and these were given the title *La Flèche d'Or*. The train between London and Dover had to wait for a while before receiving the corresponding title in English; officially it was known as the Dover Pullman Continental Express; colloquially it was termed 'The White Pullman', a reference to the fact that the cars composing it were not maroon in colour, as Pullman vehicles on the SE&CR had always been and, on the Eastern Section of the SR, in some cases still were, but had received the new Pullman colours, umber below window-level and white above.

So far the service was 'de luxe' only in regard to the trains, and there was no added quickness of travel. To make it really attractive to its élite customers a special connecting boat was needed. This was outside Dalziel's scope, but the SR authorities were moving in the matter, and its Board eventually agreed to acquire a new steamer, to be used exclusively for passengers on the Pullman service, and one was ordered from a Clydeside shipbuilder. It was launched in

December 1928, named *Canterbury*, and delivered to the railway company at Southampton the following March. Two months later it commenced service on the Dover-Calais crossing in connection with the Pullman trains. It was a fine vessel, matching the Pullman cars in luxury, possessing a special 'Palm Court' lounge, a dining saloon seating 100 people, a large number of deck cabins for those who wanted privacy, and many screened alcoves on the decks to give shelter from the wind.

However, the chief element in the provision of added comfort was the vessel's size. It was large enough (329 feet long and 47 feet across the beam) to carry over 1,700 passengers, whereas the trains that connected with it could not hold more than about 250 passengers even if all the seats were taken. So there was space in abundance during the crossing, and though in rough weather those with queasy stomachs might have to endure the inescapable discomforts of seasickness, they could at least suffer in private. Moreover, the ship was a fast one, capable of a maximum speed of 22½ knots, so the crossing time could be shortened. Paris was reached in just over 6½ hours, with a 20-minutes wait at Dover and 15 minutes at Calais. Now at last the train on the English side was given its title, to correspond with the French one, and the timetable referred to it as the Golden Arrow.

This exclusive de luxe service, in which Pullman passengers travelled in advance of ordinary passengers on a quicker schedule, lasted for only two years. The winds of adverse financial change had already begun to blow even as the *Canterbury* took her first passenger complements in the summer of 1929. The following October the share collapse on Wall Street in the United States heralded a trade depression which gradually spread to all countries and affected all classes. For the poorer elements in society it meant real belt-tightening as salaries and wages were cut. (My own salary as a junior clerk went down from £60 to £50 a year.) For the more affluent it meant that one did not so readily indulge in superfluous luxury. The patronage of the Golden Arrow declined. Only two years after its inauguration it was announced that a single sea-crossing would have to serve both the Pullman passengers and those in the ordinary boat train which preceded or followed the Arrow; the *Canterbury* now carried them all between Dover and Calais. A slight reduction was made in the all-in fare charged to Pullman passengers, and there was a small increase in journey time on the French side of the Channel, bringing passengers into Paris 5 minutes later. The service in the opposite direction was similarly decelerated.

There was worse to follow. A year later, in May 1932, the Pullman element in the service was diluted by the addition of ordinary First and Third Class coaches, and only one train was run instead of two or more. By now the trade recession was biting hard, and the number of passenger journeys being made across the Channel had dropped by over a third. Prestige had to give way to prudence. On the French side the *Flèche d'Or* element consisted of both First and Second Class Pullmans. Together with them some *Wagon Lits* sleeping cars were taken for destinations beyond Paris. On the English side the number of First Class Pullmans was reduced to allow for the addition of ordinary First and

The 'Golden Arrow Limited' makes its appearance in an advertisement that appeared in the December 1929 issue of *The Railway Magazine*.

Third Class carriages. As an all-Pullman train, the Golden Arrow, though still bearing that title, no longer existed.

Three years later a further deterioration took place. Whereas a single rake of coaches sufficed for the double journey to Dover and back on the English side, on the French side it had so far been necessary to provide two, which passed each other going in opposite directions somewhere in the vicinity of Boulogne.

Clearly economies could be effected if only one rake were used, and in October 1935 the London-bound service was re-timed to leave Paris an hour and a half earlier, at 10.30, and set down its passengers at Boulogne, there to take the cross-Channel boat for Folkestone, while the empty cars proceeded to

Calais 25 miles further on to collect the southbound passengers who had crossed on the *Canterbury*. While the Paris-bound service was not much affected by this change, that in the other direction became slower and less convenient. The crossing could not be made in the *Canterbury* but in another vessel lacking all its special appointments, and the voyage took a quarter of an hour longer. At Folkestone Harbour the rake of Pullmans and ordinary coaches was waiting, there having been plenty of time for it to be brought there from Dover, but before it could begin its passage to Victoria it had to be pushed and pulled by small tank engines up the 1 in 30 incline of the Harbour branch; the seated passenger,instead of enjoying the seaward view and the sight of the famous white cliffs, had instead the prospect of the rears of the Folkestone houses whose back yards faced the line - not quite such an inspiring sight. At Folkestone Junction the train was handed over to an express locomotive, London being reached at 5.20 pm in 6 hours 50 minutes from Paris if the boat had arrived on time. If not, the Maidstone route between Ashford and Bickley might be taken instead of the more direct way through Tonbridge, and a full 2 hours would then be required for the journey to Victoria.

This remained the pattern of operations over the next four years. In November 1938 the train underwent some alterations in external appearance. A new passenger livery had been determined upon, with a brighter green for both locomotives and ordinary coaches, though no change was made to the livery of the Pullman cars. Four 'Lord Nelson' 4-6-0s were now reserved for the haulage of the Arrow and other Continental expresses. This was the final phase in the rise and decline of the pre-War Golden Arrow. Less than 10 months later the Second World War broke out and the train was taken out of service, the Pullman cars going into store for the duration.

The first Golden Arrow was thus a train dependent on favourable economic circumstances for its success, and the times were not propitious. Not only the slump of the early 'thirties, but also the increasing use of aircraft to convey passengers from London to Paris in a third of the time that the train-and-boat service required, limited its period of exclusive 'de luxe' splendour to a mere two years.

So far as speed was concerned it was never a record-breaker. When the first 'White Pullman' began running a full 100 minutes were required for the journey from Victoria to Dover Marine; nothing faster was possible since the 4-4-0 locomotives deputed to haul it needed every second of that time even when the minimum load was taken. With the introduction of the 'King Arthur' 4-6-0s the time came down to 98 minutes, but still well below the 50 mph average. These engines could just about cope with 450-ton loads on that timing. The difficulties came principally at each end of the journey. The start from Victoria was tricky, with half a mile at 1 in 60 straight from the platform end, and some banking assistance was usually given here. Then came the climb to Penge tunnel entrance, which included some short but steep pitches. After that there was not much chance to get going again before speed had to be slackened round the curve beyond Bickley to join the SER main line from Charing Cross at Petts

The down Golden Arrow approaches Dover Marine on 22 September 1930 hauled by 'Lord Nelson' 4-6-0 No E851 *Sir Francis Drake*. LCGB, Ken Nunn Collection

Wood. The climb to Knockholt summit followed at once.

After Knockholt a good rate could be attained down the banks before and after Sevenoaks, but a severe slack for the curve before Tonbridge then followed. From there to Headcorn speed could be worked up into the sixties along a straight though by no means level main line. Rising gradients then followed to the summit at Westenhanger, with a short intermission through and beyond Ashford. No sooner had speed recovered on the subsequent downhill stretch than a prolonged slowing was necessary from the Martello tunnel all the way to Dover, along that part of the route which had been affected by the landslide of 1915. Had the boat trains been as light as at the beginning of the century, speed recovery from slacks could have been more rapid, and schedules similar to that of the 80-minute Folkestone expresses would have been possible, but they had instead to be tailored to suit much heavier trains.

In the opposite direction the going was a little easier. The restriction between Dover and the Martello tunnel was less hampering on an up grade, and there were no more service slacks before Tonbridge so that speeds in the Headcorn dip might rise into the upper seventies. The climb from Tonbridge to Knockholt, begun at a low speed, was tough - 12 miles with only one short downhill intermission, and once past the summit one was only 4 miles away from the sequence of slacks and steep banks between Bickley and Victoria.

When the train was given its name in 1929 the schedule was quickened to 95 minutes - still below the 50 mph average - but it never became any faster in pre-Second World War days. The actual times of departure and arrival did not change much except, as already mentioned, in the case of the up afternoon service from October 1935 onwards. The usual time of the southbound departure from Victoria was 11.00 am, but in 1926 during the summer months the all-Pullman train left 10 minutes earlier, and in September of that year 10.45 became the regular time. When the *Canterbury* came into service the departure time once more became 11.00 am and remained thus until the service was withdrawn in 1939. Arrival at Dover then became 12.35 and continued so. In the other direction Dover was left at 4.57 pm until May 1929, when it was delayed 3 minutes to 5.00, Victoria being reached at 6.35 pm. The later start from Paris in and after May 1931 delayed the departure from Dover to 5.25, Victoria being reached at 7.00 pm. The subsequent switch to the Boulogne route brought the London arrival time forwards to 5.20. This involved a lengthening of the time forwards from Folkestone Harbour to a full 100 minutes, but this did not really represent a slowing of the schedule; the extra time was necessary for the manoeuvring of the heavy rake of coaches, vans and trucks up the steep incline to Folkestone Junction.

In the days of the 'White Pullman' locomotive provision was at first limited by the permitted axle-loadings over the Victoria-Bickley Junction section, and rebuilt 'E.1' Class 4-4-0s of the former SE&CR were used - in pairs if the load were heavy. Once the underline bridges had been strengthened at the London end of the journey the use of newly-built 'King Arthurs' obviated the need for double-heading, and the later introduction of 'Lord Nelsons' provided a little more power, though too few of them were built to replace the 'King Arthurs' entirely, so that the schedule had always to be one which the latter could manage to keep.

Not many logs of boat train performance appear to have been published during the inter-war period, and one may suppose that not many were made, for this was not a train on which an enthusiast could travel with a day return ticket; to travel to Dover he had to book to Paris! In his book *The South Eastern & Chatham Railway* O. S. Nock mentions, however, having in his possession 36 logs of performances on Continental trains by rebuilt 'E.1s', made by a previous recorder, and says that they were tricky engines to handle in contrast to what they had been before rebuilding. He gives an example of 'E.1' performance on the 'White Pullman':

> On one occasion the 41.4 miles from Tonbridge to Folkestone Junction was covered in 41¾ minutes, with an average speed of 59 mph over the generally rising length from Paddock Wood to Sandling Junction. This was with engine No 19 and a load of 294 tons tare ... The cut-off was 30 per cent throughout, and the regulator partly open. Boiler pressure was maintained very steadily at 175 lbs per square inch from Tonbridge until nearing Ashford, but all the time the cylinders were gradually beating the boiler and water level was falling steadily. From a full glass at Tonbridge the level had fallen by 3 ins at Pluckley, but a brief closing of the regulator due to Ashford West distant signal being sighted at caution, and a couple of minutes with both injectors on, restored the water level. This procedure, however, set the boiler pressure on the downward path, though after

> Smeeth, with the end of the hard work in sight, the firing was being eased. This was a classic example of the way a steam locomotive can be run for an appreciable period beyond its maximum sustained capacity by a careful and systematic mortgaging of the boiler. The speeds during this fine spell of running were 65 mph at Paddock Wood, 69 at Staplehurst, a minimum of 57 at the top of the long gradual rise from Headcorn towards Ashford, 60 through Ashford and a final minimum of 50 mph at Westenhanger.

This gives some indication of running with this train when it was headed by a 4-4-0, with a skilled footplate crew going all-out to regain time.

Of 'King Arthur' performance on the Pullman, again there is not very much to report. When these engines were introduced to the Eastern Section main line they were at first by no means successful and had difficulty in keeping time with 400-ton loads. This was partly because the Eastern Section crews were used to running with fairly long cut-offs and partly-closed regulators, whereas the 'King Arthurs' were at their best when worked with full regulator and the cut-off well back, on favourable and unrestricted stretches of line such as abounded on the Western section, the former LSWR. Cecil J. Allen recorded a run on which, with No 771 *Sir Sagramore* and a 440-ton load, the exit from Victoria was taken easily because of a relief train just in front, speed falling to only 27 mph at Knockholt. The driver then felt able to speed up a little and attained 73 on the descent to Tonbridge; after the slack there speeds in the middle sixties prevailed as far as Headcorn. Signal checks spoiled the conclusion of the run. This, too, was on the 'White Pullman'.

By 1926 the first of the new four-cylinder 4-6-0s, *Lord Nelson*, was put into service and given a thorough testing. This type was designed to be capable of working 500-ton trains at an average speed of 55 mph. On the Western Section this indeed proved possible but not on the more slack-infested Continental route from Victoria. Opinion varies about how good or how poor the 'Nelsons' were before they were modified by Maunsell's successor O.V.S Bulleid. Allen made a footplate journey on the prototype during 1926 and wrote enthusiastically of this experience in the columns of *Trains Illustrated* 23 years later.

> Strengthening of the track and underline bridges in Southern Railway days ... permitted the introduction of 4-6-0 engines and considerable increases in loads. It was a tremendous change in 1927 for me to mount the footplate of *Lord Nelson* himself at Victoria one day ... at the head of the then 10.45 am Dover boat train - later to blossom out into the Golden Arrow - and to realise that behind our tender were nine Pullmans, a corridor first, and four six-wheelers, making up a total load of 460 tons. Owing to the presence of a special train for the President of France we were shifted from the usual No 2 platform to the opposite side of the station, and that meant no banking assistance up the 1 in 62 to the Grosvenor Bridge. But Driver Stuckey took the precaution to sand his rails as the engine backed on to the train, and that meant a grand start, even though with no more than 40 per cent cut-off and half-regulator to get us over the top ...

'Lord Nelson' 4-6-0 No E855 *Robert Blake* on the down Golden Arrow near Chelsfield in March 1930. *LCGB, Ken Nunn Collection*

> Directly this hard work was over, cut-off came back to 25 per cent, and between there and 30 per cent it stopped for all the rest of the journey, with the regulator never more than two-fifths open. Even this moderate handling took us up to Penge tunnel at 31½ mph and Knockholt at 33½, with a time of 31 min 5 sec to this point, 17.6 miles. We had gained a minute on schedule, but two permanent way slowings as we ran down to Tonbridge put us ¾ minute behind time at Paddock Wood. Then followed some fine running, for 30 per cent cut-off and half-regulator took us along the straight at a speed which rose by Staplehurst to 70½ mph and at no point fell below 61½ until we were pulled up for a third permanent way check after Ashford. The 21.3 miles from Paddock Wood to Ashford, passed in 73 min 25 sec from Victoria, were run in 19 min 40 sec. From the Ashford slack we accelerated up the hill to 46 mph at Westenhanger and reached 66 before easing to 55 through Folkestone Junction. Eventually we stopped at Dover Marine, 78 miles, in 98 min 10 sec from Victoria dead on time; the net time was 94 min. I was greatly impressed by the smooth and quiet running of the big 4-6-0, as also with the perfectly even draught in the firebox that is obtained with the 135-degree crank arrangement of a four-cylinder engine.

Allen was perhaps a bit too congratulatory; arriving 10 seconds late can scarcely be termed 'dead on time', though probably no one but himself noticed it. However, it was now plain that here was a type of locomotive that could cope with these heavy boat trains if knowledgeably handled. What a 'Nelson' could do in its original state, if put to it, is evidenced by a quotation from S.C.

Townroe's *Arthurs, Nelsons and Schools at Work*. In chapter 8 he refers to an experiment made by O.V.S. Bulleid.

> He was particularly interested in the 'Nelsons' and made a series of memorable footplate appearances on the Golden Arrow. He was convinced that the schedule between Victoria and Dover could be cut by higher speeds on rising gradients. On his instructions No 862 *Lord Collingwood* was driven in full gear up Grosvenor Road bank out of Victoria, and then at 40-50 per cent cut-off for the rest of the journey. Along the straight between Tonbridge and Ashford, with wide open regulator and both injectors working to keep the boiler water level in sight in the water gauges, speeds were between 90 and 95 mph. By the time he reached Dover the fireman ... was pretty well exhausted, but Bulleid was delighted.

One hopes that the fireman was given some compensation, either monetary or alcoholic, for his herculean efforts. One wonders, too, what the Pullman passengers made of this headlong progress.

It is of course questionable whether a minute or two lost on schedule on any ordinary workaday occasion would have been noticed by the passengers, whose concern was not punctuality in reaching Dover, but getting to Paris on time. In the opposite direction any on-time or early arrivals at Victoria would have been nullified by the usual lengthy Customs examination of registered baggage. Users of the Golden Arrow would have been more concerned with the quality of the ride and with the on-board service, and with the calmness or otherwise of the sea-crossing, than with meritorious locomotive performance.

As a prestige train the pre-Second World War Golden Arrow had only a short life, and what remained of it was discontinued after 3 September 1939. One would have been bold to predict its post-war resuscitation, for already aircraft services to Paris were presenting a challenge. In addition, another luxury rail service to the same place was vying with the Arrow - the all-sleeping car *Wagons Lits* train, the Night Ferry, from which passengers did not need to alight to cross the Channel. As it happened, both trains were restored when the war ended, and an even more splendid Pullman train that before competed with its nocturnal rival for the privilege of taking the best people to the best places.

14

The Torquay Pullman

1929-30

The brief history of the only all-Pullman train which ever appeared in a GWR timetable makes a somewhat melancholy tale, related against the background of disagreement in high places which doomed the service from the start and provided the curious phenomenon of the chief officials of a railway company seemingly trying to ensure that a new luxury express train on its system should not become a profit-maker. Deeply held prejudice can be a stronger influence than enlightened self-interest, as earlier railway history had shown more than once.

The GWR was a company which generated in the minds of those who worked for it a sentiment almost akin to patriotism. Its chief servant at the beginning of 1929 was its General Manager, Sir Felix Pole, who had risen from being a telegraph clerk at Swindon at the age of 14 to the top salaried position 30 years later. *The Dictionary of National Biography* praises his services to the company in improving its efficiency and increasing the dividends paid to shareholders:

> Receptive to new ideas, he pursued an imaginative progressive policy ... strengthening of track and bridges enabled the most powerful locomotives in the country to ... haul heavier high speed trains; higher-capacity wagons were adopted, reducing track occupation; safety techniques lowered the staff accident rate; propaganda and publicity received a new look; housing schemes were established.

In regard to publicity, it is commonly believed that when the design of the new express passenger engine *King George V* was under consideration, Pole pressed for a reduction in the diameter of the driving wheels sufficient to raise its nominal tractive effort above 40,000 lbs. This was not so much in the interests of greater haulage ability (for the alteration made very little difference to this) but because of the prestige that this could bring the company in public esteem.

The GWR was a prestige-conscious line. It had to be seen as one which pointed the way for others, rather than following their examples. In regard to locomotive design, that was indeed true while G.J. Churchward was Locomotive Superintendent (though it was probably not he who insisted on building a solitary 'Pacific' locomotive, *The Great Bear*, long before any other British railway company contemplated taking such a step). The GWR also prided itself on its high-speed expresses, such as the Cornish Riviera Limited. All this was good publicity - with just a slight touch of humbug in the background, for the run-of-the-mill services lagged well behind the few crack trains, and that between Paddington and South Wales was mediocre in regard to speed. Pole, however, was not unaware that a *Sinn Fein* - 'Ourselves Alone' - attitude had its drawbacks, and that it might sometimes be advantageous to co-operate with others. He knew that both on the Southern and London & North Eastern Railways an association with the Pullman Car Company had proved mutually lucrative, and there was no reason to think that the GWR might not similarly profit. So when the Pullman Car Company made approaches, suggesting the use of some of its vehicles on GWR expresses, Sir Felix's response was not a chilly rejection of them.

Pole had two uses in mind for Pullman cars. One was on special boat trains between Paddington and Plymouth. Transatlantic liners plying between Continental ports and the United States were beginning to call at that port to disembark or pick up passengers, and suitably appointed special fast boat trains from and to Paddington could save voyagers hours. Pole therefore negotiated a contract with the Pullman Car Company for a number of its cars to be used in such special trains.

In addition he arranged for some other cars to be supplied for making up a special weekend luxury train to link Paddington with Torquay and Paignton on the Torbay coast. These two resorts, and Torquay in particular, matched the South Coast towns of Eastbourne and Bournemouth and the Yorkshire spa of Harrogate in being 'classy' places which might, it was hoped, generate custom for a luxury train running at the weekend. The Torbay coast had a genial climate and scenic attractions, together with many opulent hotels, which attracted the wealthier classes both for holidays and for residence after retirement. An all-Pullman train might be expected to be profitable both to the GWR and to the Pullman Car Company. It was true that the former had already put on a daily fast train, The Torbay Limited, to serve Torquay and adjacent resorts, composed of ordinary vestibuled compartment stock, which ran non-stop to Exeter in a timing similar to that of the Cornish Riviera Limited. However, in those days weekend holiday traffic was markedly heavier than during the rest of the week, so if the well-known daily train were liable to be crowded, the existence of another train of luxury vehicles, in which all the seats were reservable, might well induce many of the better-off travellers to pay a little more so as to be sure of seat-occupancy, the avoidance of a crowd and refreshments on hand when required.

Arrangements were made for the new Pullman train to begin service on 8 July 1929, running on Mondays and Fridays. As it happened, however, Pole had by then already resigned as General Manager, and on that very day his successor, Sir James Milne, took over, Pole transferring himself to the Chairmanship of Associated Electrical Industries. It seems extremely likely that one reason for his departure from a railway on which he had worked for so long, and to which he was so strongly attached, was a clash with his Chairman, Viscount Churchill, over the association that had been arranged with the Pullman Car Company. Churchill, of aristocratic lineage, an old Etonian, born with a silver spoon in his mouth, no doubt found Pole, this working-class-boy-made-good, not all that easy to get on with. He had also disliked Lord Dalziel, the former Chairman of the Pullman Car Company, who had died the previous year, and the dislike spread to the business he had nurtured for so long. Pole's resignation gave the opportunity for someone who shared that dislike to be appointed in his place as General Manager. Thus the new train lost the support of the man who would have been best placed to give it.

The new state of affairs was exemplified in the events at Paddington on the morning of Monday 8 July 1929. The Cornish Riviera Express had been allotted new carriage stock and its first departure from Paddington during the summer season was accompanied by a certain amount of razmataz. Sir James Milne, in morning dress, came to see the renovated train off. It was hauled by the flagship locomotive No 6000 *King George V*, which carried on its buffer beam the large bronze bell presented when it had visited the USA shortly before, and the departure was preceded by a ceremonial ringing of it by C. B. Collett, the Chief

The Torquay Pullman at platform 5 at Paddington just prior to its unheralded departure for its inaugural run on Monday 8 July 1929. *NRM, York*

Mechanical Engineer. Press representatives were shown over the train and free souvenir brochures were handed to all the passengers. This was at 10.30; half an hour later the new Torquay Pullman left on its inaugural run almost apologetically behind a 4-6-0 'Castle'. No frock-coated dignitaries were in evidence; there were some press representatives on board, but that was all.

However, the latter included one appreciative reporter from the *Torquay Herald & Express*, which the following day published a very laudatory article on the new train. The writer was 'wonderfully struck with the smoothness with which it travelled, or rather glided over the rails. In fact it was quite an easy matter to write, and this in itself proves that its steadiness is extraordinary'. Then followed a tribute to the interior furnishings and decor of the First Class cars, and a comment that the Third Class cars were almost as well appointed. The article ended by saying that, for all this luxury, the additional supplement '...is a comparatively small matter. The Torquay Pullman Limited should become extremely popular. The enterprise of the GWR Company in initiating such a splendid service deserves success.'

A rare shot by M. W. Earley of the Torquay Pullman at speed near Twyford, taken soon before the train's withdrawal. The locomotive is No 4082 *Windsor Castle*. The train has only five Pullman cars, an additional ordinary coach being attached to the rear. *NRM, York*

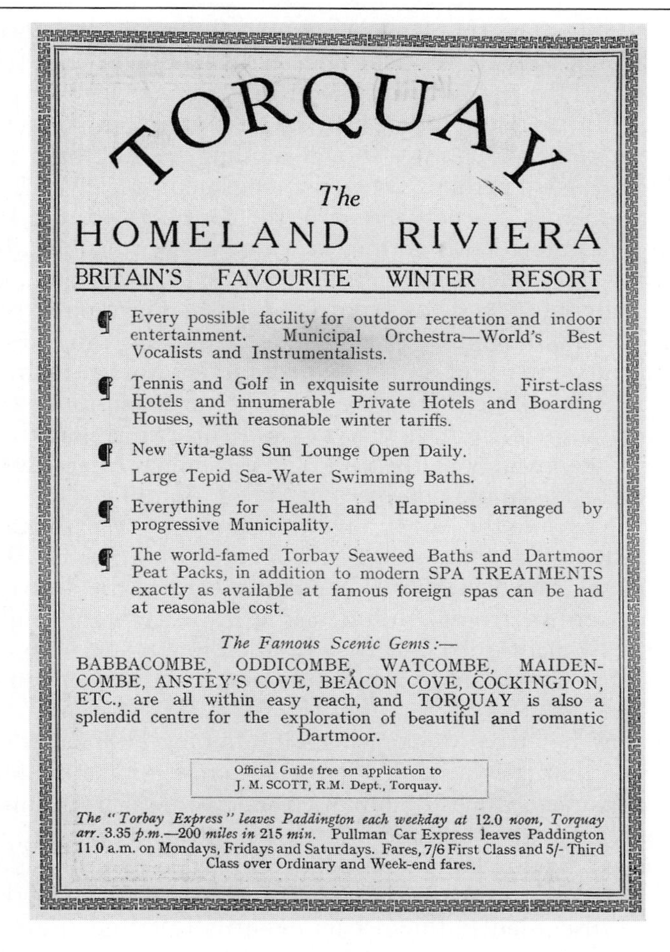
TORQUAY
The
HOMELAND RIVIERA
BRITAIN'S FAVOURITE WINTER RESORT

¶ Every possible facility for outdoor recreation and indoor entertainment. Municipal Orchestra—World's Best Vocalists and Instrumentalists.

¶ Tennis and Golf in exquisite surroundings. First-class Hotels and innumerable Private Hotels and Boarding Houses, with reasonable winter tariffs.

¶ New Vita-glass Sun Lounge Open Daily.
Large Tepid Sea-Water Swimming Baths.

¶ Everything for Health and Happiness arranged by progressive Municipality.

¶ The world-famed Torbay Seaweed Baths and Dartmoor Peat Packs, in addition to modern SPA TREATMENTS exactly as available at famous foreign spas can be had at reasonable cost.

The Famous Scenic Gems:—

BABBACOMBE, ODDICOMBE, WATCOMBE, MAIDENCOMBE, ANSTEY'S COVE, BEACON COVE, COCKINGTON, ETC., are all within easy reach, and TORQUAY is also a splendid centre for the exploration of beautiful and romantic Dartmoor.

Official Guide free on application to
J. M. SCOTT, R.M. Dept., Torquay.

The "Torbay Express" leaves Paddington each weekday at 12.0 *noon, Torquay arr.* 3.35 *p.m.*—200 *miles in* 215 *min.* Pullman Car Express leaves Paddington 11.0 a.m. on Mondays, Fridays and Saturdays. Fares, 7/6 First Class and 5/- Third Class over Ordinary and Week-end fares.

A brief mention of a 'Pullman Car Express' tucked away at the foot of an advertisement for the resort of Torquay. *The Railway Magazine*

The last sentence in retrospect sounds ironical. Had Pole remained as General Manager the train's fortunes might have been more favourable. It was probably a mistake to run it so closely ahead of the existing Torbay Limited and to give it so similar a title. The latter train was somewhat faster, charged no supplement and was already well established in the public mind. The Pullman left Paddington on Mondays and Fridays at 11.00, ran non-stop to Newton Abbot, arrived at Torquay at 2.40 pm and Paignton at 2.50; it returned at 4.30 pm from Paignton, 4.40 from Torquay and reached Paddington at 8.30 pm. Times such as these were dictated by the Pullman Car Company's wish to base its employees at London, but they were not entirely convenient either to residents or holidaymakers, particularly the schedule of the return train, whereas the midday departures of both the down and up Torbay Limited expresses were much more suitable. The supplementary fares chargeable, too, were, for the period, on the high side. This could have been justified if the schedule had been quickened and the train made a real 'flyer'.

As it was the Torbay Limited beat it by 10 minutes in both directions. In the winter timetable of 1929-30 it was shown running on Saturdays as well as on Mondays and Fridays, so perhaps some encouragement was given by the extent of the summer bookings - or perhaps, since the contract with the Pullman Car Company was still in force, preventing the train's discontinuance, the additional Saturday run was an attempt to scrape up a little more custom. However, the latter did not materialise, and the following July the make-up of the train was altered. Only five Pullman cars were included instead of the previous seven, and some ordinary First and Third Class coaches were attached to them, together with a restaurant car. The result was to divert custom away from the Pullman element in the train, and it was not surprising that the latter was taken out of service entirely at the end of the summer, as also were the First Class cars which had been used on the special boat trains.

It is interesting to note the sort of advertisement the GWR tolerated to bring the train to public notice. One issue of *The Railway Magazine* in 1929 carried a full-page display inserted by Torquay Council. It featured the Torbay Limited as the main train service from London, using italic type for emphasis. The Pullman was briefly mentioned underneath, in ordinary type, with no reference to its title, and care was taken to inform readers that a supplementary fare was payable.

The GWR may not have welcomed its interloping Pullman train, but it is interesting to see that they accorded it the sincerest form of flattery, building subsequently a number of quasi-Pullman coaches of their own, similar in style to the Pullman cars and with names on their waists; internally, too, they were similarly furnished, having individual tables with table lamps beside large windows. These were used on the special trains connecting with the liners at Plymouth. The discarded Pullman cars eventually found their way to the Western Section of the Southern Railway.

15

The Bournemouth Belle

1931-67

The decision to introduce an all-Pullman train on the Waterloo-Bournemouth service was something of a gamble on the part of the Southern Railway Board. They had already been made aware that such a train was not a profitable proposition on the line between Victoria and the Thanet resorts, for the Thanet Pullman, which had run only on Sundays, had had a precarious existence, and even before the recession had begun to show its effect in this country it had been taken off. Bournemouth was not as populous as the three Thanet resorts taken together; it was considerably further from London than the day tourist was then accustomed to travel; and it lacked the popular attractions of Brighton or Margate. It was a place for rest and recuperation and, though not a place where one could 'take the waters', had some of the qualities of a spa. Many nursing and convalescent homes were sited there. Affluent people retired to spend the evenings of their lives among its pine trees. Its whole atmosphere differed from that of Brighton; its culture was that of the symphony orchestra rather than the music hall. A luxury out-from-and-back-to-London train would not be of much use to those who already lived there, since it could not offer them day return facilities to the capital as the Southern Belle could to the people of Brighton. Furthermore, the trade recession was now affecting British economic life, and an extra-fare train was not going to be much of an attraction to those who had suffered a salary cut.

However, it was not at first proposed to serve only Bournemouth. As first envisaged, the train was to continue through Poole, Wareham and Dorchester to Weymouth, and during the three summer months was to run on weekdays as well as Sundays (though on the latter day terminating at Bournemouth West). Furthermore, it would be necessary to stop the train at Southampton in either direction to replenish the engine's water supply, since the train would be heavier than the Bournemouth Limited which managed to do the journey without a stop. The SR had no water troughs, and even the large eight-wheeled tenders used by the express engines on the Western Section could not be guaranteed to hold sufficient water for a run of more than 100 miles with a train of over 400 tons. The Southampton stop would make a virtue of necessity during the week; a businessman from London would have time to put in an afternoon's work and travel restfully in both directions.

It was not to be an exclusively First Class service. The revolution begun by the LB&SCR when it introduced Third Class cars on the Southern Belle had been spreading. The LNER's all-Pullman trains served both classes, taking their patrons much greater distances than those between London and any of the South Coast towns. If one got the mixture right, with a preponderance of Third Class seating for a moderate supplementary fee, any shortage of First Class custom might be made up. In any case, running a prestige train would generate useful publicity.

The Pullman Car Company provided three First Class and seven Third Class cars for use on the service. The former, *Flora*, *Montana* and *Aurelia*, had already seen service on the 'White Pullman' and Golden Arrow on the Eastern Section, the latter having now shed much of its Pullman complement so that there were cars to spare. Of the Third Class cars, four were newly built; the other three had already been used on the LNER. The whole train had 314 available seats - more than any previous all-Pullman train had supplied. Supplements varied from 1s 6d Third Class between London and Southampton to 4 shillings First Class all the way to Weymouth. As far as Bournemouth the timetable of the new Bournemouth Belle, on every day of the week, was as follows:

Down:		Up:	
Waterloo	dep 10.30	Bournemouth West	dep 16.50
Southampto	arr 11.59	Bournemouth Central	arr 17.00
	dep 12.01		dep 17.10
Bournemouth Central	arr 12.39	Southampton West	arr 17.45
	dep 12.43		dep 17.48
Bournemouth West	arr 12.50	Waterloo	arr 19.18

The down train divided at Bournemouth Central, the front portion going on to Weymouth, reached at 13.45; it returned at 16.00 to rejoin the rest of the train at Bournemouth Central. The schedule was not very fast, but the heavy formation, and the fact that haulage by 'King Arthur' 4-6-0s as well as by the more powerful 'Lord Nelsons' was envisaged, made it necessary for the timings to be easier than that of the lighter Bournemouth Limited.

The inaugural run was made on Sunday 5 July 1931, the engine being No E870 *Sir Persant*. As a publicity occasion it was rather spoiled since delays *en route* caused a late arrival; on the return journey, however, Waterloo was reached a minute early. Nine weeks' subsequent daily running justified the company's expectations in regard to both weekday and Sunday patronage as far as Bournemouth, but on weekdays so few people proceeded further that it was decided to terminate the service at Bournemouth. The autumn, winter and spring months saw the train running only on Sundays, but the following July it became a daily service again, and the departure times from the West and Central stations in the up direction were put back by 1¼ hours, with an arrival at Waterloo at 8.30 pm to allow more time for the day tourist. The pattern was

An early view of the down Bournemouth Belle near Malden behind 'King Arthur' No E777 *Sir Lamiel* in August 1931. *LCGB, Ken Nunn Collection*

now settled for the train's continuance every Sunday throughout the year, with a weekday service during the summer months, and this lasted until the end of 1935.

By then the recession had run its course and things were looking better for the economy, so it was decided that as from 1 January 1936 it would be a daily train all the year round. When the summer timetable came out that year the general tendency towards acceleration on other railways was reflected in the Bournemouth Belle's running in the up direction; it was given a 2-hour timing to Waterloo, inclusive of the Southampton stop. The time of the weekday arrival at Waterloo now became 6.45 pm. In July 1937 the timings of the up Sunday train were put back by a further 2 hours, with a Waterloo arrival at 8.45 pm. Schedules remained thus until the outbreak of the Second World War in 1939, when the train was withdrawn and the cars went into store for the duration.

Once the war had ended no time was lost in getting the train back into service. Its re-appearance was welcomed in October 1946, for after wartime neglect much of the SR's ordinary coaching stock was in a poor state, and to travel in a train that was not only luxurious but clean, with bookable seats and refreshments to hand, was an experience which made the modest supplement seem negligible. When running in full capacity the train was again made up of three First and seven Third Class cars, though not the same ones as before, and during the remainder of its life there were further changes, the number of First

Class cars in the rake extending to a maximum of four, with an additional Third Class car being added in 1958. All but one were 12-wheelers. Thus from the summer of that year the train's weight could rise to 485 tons - well over 500 tons when carrying passengers and luggage - and became the heaviest Pullman train in the country, a position previously held by the Devon Belle which had ceased to run in 1954.

Rather surprisingly the re-introduced train went straight back to its 1939 schedule, though the arrival and departure times were not the same. At first it ran as follows:

Down:		Up:	
Waterloo	dep 12.30	Bournemouth West	dep 19.15
Southampton	arr 13.57	Bournemouth Central	arr 19.23
	dep 13.59		dep 19.25
Bournemouth Central	arr 14.35	Southampton	arr 19.58
	dep 14.37		dep 20.00
Bournemouth West	arr 14.46	Waterloo	arr 21.25

This timetable applied both on weekdays and Sundays, and having regard to the weight of the train and the not inconsiderable gradients *en route* the schedule in the up direction was among the fastest in the country at that time. The train now offered the day excursionist nearly 5 hours in Bournemouth itself.

The Bournemouth Belle in very early British Railways days passing Vauxhall in June 1948 with unrebuilt Bulleid 'Pacific' No 35013 *Blue Funnel Line* in charge. *Steamchest*

However, at the beginning of the summer season of 1947 the up train's timings were brought forward by 2 hours and 40 minutes, so that a return journey by it on the same day was no longer possible if one wished to see anything of Bournemouth as well. Departure from Bournemouth Central now became 4.45 pm.

A year later the train was slowed by 5 minutes in either direction, the pattern otherwise remaining the same. Not until 1963 was the 2-hour timing restored, and then only for a couple of years, since in 1965 work began to prepare the route for electrification and the train had to be decelerated again to allow for the inevitable permanent way slowings. From September 1965, too, Bournemouth West station ceased to be used and the train ran only to Bournemouth Central. The summer timetable of 1967 saw the introduction of the new electrified service, much faster and more frequent than before, but no electrified Bournemouth Belle took the place of the locomotive-hauled one; the Pullman made its last run on Sunday 9 July of that year.

As a passenger experience, travel on the Bournemouth Belle was more rewarding than on any other possible Pullman journeys in southern England. One got clear of London at Surbiton; the train then passed through urban areas only briefly, at Woking, Basingstoke and Winchester, for some 60 miles, and one had the pleasanter prospects of the pinewoods of western Surrey and the chalk downlands of Hampshire. At Southampton, as the train slowed to a stop, a glimpse might be had of the tall funnels of some transatlantic liner and one could try to guess which one it might be. After the re-start the line ran through the New Forest, where deer or wild ponies might be observed grazing. Finally one crossed the estuary at the confluence of the Avon and Stour rivers, with its many small boats and the view of the impressive outline of Christchurch Priory. For a journey twice as far as from Victoria to Brighton one certainly got more than twice as much scenic interest. Meanwhile one could sip one's morning coffee appreciatively during the outward journey (or, after 1946, enjoy a Pullman lunch) and regale oneself with dinner on the return.

Locomotive provision for the Bournemouth Belle between 1931 and 1939 was generally a 'Lord Nelson', but there were only 16 of these engines on the whole SR system, so at times of shortage a 'King Arthur' had to be used. Such a heavy train, if running with its full load, was a tough proposition for one of the latter, which would not have had much more than 5 minutes to spare even on the earlier un-accelerated schedule, so a 'Nelson' was employed wherever possible. On its 2-hour up timing, the Belle between 1936 and 1939 was possibly the hardest assignment anywhere on the SR when the complete load of 10 Pullmans was taken. The most trying part was the long drag from sea level at Southampton to the summit at Litchfield, most of which was continuously at 1 in 252. As will be seen later, some drivers preferred to take this ascent easily and make up time on the downhill stretch beyond if a clear run could be obtained.

Locomotive performance at the head of the pre-war Belle was usually of a high order. In the winter, when only eight vehicles might be run, it was com-

A pre-war view of the Belle in about 1935, leaving Bournemouth behind 'Lord Nelson' No E856 *Lord St Vincent*. *Steamchest*

paratively easy to keep time, but the full 10-car load could extend the engine. Drivers who had been trained under the regime of Dugald Drummond would generally use the technique of keeping the regulator open for much of the way and varying the cut-off according to the gradient, and the Western Section main line, with its freedom from service slacks and its long and steady gradients, favoured this method of driving. Generally speaking, Western Section crews coped better with the 'Nelsons' that their counterparts on the Eastern Section, though it was not until O. V. S. Bulleid had given these big engines improved steam passages at their front ends, and the better draughting that Lemaître multiple jet exhausts made possible, that really remarkable performances began to be seen.

What must have been a record run with a 'Nelson', hauling the full Bournemouth Belle rake of 10 cars (though not actually on the Belle itself), was achieved early in 1938 during a special test run during the period when Bulleid was experimenting with these locomotives before modifying their front ends. A test schedule of 100 minutes had been laid down for the 107.9 miles from Waterloo to Bournemouth, and this was kept with a few seconds to spare, 100 mph being just reached near Winchester. In actual daily practice it was rare for 80 mph to be much exceeded with the unmodified engines. From 1938 they became much more free-running.

In his book *Maunsell's Nelsons* D. W. Winkworth includes logs of runs on the Belle which demonstrate this. Net times of 85-86 minutes on the down run to Southampton with full loads were succeeded by those of 79-82 minutes after the re-designed cylinders and Lemaître blast pipe had been fitted. It now became more usual for a fast climb to be made with the up train between Southampton and Litchfield, even with a 500-ton train. On one occasion the newly-modified No 865 *Sir John Hawkins* took a train of this weight up the bank, actually accelerating from 52 mph at Shawford to 55 at Litchfield, and despite comparatively easy running onwards, with a speed no higher than 76, nevertheless ran into Waterloo 4 minutes early. Before the train was suspended on the outbreak of the Second World War the 'Nelsons' were equalling the later feats of Bulleid's 'Pacifics' as hill-climbers.

In 1937 I made a journey on the up Belle on a summer Saturday travelling in the front Third Class car when the full load of 10 vehicles was taken. There was a 'Nelson' at the head - which one I cannot remember. I positioned myself carefully in a forward-facing seat on the left-hand side of the train so as to be able to sight the mileposts - something easier to achieve in a Pullman car as the large windows were so low, well below the level of the tables. This was my first journey behind a 'Lord Nelson' and I hoped for a good performance. In fact, from the operational point of view it was an excellent performance, though at the time I did not realise this. Once we had got on the move we appeared to be in no great hurry, never reaching 50 mph at any point before the foot of the 1 in 252 and going so gently up through Winchester and Micheldever that when we passed the summit we were 2 minutes down. I began to think that something was wrong with the engine and regretted the money I had expended on a day return ticket and Third Class supplement. However, the locomotive crew knew what they were about. They were aware that there were no out-of-course slacks to be encountered; they also knew that on a summer Saturday line occupancy was at its greatest and that running ahead of time might cause signal delays. Once past Worting Junction speed rose rapidly into the 80s, and we bowled merrily along with nothing to hinder our progress. I began to hope for a punctual, perhaps early, arrival. What happened was that we made a moderately slow approach to Waterloo and stopped at the platform exactly 1 second over the allotted schedule time. It was an exhibition of precision working, with due account being taken of all the prevailing circumstances. One could scarcely grumble - though I did regret that lost second.

Post-war performance on the restored Bournemouth Belle showed more sparkle and some astonishing maximum-quality achievements, displaying the abilities of Bulleid's 'Merchant Navy' 4-6-2s both to produce steam as required and to use it. While the train's schedule was not for a long while what it had been in 1939, thrills for a train-timer were probably more frequently offered. In his book *Bulleid's Pacifics* D. W. Winkworth gives a number of logs showing performances on the Waterloo-Southampton-Bournemouth route. They bear witness that in the down direction it was not at all unusual to travel in a heavy train behind a 'Merchant Navy' or 'West Country' 4-6-2 without the speed falling below the mile-a-minute rate at any point east of Worting Junction, and achieving rates of 70 or more on the slightly adverse grades. In the opposite direction topping Litchfield summit at well above 50 was now par for the course.

The down Bournemouth Belle leaving Southampton West, hauled by rebuilt Bulleid 'Merchant Navy' 'Pacific' No 35018 *Belgian Marine* in June 1956. *LCGB, Ken Nunn Collection*

On one exhilarating occasion driver Hooper, on the up Belle, with 445 tons behind the tender of No 35012 *United States Lines*, in its modified form after rebuilding, made, on instructions, what Winkworth calls 'a deliberate attempt to extend the locomotive from start to finish'. It probably ranks with the run on the Golden Arrow, made when Bulleid was on the footplate of a 'Lord Nelson', as recounted in the last chapter but one, as one of the two most spectacular performances ever accomplished with a Pullman train in the days of steam. The exit from Southampton round Northam curve was taken with caution, but after that Hooper just went on accelerating uphill. The 60 mark was reached before Eastleigh, the 70 mark just after Winchester, going all out up the 1 in 252, and at the top of the incline the speed had reached 76. So far from easing the engine after this almost incredible effort, the driver kept at it and passed the 80 mark before Worting Junction, there to be seriously checked by signals. Undeterred, he quickly brought the speed up again into the 80s, reached 92 near Winchfield and 93 at Brookwood, and kept up the headlong progress as far as New Malden. Two signal checks between Clapham Junction and Waterloo marred the conclusion, but the actual time taken from Southampton to London was over 11 minutes less than booked, and the net time 15 minutes less.

The up journey between Bournemouth and Southampton could also occasionally provide excitement. The 28½ miles were allowed 32 minutes on the Belle, and this was not an easy booking since there were a number of short but stiff banks to be climbed - in particular the 4 miles after Christchurch which

Non-Bulleid 'Pacific' haulage of the Bournemouth Belle included stints by the new Standard 'Britannia' 4-6-2s. Here the train passes Clapham Junction behind No 70009 *Alfred the Great* in June 1951. *Brian Morrison*

ended with a mile at 1 in 119/103. On one occasion, on a damp day with a wet rail, drive Pope, with the full load of 12 cars and No 35016 *Elders Fyffes*, actually managed to beat even time from Bournemouth to passing Redbridge, and nearly did the same to the Southampton stop, reached almost 3 minutes early. Speed fell to 55 mph after Hinton Admiral following the slack at Christchurch to 60, and then quickened rapidly, with three most unusual successive maxima of 80 in three successive dips in the New Forest.

Both the above runs, by drivers Hooper and Pope, were made during the last days of steam on the SR, and the Belle's concluding runs were behind Class 47 Brush/Sulzer diesel-electric locomotives. With electrification of the line the Belle's cars disappeared into limbo, some being demolished and others sold. The subsequent electric service was to be faster, and the newest stock on the line, resplendent (if that is the appropriate word) in Network SouthEast livery, is as comfortable to travel in as the Pullmans ever were. But one sighs, no doubt unreasonably, for the former opulence and occasional excitements which the Bournemouth Belle provided for its patrons. A railway enthusiast of my generation cannot help, sometimes, being (as Cecil J. Allen, that inveterate user of Latin tags, might have said) a *laudator temporis acti* ('one who praises past times'), and reminiscing sadly about the days that are gone.

16

The Brighton Belle

1933-72

The new all-Pullman train which took the place of the steam-hauled Southern Belle[1] on 1 January 1933 was unique at the time of its introduction and has remained so to the present day, as the only all-Pullman express train to be powered by electric current taken from a third rail, and driven by motors within the train itself and not in a separate detachable locomotive. Third rail electrification at 660 volts had been the method selected by the LSWR and SE&CR for their suburban services, and the SR continued it, to cover a greater and greater mileage of track during the 'twenties and 'thirties, using multiple unit trains. The new Pullman was a specialised version of the vestibuled six-car sets of coaches introduced on the Brighton and Worthing services at the same time.

It would have been possible for the train to have been hauled by electric locomotives and to have been composed of the same sort of stock as before, since no rapid turn-rounds at either Victoria or Brighton were envisaged. Nevertheless the multiple unit method had the advantage of economy in operation when only a few cars were needed; it would not be necessary for the traction system to be additionally burdened with the weight of a locomotive which might amount to that of two of the cars it hauled.

Each end coach in the standard six-coach unit, in which only one composite First and Third Class Pullman car was included, had two 225 hp engines driving directly on to each of the powered bodies, and the same arrangement was provided for the end cars of each new five-coach Pullman unit, of which there were three built. Each was given a rounded-off nose-end with the Pullman Car Company's coat-of-arms placed centrally beneath the edges of the forward-facing windows, the driver's seat and controls being behind the left-hand window. To the rear of the driving compartment was another space for luggage and the accommodation of the guard. All this took up the extreme end of each motorised vehicle, the rest of it containing Third Class Pullman seating.

The disposition of this Third Class seating, and of other amenities in each

[1] It retained the title Southern Belle for a further 18 months before being renamed in response to requests in Brighton.

five-car unit was as follows:

Front (motorised) car: 48 seats in a saloon with 2 + 2 seating, toilet compartment and luggage racks.

Second car: 56 seats in saloon with 2 + 2 seating, with two toilet compartments and luggage racks.

Third car: Eight First Class seats in each of two saloons, with 1 + 1 seating, and four seats in a coupé compartment, together with kitchen and pantry at one end and a toilet compartment at the other.

Fourth car: As third car, but ends reversed.

Fifth (motorised) car: As front car, but ends reversed.

Total seating: 40 First Class and 152 Third Class.

All five cars were vestibuled together, but the front and rear ends had no vestibule connections.

Usually two five-car units were used together, but when traffic was light one sufficed. The third unit was kept on stand-by but took its turn with the others. Each unit therefore did eight months' service during the year, and necessary maintenance could be done during the other four.

Externally each unit was in the characteristic Pullman livery, the Third Class cars being numbered and the First Class cars being given feminine names - *Hazel* and *Doris*, *Audrey* and *Vera*, *Gwen* and *Mona* - as were all the composite

The all-electric multiple unit Southern Belle passing Clapham Junction in April 1933. At this stage it had not yet been renamed the Brighton Belle. Note that two five-car sets are being used together. *Steamchest*

A single five-car unit approaching Merstham. The shadows on the track suggest that it is the afternoon service from Victoria. ***Author's Collection***

cars built at the same time and used singly in six-coach units. The interiors of the First Class cars were arranged as was then customary, with a pair of armchairs on either side of each window and a glass-topped table with a brass table lamp between. The decor varied from car to car according to the practice of different interior decorators; in *Doris*, for example,

> ... the interiors of the saloons are treated with fine English walnut of three varieties of figures, and the panels are quartered and cross-banded. The decorative effect is obtained by the use of Convex Eagle mirrors, cut in fine boxwood with black beaded rims, and also by the introduction of etchings mounted in black mouldings. The carpets are of rich deep pile in tones of green. The chair and seat coverings are in moquette velvet, in tones of brown, red and fawn.[2]

Whereas in *Gwen*,

> ... the main panel work is in figured English walnut with lace wood and laurel lines. Marquetry work is introduced in the principal panels, and carried out in boxwood, weathered sycamore and red and white natural pear wood. The metal work is finished in satin silver. The carpet is of Wilton pile, in tones of blue, whilst the chairs are covered in velvet moquette in blue and mauve tints.[2]

The Third Class cars, however, differed from other such Pullman vehicles in

[2] *The Locomotive*, 14 January 1933

having 2 + 2 seating, so that each bay held twice as many persons as a First Class one. Fair enough, it might be said, in view of the fact that the Third Class supplement was only half that of the First Class, but it was much less generous than on the other British Pullman trains, and for an amply-proportioned person must have been somewhat uncomfortable, as the arm rests were fixed. I have a personal memory of an up journey made in the Belle in 1935, on a Saturday when almost every seat was taken, when I was wedged awkwardly into a corner with no room to stretch my legs without disturbing those of a severe-looking woman sitting opposite. A further disadvantage most Third Class passengers had to face was that in the front and rear cars there was a very insistent vibration from the motored bogies below. One was accustomed to this in ordinary electric stock, but then one was not paying extra to ride in it. So far as comfort was concerned, the words 'de luxe' needed to be heavily qualified when applied to journeys in the front and rear cars of the Brighton Belle.

With the introduction of the electric units the number of double journeys between Victoria and Brighton went up to three on weekdays, remaining at two on Sundays, when for the first time Third Class passengers were able to use the train. The schedules and timings in force throughout most of the train's subsequent operations were:

Down:				
Victoria	dep	11.00	15.00	19.00
Brighton	arr	12.00	16.00	20.00
Up:				
Brighton	dep	13.25	17.25	21.15
Victoria	arr	14.25	18.25	22.25

It will be noticed that no acceleration of the train was attempted, despite the fact that the electric motors enabled speed to be attained more rapidly after stops, and faster climbs to be made up the banks. In fact, the standard non-stop timing for all the Victoria-Brighton trains remained at 60 minutes. This gave better opportunity for arriving punctually and also allowed for the general speed limit of 75 mph over the whole Central section, which had not applied before. On an unchecked run the Brighton Belle could keep its scheduled time without exceeding 70 mph.

During the years 1933-39 the thrice-daily journey was done uninterruptedly each weekday, with either one or two five-car units, and, in spite of the tendency of the motor vehicles to vibrate, it was popular and well patronised. With the coming of the Second World War, however, it was withdrawn, and the units were stored. One had the misfortune to be damaged in an air raid, but it was repaired and ready for use when the war ended. In October 1946 the units were put back into service and the pre-war timetable was re-introduced and adhered to for several years. In September 1963, however, an extra double trip was provided each weekday.

The Brighton Belle just north of Patcham tunnel on the early evening return run to Victoria in June 1935. ***LCGB, Ken Nunn Collection***

The overnight stabling was removed to Brighton, and the first daily service was an up run to Victoria at 09.26; then, after the performance of the usual treble stint, the train went back to Brighton at 23.00. By now, too, the late evening up run had been advanced to leave Brighton at 20.25, so that there was time to service the cars and then bring them into the platform at Victoria in time for passengers who wished to begin a late dinner before the train left. On this late run an intermediate halt was made, for the first time in the train's history, at Haywards Heath, to set down passengers for stations beyond. By now the Brighton Belle was achieving during its seven-day week a total of over 2,600 miles weekly, fractionally more than the Queen of Scots between London and Glasgow, though not quite as much as the Tees-Tyne Pullman with its five-days-a-week double journey from Newcastle to King's Cross and back.

In 1967 the three units underwent a complete change in their appearance. The Pullman Car Company had now been acquired by British Railways, and the decision was made to alter the livery of the cars so that, while still distinctive to the eye, they matched that of other BR passenger vehicles, which were now being turned out in light grey and blue. The Brighton Belle was the first all-Pullman train to be given this treatment, the newly-introduced Manchester

Right **Reliveried and in the last month of its career, April 1972, the Brighton Belle waits to leave Brighton with the 17.45 service to Victoria. Note the yellow-painted nose and warning horns above the cab. All the cars now carried the train's title instead of names and numbers.** ***both Hugh Ballantyne***

3052
4
BRIGHTON BELLE

BRIGHTON BELLE

Pullman, with a similar livery, beginning its career shortly afterwards; the Pullman trains on the East Coast Main Line gradually changed to match, as well as the Golden Arrow in its final days. The characteristic Pullman coat of arms disappeared from the cars, to be replaced by the now familiar BR 'double arrow' logo. A broad band of blue was applied to the cars' sides below the waist-line, with light grey above, except for the doors which, where not glazed, were entirely blue. Both bands were neatly lined out. The First Class cars lost their names and the Second Class[4] cars their numbers; in their places the name of the train appeared. Unfortunately, from the point of view of appearance, though no doubt desirable from that of safety, the nose at each end of the unit was painted bright yellow - a feature to become universal on all trains. The roofs were painted dark grey and the fixing slots where the nameboards had been set were removed, being unnecessary when the train's title was clearly displayed on each car side and across each nose-front. New two-tone alarm horns were fitted to the roofs above the front windows, facing forward like a pair of trumpets.

The interiors were also much modified. The walls retained their marquetry panels, but the seats were re-upholstered, the First Class in charcoal and grey check, the Third Class in blue and green check, with navy blue arm rests and hand rests. Now mustard-coloured carpets covered the floors and orange window-curtains were fitted, with green sun-blinds behind them. The brass table lamps were retained, though there seems to have been an intention to remove them, perhaps given up because they were popular with the train's regular clientèle.

No alterations were made to the engines, but there was some modification of the bogie springing in the hope of improving the riding. This was a matter about which BR was sensitive, after its experience with the 'Blue Pullmans', alluded to in a later chapter, which were by then being phased out.

The last five years of the Brighton Belle saw a quickening of the schedule and some alterations in some of the timings. In 1967 new main-line vestibuled electric stock replaced that of 1933 on the Central Section of the Southern Region, which had more powerful motors permitted to operate at 90 mph. The non-stop schedule between Victoria and Brighton was accordingly cut to 55 minutes, and the Belle, which did not have the benefit of the more modern traction, had to match what the others did on most, though not all, of its runs. From July 1967 the timings were as follows:

Monday-Friday					
Down:					
Victoria	dep	11.00	15.00	19.00	23.00
Brighton	arr	11.55	15.55	19.56	23.58
Up:					
Brighton	dep	09.25	13.45	17.45	20.45
Victoria	arr	10.24	14.40	18.40	21.40

[4] From 3 June 1956 all Third Class vehicles on BR were re-designated Second Class.

Saturday					
Down:					
Victoria	dep	11.00	15.00	19.00	23.00
Brighton	arr	11.55	15.55	19.55	23.58
Up:					
Brighton	dep	09.20	13.45	17.45	20.45
Victoria	arr	10.18	14.40	18.40	21.40
Sunday					
Down:					
Victoria	dep	11.00	19.00		
Brighton	arr	11.55	19.56		
Up:					
Brighton	dep	09.45	17.45	20.45	
Victoria	arr	10.40	18.40	21.40	

It will be noted that the 25 minutes past the hour return departure time for all the up services was now broken, and also that on Sundays there were only two down services though three in the opposite direction; presumably a journey was made empty to get the cars back to Brighton for Monday morning.

Many minor alterations were also made during the next few years, among which was a deceleration of some of the services by 1 minute - a sign that the Belle's ageing motors were not really up to the 55-minute schedule. More ominous was the cropping of any reference to the train's title in the timetables of 1970 and 1971, it being merely referred to as a 'Pullman Limited Train'.

The Southern Region was now doing some hard thinking in regard to the train's continuance. The stock was almost 40 years old. The motors were limited to 75 mph, which made time-keeping difficult when there were out-of-course delays. The question of whether to run Pullman trains at all was beginning to exercise the minds of the BR authorities. Clearly the whole train had to be replaced by a more modern one, or it had to disappear entirely. In the interest of the maximum utilisation of stock the latter course was finally chosen. It is true that the train was popular with its users - indeed, it had become something of a national institution. It carried regularly in its First Class saloons famous members of the theatrical profession. On one occasion it was even used by the Queen Mother to fulfil an engagement. Nevertheless its doom was sealed, and it made its last journey on 30 April 1972.

There was widespread opposition when it was learned that the cars would be disposed of to the highest bidders, even if the latter were from abroad. It was as if it had been proposed to sell St Paul's Cathedral to be re-erected in the USA. Angry letters were written to the Press. But in fact none of the 15 cars were sold abroad. Some, removed from their bogies, became bungalows or public houses. Some were preserved as they were by private people. Two of the latter, the First Class cars *Audrey* and *Gwen*, were bought back from their first purchasers and used in the fleet of restored Pullman vehicles owned by the Venice-Simplon-Orient Express company, seeing further service in the journeys made

The front end of one of the units of the Brighton Belle after it had been taken out of service quietly mouldering in a siding near Manningtree, Essex, in May 1977, as a Liverpool Street-Norwich express runs past. ***Brian Morrison***

from London to Folkestone Harbour and back on the English leg of the journey to Venice, and in various excursions to places as far from their former route as Bath, Bristol or Salisbury. These two cars were included in a commemorative return journey to Brighton made in September 1991, along with several other preserved vehicles making up a 400-ton train hauled by a diesel locomotive, so that, probably for the last time, they revisited the haunts of their youth.

17

The post-war Golden Arrow

1946-72

Very soon after the Second World War had ended the Golden Arrow was re-introduced, on 15 April 1946. Although air services between London and Paris had been established during the inter-war period, the 'short sea route' was still the accepted one between the two cities, taken by most travellers, and both the British and the French Governments were anxious to bring it back into use as quickly as possible.

However, there were some inevitable causes of delay. The French permanent way needed some months of work to put it in order after the ravages of wartime, and the *Canterbury*, the dedicated vessel for Arrow passengers during 1929-38, had been taken over by the Government during the war and was in need of a

In its first month of operation following re-instatement, April 1946, the down Golden Arrow is seen at Petts Wood hauled by 'light Pacific' No 21C119 *Bideford*. *LCGB, Ken Nunn Collection*

refit. Another boat had been ordered before the war began, but had not yet been delivered. In Kent the railway track was in a better state than in France, and the necessary vehicles needed only to be released from storage. The French, on the other hand, did not have enough Pullman cars in usable condition to make up a complete train, and those they did have were all First Class ones. So on their side of the Channel the Golden Arrow was only partly a Pullman train; the rest was made up of ordinary First and Second Class stock. The SR, on the other hand, was able to assemble an all-Pullman train with vehicles of both classes. Second Class passengers had to resign themselves to enjoying 'de luxe' accommodation only between London and Dover.

The schedule of the re-introduced Golden Arrow was as follows:

Southbound:		Northbound:	
Victoria	dep 10.00	Paris (Nord)	dep 11.35
Dover Marine	arr 11.40	Calais Maritime	arr 15.30
	dep 12.30		dep 16.30
Calais Maritime	arr 13.50	Dover Marine	arr 17.50
	dep 14.47		dep 18.50
Paris (Nord)	arr 18.45	Victoria	arr 20.30

The *Canterbury* was used in both directions until the end of the summer. A total time of nearly 9 hours between the two capitals compared poorly with less than 7 hours in the summer of 1939.

The deceleration was due principally to the much greater time needed for the journey between Calais and Paris, but also to longer periods being allowed for embarkation and disembarkation; the Kentish leg of the journey took only 5 minutes longer than before, and the time actually spent at sea remained the same.

The number of cars used in the train on this side of the Channel varied between eight and 10 according to demand. Seven First Class and three Second Class vehicles formed the pool from which they were drawn. One was fitted out with a bar counter and was known as the Trianon Bar (though the actual vehicle was called *Pegasus*). This was an innovation, no such vehicle having run in any previous Pullman train; two more were to make their appearances in later years on the Tees-Tyne Pullman and the South Wales Pullman. The practice was not perpetuated but died with the disappearance of the trains concerned. One finds it a little strange that all that extra weight of coach (over half a complete car) should have been set aside for the convenience of drinkers who wished to take their drinks standing up; they could have had them at any time in their seats. The Trianon Bar broke with Pullman convention in its layout and decor; glossy plastic in pink, grey and cream replaced the usual marquetry and brass. A true Pullman fan must feel it was an unhappy intrusion, like building a small supermarket inside a venerable cathedral in order to sell ecclesiastical mementoes. All the cars were decorated exteriorly with a special device, two arrows pointing in opposite directions on either side of the name or num-

The morning Golden Arrow has just arrived at Dover Marine, and passengers are making their way to the stairway at the platform end which gives access to the boat gangway. Note that the train has no roof-boards - scarcely necessary when each coach had golden arrows on its side. *NRM, York*

ber panel along the waist of each car; they were removable, so that the car could if necessary be transferred to another train. The engine, too, sported its own special device, to be mentioned later.

In mid-October 1946 some alterations were made to the service. On the French side the Second Class coaches were removed from the train, so that Second Class passengers had to proceed from Calais to Paris by a following train, and so reached the capital a good deal later - and, similarly, in the opposite direction had to leave a good deal earlier. There was also some re-timing, Victoria being left at 9.00 and Paris at 12 noon; the journey times were approximately the same as before. The *Canterbury*, too, was now taken out of service, and the newly-delivered *Invicta* replaced it and continued the 80- minute crossing time.

The service continued thus during the winter, but evidently neither the SR nor the French company believed they had the right times and train composition for maximum patronage. In May 1947 Second Class passengers were excluded altogether from the train. The three Second Class cars on the English side were replaced by First Class ones; the French at the same time put on a

Exterior and interior views of *Pegasus*, the Golden Arrow car which contained the Trianon Bar. In utter contrast to the usual Pullman style of interior decoration, the Bar flaunted its up-to-datedness. *Both NRM, York*

train of First Class cars only. This arrangement continued for a year. Then, at the end of October 1948, the departure times from London and Paris became 9.30 am and 12.15 pm respectively; the journeys took more or less the same time as before but were distorted by the timetable, which now allowed for the one hour's difference between British and French time.

Two and a half years later Second Class cars were re-introduced on both sides of the Channel, the French adding ordinary stock as well, and the train was accelerated to something like its 1939 timing, with a 95-minute run between Victoria and Dover in both directions. Departure from London was now also back to the pre-war time of 11.00 am with a return arrival at 7.30 pm. A year later BR put a new train into service to mark the fact that it was the year of the Festival of Britain. Seven cars were newly-built - all First Class, including a new bar vehicle, the second Trianon Bar, and three which had kitchen equipment; an eighth First Class car and two Second Class ones were rebuilds. With one or two subsequent changes these became the regular pool of vehicles from which the train was always made up. The new First Class cars had oblong windows with rounded corners for the toilet compartments in place of the former oval windows, and so could be readily distinguished; all later Pullman cars of the traditional style were thus fitted. The use of leaded glass, however, continued, with a diamond-shaped central pane as before.

In October 1952 it was decided to alter the timing of the southbound service to give a lunchtime departure from London. The ostensible reason was that it was more convenient for the businessman, who could now put in a morning's

New stock on the Golden Arrow; the down train approaches Dover in July 1951 behind No 35027 *Port Line*. *LCGB, Ken Nunn Collection*

work before leaving for Paris, but the convenience of the French railway company was certainly also a factor in bringing about the change, since, as in 1935, on the Continental side it was now possible to use the same rake of vehicles in both directions. Calais continued to be the port used on the French side, but on the English side it had for operational reasons to be Folkestone, not Dover, with a French boat, the *Côte d'Azur*, making the crossing. In the other direction the *Invicta* continued to be used and Dover was the port, as before.

The southbound service took rather more time, since Folkestone is several miles more distant from Calais than Dover, and the journey from Victoria to Folkestone Harbour took longer than to Dover because of the need for the train to stop at Folkestone Junction, be detached from its engine and then be cautiously taken at slow speed down the steep branch to the waterside. All this, and extra waiting time at both ports, made the southbound trip 34 minutes slower than the Dover-routed one in the opposite direction, in which for the first time a 92-minute schedule to Victoria called for some hard work from the locomotive, with speeds of up to 80 mph being attained in the Headcorn dip beyond Ashford.

Between Folkestone Harbour and Dover Marine stations, in the couple of hours between outward arrival and return departure, a good deal of manoeuvring was necessary. The heavy train needed between three and four small tank engines, disposed at either end, to lift it up the bank to Folkestone Junction, where the locomotive that had hauled it from London was waiting, duly coaled and watered and turned on the turntable, to haul it tender-first to Dover Marine and then run around it to couple on to the other end.

Golden Arrow cars being brought down from Folkestone Junction to Folkestone Harbour during the period when the southbound service was routed by way of Folkestone and Calais. At this stage in its journey the tank engine was not so much hauling the cars as holding them back on the steep gradient. ***Steamchest***

This continued to be the pattern of operation for the next 7½ years, but meanwhile it gradually became plain that the afternoon service was being less and less used. The time of arrival in Paris was too late for those who wished to travel further - even if one were occupying a sleeping berth from the Gare de Lyon or the Gare d'Austerlitz, the connection was tight - and by now businessmen were increasingly going by air. So at the end of May 1960 there was a reversion to the former departure time, and the schedule was as follows:

Southbound		Northbound:	
Victoria	dep 11.00	Paris (Nord)	dep 12.45
Dover Marine	arr 12.37	Calais Maritime	arr15.55
	dep 13.05		dep 16.20
Calais Maritime	arr 14.25	Dover Marine	arr 19.50
	dep 14.52		dep 18.13
Paris (Nord)	arr 18.10	Victoria	arr 19.50

The deceleration of the train on the Kentish side by 5 minutes was due to engineering works on the main line through Tonbridge and Ashford consequent on electrification. Indeed, the service sometimes had to be diverted by way of Chatham, which made time-keeping impossible. On the French side, however, electrification had been completed from Paris to Amiens, and a little acceleration was possible with the Calais-bound train despite the need to change from electric to steam traction *en route*.

Further alterations were not long in coming. By the beginning of June the whole line from Victoria to Dover had been electrified and newly-built electric engines took the place of the steam ones. With their increased ability of accelerating and greater power available for climbing banks they were able to maintain much better timings than ever before. From 11 June a whole quarter of an hour was knocked off the existing southbound schedule, and nearly as much northbound. The following timings now obtained:

Southbound:		Northbound:	
Victoria	dep 11.00	Paris (Nord)	dep 12.39
Dover Marine	arr 12.22	Calais Maritime	arr 15.45
	dep 12.50		dep 16.10
Calais Maritime	arr 14.10	Dover Marine	arr 17.30
	dep 14.40		dep 18.10
Paris (Nord)	arr 17.50	Victoria	arr 19.35

Thus things continued until May 1966, with minor changes in the departure time from Paris and necessary adjustments when the dates for adopting summer and winter alterations of the clock for daylight saving were different in both countries.

In 1965 BR withdrew the Second Class Pullmans between London and Dover and substituted ordinary Second Class accommodation, two coaches usually being sufficient, so that the visual effect of the train was somewhat spoiled. Two years earlier the car with the Trianon Bar had also been removed. In 1966 the final timetable change was made, departure from Victoria being advanced to 10.30 with a Paris arrival at 17.25 in the periods when the day-light-saving arrangements were similar.

On 31 May 1966 the Golden Arrow, as a Pullman service, ceased to exist on the French side, ordinary First and Second Class carriages replacing the Pullman cars. The latter were retained here, but the characteristic Pullman livery now disappeared, the First Class cars being given a blue-and-light-grey colouring similar to the rest of BR's express passenger stock. The cars lost their names and the detachable longitudinal arrows; each merely had the words Golden Arrow in the middle of each coach side. Meanwhile the number of them in the train was diminishing, until in 1969 they composed less than half of the train's formation, four Second Class coaches (including a buffet car) and two luggage vans accompanying four Pullman cars. The other First Class cars were held in reserve.

The end was now in sight. Pullman services were vanishing in other parts of Britain, except between London and Manchester; BR was preparing something very different to attract passengers from the provision of special extra-fare luxury trains. Paris was now only two hours from London by air and more and more people chose to go that way. The train's final journey was made in September 1972 and a piece of railway history begun almost half a century earlier came to an end.

Golden Arrow locomotive adornments - No 34039 *Boscastle* displays the name-board and arrow, the French and Union flags, and the large golden arrow on the 'air-smoothed' boiler casing. *LCGB, Ken Nunn Collection*

In regard to locomotive work on the train, and its performance, the second Golden Arrow was more distinguished than the first, since at last engines of adequate power were available to haul it. During the Second World War O. V. S. Bulleid, the SR's Chief Mechanical Engineer, fluttered a few dovecotes by his unconventional locomotive designs, notably by the so-called 'Mixed Traffic' 4-6-2s (thus described to avoid criticism; one could hardly justify building express passenger engines in wartime, but that was what in fact these locomotives were - or why else where they given names?). This is not the place to dwell on the pros and cons of these rather remarkable engines; enough to say that nothing of similar tractive power had ever been seen on SR metals before. The 'Nelsons' of 1926/1928 had been built to enable the haulage of 500-ton trains at average speeds of 55 mph; this they could only just manage to do. The Bulleid 'Pacifics' did it easily, as the following chapter on the Devon Belle indicates.

Such a locomotive, either of the larger 'Merchant Navy' Class or of the slightly smaller but equally competent 'West Country' Class, was assigned to haul the Golden Arrow for most of the years when it was steam-operated. On these occasions they were specially decorated. A circular plate with the name of the train across it was fixed to the front of the smokebox, in front of which a large golden arrow pointed obliquely downwards; another similar arrow, pointing forwards, decorated the side of the boiler sheeting. Above the buffer beam were two short flagpoles arranged in a V, one bearing the Union Flag, the other the French Tricolour. All the steam locomotives selected to haul the Golden Arrow were adorned in this way.

Later, however, when electric locomotives took their place, the scheme was much modified: a single board with the name of the train on it and an arrow between the two words sufficed, and the two flags and side-arrows disappeared; the effect was much less impressive. The change was necessary because of the need for the driver to get a clear view through his front driving window. Other kinds of locomotives other than Bulleid 'Pacifics' did occasionally head the train before electrification was completed between London and Dover. During two separate weeks in the late winter and early spring of 1955 two of BR's experimental diesel-electric locomotives each took a turn. There were also periods during 1961 when smaller diesel locomotives working in pairs took the train by the Chatham route while the main line through Tonbridge was temporarily unusable because of electrification works.

But the chief alternative locomotive type, used continuously for 6½ years apart from a few short breaks (as when the two diesels mentioned above were used, and once when an accident occurred to the designated engine) was a newly-built Class 7 Standard 4-6-2 of the 'Britannia' design. No 70004 *William Shakespeare*, after being exhibited at the Festival of Britain site near Waterloo Bridge during the summer of 1951, was sent to Stewart's Lane depot together with No 70014, *Iron Duke*, and one of the two, usually the former, was given the regular task of hauling the Arrow in both directions until June 1958.

I have not been able to discover any records of performance by either of

During one of the short periods when it was diesel-hauled, the Golden Arrow passes Brixton on its way to Dover headed by Nos D6527 and D5013 in March 1961. *Hugh Ballantyne*

these two locomotives with the Golden Arrow, but the fact that they ran with it for such a long time suggests that they were well up to the job. So far as power was concerned each was equivalent in tractive effort to a 'West Country' 4-6-2 and did not have the same tendency for things to go wrong. They were well able to keep time with similarly scheduled 400-ton trains on other parts of the BR system. As to the work of the Bulleid 'Pacifics' before and after the 'Britannia' interlude, there is a fair amount of information available. What strikes one, when logs of performance on the pre-war and post-war Arrow are compared, is the greater ability of the newer engines to hurry with this train when the time needed to be recovered. In theory a 'Nelson' was slightly more forceful than one of Bulleid's smaller 'Pacifics', but the latter had a far better boiler. With all their faults (and they had many) the Bulleid engines in their unrebuilt state could steam well, even on inferior coal, of which drivers on the SR got more than their share.

Two logs of down journeys, appended overleaf, display typical performance on the Golden Arrow during a period when a Bulleid 4-6-2 was in charge. In the first, on the earlier 100-minute schedule with a 14-vehicle load (some of which were of course vans), time was steadily gained to Tonbridge by No 34091 *Weymouth*, with (for this train) a high speed at Hildenborough; beyond

No 70004 *William Shakespeare* is a stirring sight at the head of the Golden Arrow near Bickley in July 1955. *Brian Morrison*

Tonbridge a permanent way check cost something like half a minute, but the engine recovered quickly to maintain between 66 and 76 all the way on the generally rising stretch to Ashford, where it was 4½ minutes early; at Folkestone, despite easy running, this had increased to 6 minutes; Dover was reached almost 7 minutes before time. In the second run tabulated the extra power of a 'Merchant Navy' Class engine is evident. *Clan Line*, on the faster 95-minute schedule, arrived 3¼ minutes early despite four checks *en route*. The exit from Victoria was more rapid, the climb to Knockholt more vigorous, and the unusually high maximum of 71 before Sevenoaks took the train through Tonbridge 2½ minutes early. With no checks thenceforward until Ashford had been passed, the train was 4½ minutes early at the latter point, and despite the permanent way slowing before Smeeth and the signal checks after Folkestone, Dover was reached well before time.

In the up direction the Arrow's progress over the fast stretch from Westenhanger summit to Tonbridge frequently resembled - indeed, sometimes bettered - that of the 80-minute Folkestone to London expresses at their best.

Bulleid 'Pacifics' on the Golden Arrow - down

Locomotive		34091 *Weymouth*			35028 *Clan Line*		
Gross load in tons		455			445		
Miles		**min**	**sec**	**speed**	**min**	**sec**	**speed**
00.0	Victoria	00	00		00	00	
04.0	Herne Hill	09	48	37	08	52	39
05.7	Sydenham Hill	13	37	24	11	53	33
						pws	28
08.7	Beckenham Junc	17	58	58	16	32	50
10.9	Bromley South	20	31	57	19	12	57
12.6	Bickley Junc	23	00	30	21	32	32
						sigs	38
14.9	Orpington	27	13	42	25	29	33
17.6	Knockholt	31	38	32	30	05	34
21.7	Dunton Green	36	25	66	34	29	71
23.2	Sevenoaks	37	52		35	49	
				54			60
28.1	Hildenborough	42	27	78	40	20	71
30.6	Tonbridge	45	13	33	43	02	40
			pws	35			
35.0	Paddock Wood	52	24		48	35	
40.5	Marden	56	25	71	52	35	73
43.0	Staplehurst	58	34	66	54	51	63
46.3	Headcorn	61	15	76/67	57	44	72/62
51.5	Pluckley	65	40	73	62	25	68
55.1	Milepost 54	68	44	66	65	35	64
57.2	Ashford	70	32	74	67	25	73
						pws	
61.5	Smeeth	74	27	60/63	71	07	48
65.3	Westenhanger	78	16	54	75	26	54
66.5	Sandling Junc	79	36		76	47	67
72.0	Folkestone Junc	85	03	60/65	89	59	56/58
						sigs	
78.0	Dover Marine	93	10		91	45	

One may cite a run made in August 1951, when *Weymouth* again distinguished itself at the head of a very heavy train. There was some slipping at Folkestone, so that Sandling Junction was passed 1 3/4 minutes late on the 100-minute schedule, but then followed a headlong dash for Tonbridge with three separate maxima of 80 or more, one being not far short of 90 at Headcorn, until a bad permanent way check at Marden caused Tonbridge to be passed half a minute

Bulleid 'Pacifics' on the Golden Arrow - up

Locomotive		34091 *Weymouth*		
Gross load in tons		470		
Miles		**min**	**sec**	**speed**
00.0	Dover Marine	00	00	
06.0	Folkestone Junc	12	52	
11.5	Sandling Junc	20	49	
12.7	Westenhanger	22	24	28
16.5	Smeeth	25	59	69/66
20.8	Ashford	29	25	80
22.9	Milepost 54	31	05	73/80
26.5	Pluckley	33	51	74
31.7	Headcorn	37	37	88
35.0	Staplehurst	39	58	78
37.5	Marden	41	49	
			pws	13
42.1	Paddock Wood	49	56	57
47.4	Tonbridge	55	36	48/52
49.9	Hildenborough	58	46	
52.2	Sevenoaks tun'l S	62	30	37
54.8	Sevenoaks	66	39	
56.3	Dunton Green	68	14	65
60.4	Knockholt	72	26	49
			sigs	28
63.1	Orpington	76	00	45
65.4	Bickley Junc	79	26	40
67.1	Bromley South	81	50	49
69.3	Beckenham Junc	84	44	
			sigs	
74.0	Herne Hill	96	36	
			sigs	
78.0	Victoria	105	02	

late. A good climb, with this load, was made to Sevenoaks tunnel, and a still better one to Knockholt, so that the train was half a minute early at Orpington, but signal checks then made the train late into Victoria. Running of this sort was never seen on the Golden Arrow in pre-war days, except when some special effort was made - as on the occasion of Bulleid's celebrated footplate trip, mentioned above in Chapter 13.

18

The Devon Belle

1947-54

When at the commencement of the summer season in 1947 the SR decided to put into service an all-Pullman train to the West of England, to run during the summer months, they were flying in the face of previous omens. The short career of the GWR's Torquay Pullman 17 years earlier had suggested that there was not much demand for such a train from those going on holiday in the West Country, and from day tourists there could of course be none at all over such a distance. However, there were special circumstances which afforded hope that such a train might prove profitable, both to the railway company and to the Pullman organisation.

The accepted route for travel to Devon and Cornwall might seem to have been that of the GWR, whose trains in 1939 had been reaching Exeter in less time than the Southern's, and Plymouth in very much less time - 4 hours by the Cornish Riviera Express. However, there were some parts of Devon which were more conveniently reached by the former LSWR route, which the Atlantic Coast Express had long been serving, and it was decided to make Ilfracombe the new train's main destination, while also including a portion for Plymouth.

The latter decision on the face of it seemed surprising, for although the GWR's 4-hour run to that city had not yet been restored, that line could still make the faster time over a somewhat shorter and (except west of Newton Abbot) very much easier route. The explanation lies in bookability of seats. After six years of wartime discouragement from travel, when the public was being continually asked 'Is your journey really necessary?', this facility had not yet been re-introduced for ordinary travellers, but with Pullman Car services it was immediately available, since it had always been part of what was offered in return for the supplement. Not only so, but in general the Pullman cars, which had been for the most part out of use and in store since 1939, and (so to speak) mothballed, were in good condition, whereas much of the railways' ordinary rolling-stock was not. Thus, so far as offering merely guaranteed comfort, let alone luxury, was concerned, the Pullman car had a built-in advantage. The traveller could be sure of his seat, and if he wanted refreshments they could be brought to him as he sat there.

A special Pullman train from Waterloo to the West of England could therefore offer certain attractions, at any rate for a short while, to anyone going

The Devon Belle heads west away from the capital near Clapham Junction behind an unidentified 'Merchant Navy' 'Pacific'. ***Steamchest***

there on holiday, whether to Ilfracombe and thereabouts, or to Plymouth and its vicinity, or to that part of the South Devon coast east of the Exe estuary which the GWR had never served. A time of $5\frac{1}{2}$ hours to either destination, while slow compared with what the latter company could offer in 1939, was not so excessive in comparison with existing GWR timings. As to comfort, the special wide-bodied stock built for the Cornish Riviera Express was not now, after 18 years of use, six of them in wartime conditions, what it had been. The little extra time spent in surroundings where one could sit back and relax in the ambience of polished brasswork and marquetry was not likely to be a matter of much concern when one was going on holiday and had all the time in the world.

As if to emphasise that it was indeed a holiday train, the railway company and Pullman Car Company between them took a leaf out of the pre-war LNER's practice in regard to its luxury Coronation express between King's Cross and Edinburgh, and added to each of the two rakes of cars a specially made Observation car. These two vehicles were not newly built for the purpose, as the Coronation's 'beaver-tail' cars had been, but were rebuilt from old Third Class cars of First World War vintage; steel underframes were fitted, and above the floor-level the front three-eighths contained a refreshment buffet with a small pantry and kitchen, while the rear five-eighths had swivelling seats, single armchairs and double settees, which could be swung to any angle, and an almost continuous wall of window-glass on either side and at the end, with only very narrow uprights between the panes to support the roof. No charge was

L M A N
AR Nº27 THIRD CLASS
PULLMAN OBSERVATION CAR

SAVONA

Left **The Observation car at the rear of the Devon Belle photographed somewhere in the London area. The vehicle's buffet section is situated behind the small high windows.** ***Herbert Collection, NRM, York***
Below left **Interior of the Observation car. Note the clear views obtainable to the side and rear of the train, the swivelling seats and the double-seats.** ***NRM, York***

made to passengers visiting the car during the journey; the idea seems to have been that they should supply themselves with drinks from the buffet and sit down and consume them while viewing the receding landscape. A certain amount of low cunning was shown by the designers, who made sure that the seats were markedly less comfortable than those in the main part of the train, so that no one would want to remain there too long; after the initial excitement of seeing the track and linesides disappearing backwards at high speed for a few minutes, the memory of superior comfort in the seats they had vacated, and for whose occupation they had paid good money, would re-assert itself and they would make room for others.

The train, like the ill-fated Torquay Pullman, was not to run daily, but on Mondays, Fridays, Saturdays and Sundays in each direction during its first summer, and additionally on Thursdays down and Tuesdays up from 1948-51; during these four years it was making as many journeys a week as a Mondays-to-Fridays train such as the Tees-Tyne Pullman, and with a greater number of cars. The schedule of the train in both directions was as follows, weekdays and Sundays alike

Down:		Up:	
Waterloo	dep 12.00	Ilfracombe	dep 12.00
Sidmouth Junc	arr 15.16	Mortehoe	dep 12.12
Exeter Central	arr 15.36	Braunton	dep 12.23
		Barnstaple Town	dep 12.32
Exeter Central	dep 15.39	Barnstaple Junc	dep 12.37
Exeter St Davids	dep 15.45	Exeter St Davids	dep 13.33
Okehampton	dep 16.27	Exeter Central	arr 13.38
		Devonport	arr 17.16
Plymouth North Road	arr 17.15	Plymouth Friary	dep 11.30
Plymouth Friary	arr 17.36	Plymouth North Road	dep 11.40
		Devonport	dep 11.47
Exeter Central	dep 15.48	Okehampton	dep 12.45
Exeter St Davids	dep 15.48	Exeter St Davids	dep 13.23
Barnstaple Junc	dep 16.51	Exeter Central	arr 13.27
Barnstaple Town	dep 16.55		
Braunton	dep 17.05	Exeter Central	dep 13.40
Mortehoe	dep 17.23	Sidmouth Junc	dep 14.03
Ilfracombe	arr 17.32	Waterloo	arr 17.20

Compared with the schedule of the Atlantic Coast Express which preceded it both from Waterloo and Exeter, this was not particularly impressive in terms of speed; the ACE, progressively accelerated, was half an hour faster than the Belle going down to Exeter, and also coming back, in 1954; the Pullman retained the same timings throughout its existence. There were two good reasons why it was so slow. In the first place, it had to make a stop to change engines at Wilton, 2½ miles west of Salisbury, since the SR had no water troughs anywhere on its system, and even the large tenders of the locomotives used could not have lasted out as far as Sidmouth Junction, let alone Exeter. It was usual for engines to be changed at Salisbury; in the case of the Belle it was operationally more convenient to do this at Wilton. Allowing for stopping and starting, uncoupling and recoupling, this in itself used up the best part of 10 minutes.

Secondly, the Devon Belle was always a heavy train, and sometimes extraordinarily heavy. The minimum formation was 12 cars, three Thirds and a First for Plymouth, four Thirds and three Firsts plus the Observation car for Ilfracombe. On occasions of heavy traffic the latter portion could be strengthened by two more cars. This meant a regular load exceeding 500 tons, which might on occasion reach 570 tons or more. No other Pullman train in the country ever approached such a loading as this. Although the locomotives provided between Waterloo and Exeter were always the most powerful that the SR, and later the Southern Region of BR, possessed - 'Merchant Navy' 4-6-2s - it simply would not have been possible to accelerate the train without lessening the load.

Such a train was of course a magnificent occasion for publicity - something like the equivalent of being the largest Atlantic liner afloat - and the authorities saw that it was adequately placarded. Every car except the Observation car bore its title on headboards along the roof edges, and there was also an oblong headboard on the locomotive smokebox. In addition, for most of its period of service it also carried a wing-shaped board fixed to each smoke deflector, marked DEVON BELLE in very large letters. Only the Golden Arrow advertised itself more splendidly. However, the wing-boards were eventually removed after one of them came adrift through air-suction as the up train was passing the down Atlantic Coast Express near Honiton and struck the engine that was hauling it.

Of all the trains dealt with in this book, the Devon Belle probably offered the best lineside viewing from its windows, and from the Observation car the prospect must have been even more alluring, could one have endured the uncomfortable seating for long enough. The section beyond Wilton, with its many up-and-down gables, on the declivities of which speeds in the 80s would regularly be reached, must have offered the railway equivalent of a helter-skelter through the extremely attractive Dorset, Somerset and East Devon scenery. The choicest parts would have been the last few miles at the westward end of the main train's journey, along the Taw estuary and northwards to Ilfracombe, with occasional glimpses of the sea, with Baggy Point and Mortehoe Point (the wickedest headland in England, cause of many wrecks) along the shore, and Lundy Island on the horizon.

The winged nameboard of the Devon Belle being worn by a 'Merchant Navy' 'Pacific'. This locomotive has been detailed to work the train from Exeter to Wilton, and stands at Exeter Central waiting to couple on to the rake, which can be glimpsed beyond the smokebox. ***Steamchest***

As already mentioned, locomotive provision was always a 'Merchant Navy' 4-6-2 east of Exeter; to the west both the Plymouth and the Ilfracombe portions usually had one of the somewhat smaller 'West Country' 4-6-2s, of which the Southern Region had an adequate, and in later years almost an over-adequate, supply. The timings beyond Exeter were not demanding and one wonders how often a 'West Country' hauling the four coaches of the Plymouth portion needed to make up time lost east of Exeter by running hard over Meldon summit. Between Waterloo and Exeter the hardest work was that needed between Wilton and Sidmouth Junction, $73\frac{1}{2}$ miles, for which 83 minutes were allowed. In the opposite direction the timing was 89 minutes, but the start from Exeter was frequently late, since only 2 minutes were allowed for coupling the two portions together, so that hard running in the up direction must also sometimes have been required.

Although not many recordings seem to have been made of locomotive performance on this train, one made by Mr A. J. Baker in August 1949 is worth mentioning at length. The engine was No 35008 *Orient Line*, in its unrebuilt state, and the load was 575 tons full. The start from Wilton was not easy, a mile at 1 in 144 having to be tackled almost from the platform end; beyond that were a number of summits preceded by heavy grades of varying lengths, culminating in the rise to Honiton tunnel after a 7-mile climb out of the valley of the Axe, a long slog at between 1 in 132 and 1 in 80 with a half-mile midway at 1 in 70 - one of the toughest climbs in the whole country and no joke with 14 Pullman cars behind the tender. To gain nearly 3 minutes on schedule despite such a load and the handicap of a permanent way check before Crewkerne was a most meritorious achievement - and the engine then went on to gain a further $1\frac{1}{4}$ minutes on the short run into Exeter. Maximum speeds were 79 at Gillingham, 78 before Templecombe, 83 at Sherborne, 87 after Axminster and 80 before the stop at Sidmouth Junction; minima were 46 at Semley, 57 after Gillingham, 47 before Milborne Port, 54 up Sutton Bingham bank followed by a slowing for track repair to 26, 31 at milepost $113\frac{1}{4}$ after a recovery to 60 at Crewkerne, 30 at the top of the steepest part of the rise to Honiton tunnel, and 34 at the tunnel's exit. The total time for the 73.4 miles was 80 minutes 10 seconds.

On another occasion, similarly loaded and without any check, No 21C7 in the former SR numbering, *Aberdeen Commonwealth*, beat this by almost 2 minutes, with maximum speeds exceeding 80 mph on six occasions, one of them, at Sherborne, being a 90. The gain on time would have been greater than it was if the engine had not started slipping on the ascent to Honiton tunnel, with the consequence that speed fell to 22 mph. The total time taken was 78 minutes 19 seconds.

Seen from the rear, the Devon Belle storms through Surbiton in mid-June 1947. ***Herbert Collection, NRM, York***

For a while the SR's hopes in regard to the Devon Belle were fulfilled, Ilfracombe in particular attracting passengers on Saturdays, so that additional cars were then required. The Plymouth portion was less well patronised once the Western Region was able to offer a really fast service from Paddington. From operating for five days a week during the summers of 1948-51 the Belle fell to three the following year: Fridays, Saturdays and Sundays outwards, and Mondays, Saturdays and Sundays returning. From 1950, also, the front four cars ceased to run to Plymouth, being detached at Exeter Central and returning on the up train the next day.

In 1954, in an attempt to attract further custom, a radical acceleration of the westbound service on Fridays was made, together with a change in the departure time from Waterloo to 16.40. Additional stops were made at Salisbury (where water was taken, the same engine then continuing to Exeter and not stopping at Wilton as before) and at Axminster, where a connection could be made for Lyme Regis. For the first time a fast schedule was established as far as Salisbury, reached in 85 minutes from Waterloo, and (considering the gradients) this was followed by an equally fast one of 66 minutes thence to Axminster. The result was that without any further speed-up Ilfracombe was reached at 21.48, after a journey almost 20 minutes quicker than before. This may have been a try-out, to see whether similar accelerations were possible on other days of the week, and in both directions. At the end of that summer no firm decision had been made on whether or not to abolish the service. But it did not appear again in the following summer's timetable; it had evidently been written off as no longer a profitable venture. So, like the Torquay Pullman before it, but after a longer spell of service, it passed into limbo.

19

The Thanet and Kentish Belles

1948-58

Besides re-introducing the Golden Arrow, Brighton Belle and Bournemouth Belle, the Southern Railway, before it went into public ownership together with the other three of the 'Big Four', had been planning another all-Pullman service to Thanet. The earlier one, as described in Chapter 8, had not been economically successful, and even while it lasted had only run on Sundays. Post-war optimism showed itself in the mooting of a similar service to the resorts of the North Kent coast, from Whitstable to Ramsgate, during the summer season, which would run both on Sundays and weekdays. A 10-car train was planned, of which only two were First Class; the service was aimed at a popular market, whereas the Thanet Pullman had been First Class only.

The Thanet Belle made its first out-and-back journey on 31 May 1948, five months after the SR had been merged into British Railways. The timetable was as follows:

		Mon-Fri	Sat	Sun
Victoria	dep	11.30	15.05	11.30
Whitstable	arr	12.52	16.30	12.52
Herne Bay	arr	13.01	16.39	13.01
Margate	arr	13.17	16.56	13.17
Broadstairs	arr	13.28	17.07	13.28
Ramsgate	arr	13.34	17.15	13.34

and in the reverse direction:

Ramsgate	dep	17.05	18.15	18.15
Broadstairs	dep	17.10	18.20	18.20
Margate	dep	17.18	18.27	18.27
Herne Bay	dep	17.35	18.48	18.48
Whitstable	dep	17.44	18.57	18.57
Victoria	arr	19.10	20.20	20.20

This pattern was exactly repeated the following summer, but in 1950 the Saturday timings were changed. This was perhaps associated with the spread of

The down Thanet Belle near Bickley in the summer of 1948. The locomotive is 'light Pacific' No 21C268 *Kenley*. *LCGB, Ken Nunn Collection*

the five-day week, which tended to give people whole Saturdays free from work. On this day the train ran outwards from Victoria at 7.55 am - the earliest departure time of any all-Pullman train anywhere in Great Britain up to that year - and began its return journey before midday. The timings were:

Outward:		Return:	
Victoria	dep 7.55	Ramsgate	dep 11.15
Whitstable	arr 9.23	Broadstairs	dep 11.22
Herne Bay	arr 9.34	Margate	dep 11.32
Margate	arr 9.53	Herne Bay	dep 11.52
Broadstairs	arr 10.05	Whitstable	dep 12.03
Ramsgate	arr 10.13	Victoria	arr 13.28

Except during 1952, when the Saturday trains returned to their 1948 timings, this remained the pattern on that day. From 1952 the Monday-Friday and Sunday timings in both directions were what they had been in 1948, with the exception that the morning down train ran 5 minutes later throughout, while in 1957 and 1958 a stop was made at Dumpton Park, between Broadstairs and Ramsgate, by the up service between Monday and Friday and on Sunday, and a 3 minutes earlier departure was made from Ramsgate in consequence.

Like the Southern Belle and Bournemouth Belle, this train was for those going on holiday, not for businessmen, though no doubt some of the latter used it on its way back from the coast and helped to fill the First Class seats. One cannot help remarking how leisurely the timings were, especially on Saturdays. This is no doubt partly to be accounted for by the difficult gradients, and partly by the weight of the train, but undoubtedly one contributory cause was the provision of locomotive power. The SR, and the Southern region of BR after it, did not dispose of as large a number of steam express passenger engines as did the other three regions in 1948. O. V. S. Bulleid had begun the rapid construction of his 'light Pacifics', of which there were eventually as many as 110, and had they always been available the haulage of a 400-ton train over the former Chatham line would have been feasible on faster timings than the ones laid down, even on a schedule equivalent to the former non-stop 90-minute Victoria-Margate timing of the former Thanet Sunday Pullman.

However, the schedules had to be tailored to meet the Region's special needs, especially the exigencies of summer Saturdays when heavy boat trains between Victoria and Folkestone or Dover might have to be run in duplicate or triplicate. On such occasions there might very well not be a 'Pacific' available and a smaller engine would have to be supplied. It was not uncommon for a 'U' Class mixed traffic 2-6-0 to appear at the head of the train. Another possibility was a 4-4-0 'Schools'. There were even occasions when an 'L' 4-4-0 of 1914 vintage had to be used, and with the full load of Pullman cars such an engine would need every minute of the generous Saturday schedule in order to keep time. Probably the extra minutes taken on the journey did not matter very much to persons who regarded their occupation of a Pullman car seat as part of their holiday or day's outing. Certainly the Pullman attendants, serving main meals

The down Kentish Belle hauled, for a change, by a 'Schools', No 30938 *St Olave's*. *Steamchest*

to passengers in both directions, must have been glad of the extra time.

1951 was a special year, that of the Festival of Britain, the centenary celebration of the Hyde Park Exhibition in the Crystal Palace. Festivities were officially encouraged, and it was hoped that foreign visitors would be attracted to this country in large numbers. An obvious goal for tourists was Canterbury, with its famous cathedral and historical associations. It was decided that during that summer the Thanet Belle should carry a Canterbury portion of two or three cars between Monday and Friday, and that the train should stop at Faversham in either direction to detach or attach them. Since Canterbury was not in the Isle of Thanet, the train's title was altered to the Kentish Belle, which it kept thenceforward even after it ceased to serve Canterbury in subsequent years.[1] The 1951 schedules between the weekends were as follows:

Outward:		Return:	
Victoria	dep 11.30	Ramsgate	dep 16.55
Faversham	arr 12.43	Broadstairs	dep 17.01
		Margate	dep 17.10
Canterbury	arr 13.06	Herne Bay	dep 17.27
		Whitstable	dep 17.36
Whitstable	arr 12.56		
Herne Bay	arr 13.06	Canterbury	dep 17.30
Margate	arr 13.33		
Broadstairs	arr 13.33	Faversham	dep 17.58
Ramsgate	arr 13.40	Victoria	arr 19.05

As things turned out, the Canterbury portion was never well patronised and almost certainly did not pay; there appear to have been occasions when the cars for that city ran completely empty. One peculiarity of this short journey, from Faversham, was the locomotive provision. Any engine that was handy would do. While the train went grandly on behind its customary 'Pacific', the portion for the cathedral city was trundled over the gable between Faversham and the Stour valley by some locally available locomotive, which might be a Standard 2-6-4 tank engine of recent build or an ancient 50-year-old Wainwright 'D' 4-4-0.

In general, apart from the unsuccessful Canterbury venture, the Kentish Belle was a success, though never a money-spinner. In 1959 electrification of the main line from Victoria to Thanet by way of Chatham was complete, and multiple unit trains provided a regular interval service; they were vestibuled and had refreshments facilities, but no Pullman cars. It would have been possible to retain the Kentish Belle, just as the Golden Arrow had been retained, since a number of electric locomotives had been built for the haulage of Continental and other special trains, and for freight work. However, it would

[1] A purist would regard the new title as a misnomer. By tradition the people of Kent are known as 'Men of Kent' east of the Medway and 'Kentishmen' west of it. Belle of Kent would therefore have been a more correct title. But no one seems ever to have complained.

A fine portrait of the Kentish Belle between Bickley and St Mary Cray in July 1955, No 34067 *Tangmere* in charge. *Brian Morrison*

have been inconvenient fitting it into the regular-interval pattern. At this time, too, British Railways was re-thinking its whole attitude to the provision of special luxury trains, which in future were angled in the direction of the needs of the business traveller. It was therefore decided to run the Kentish Belle no longer once the third rail system had reached Ramsgate, and its last journeys were made on 14 September 1958.

20

Post-war restored Pullman trains from King's Cross

While each of the restored all-Pullman services into and out of King's Cross could have been considered separately, it seems more convenient to treat all three together, since their fortunes were in many respects similar, and had each been dealt with singly it might not have needed more than a few paragraphs.

It may seem surprising that the streamlined trains of 1935-9 were not brought back, but a few moments' reflection will explain this. They had not been mothballed during the war, but had seen service of one sort or another. Furthermore, they had been built to work in specially fast services, which until the permanent way all over the country had been brought into thorough repair could not be restored. To have run the Silver Jubilee from London to Newcastle in 5 hours instead of the pre-war 4 would merely have emphasised that things were not what they had once been. Moreover, the former names now smacked of past history. Pullman trains, on the other hand, suggested comfort rather than speed and were acceptable on that ground. So it was the Queen of Scots, the Yorkshire Pullman and the Harrogate Sunday Pullman which came back into service again, to be followed by other all-Pullman services which had not run before, and which merit description in the chapter following this one.

The restored services resembled the former ones as to the times when they ran, approximately, and in appearance, except that more cars were included in each rake, and that, between Yorkshire and London, the once-familiar Ivatt 'Atlantics' were no longer to be seen hauling them. The latter engines had now either been withdrawn or were about to be, and such as survived had worn themselves out during the war and were now only fit for light duties. 'Pacifics' took their places. On the LNER there were now four types of these: the 'A1s' and 'A2s' built by Gresley's successors, Thompson and Peppercorn; the 'A3s' built by Gresley, to which his former 'A1s' had now all been assimilated by rebuilding; and the streamlined 'A4s', which had been slightly altered in appearance by having the valances beneath their curved running plates removed.

The re-introduced Pullman cars were at first all of pre-war design, though as time went on these were gradually replaced by new cars whose interior arrangements were different; there was less concern to gratify the eye with marquetry and brasswork, but more attention was paid to bodily comfort (First Class passengers being given seats whose backs were adjustable, so that one could semi-recline if one wished).

So far as journey times were concerned, all the restored services had a common feature. Necessarily slow at first, they were accelerated by degrees to about 1955, after which they remained about the same, or slowed a little, so far as travel to or from Yorkshire was concerned. As long as steam traction was employed the average speeds reached in 1939 were not re-attained.

* * *

The Queen of Scots came back in 1948 with a regular formation of 10 cars, of which two proceeded no further than Leeds. The usual locomotive provision was an Peppercorn 'A1' 'Pacific' both to Leeds and onward. As far as Leeds the schedule was considerably slower than the 191 minutes down and 190 minutes up of the 1939 service, being as follows:

Northbound:		Southbound:	
King' Cross	dep 11.30	Glasgow	dep 10.15
Leeds	arr 15.12	Edinburgh	dep 11.25
Harrogate	arr 15.53	Newcastle	dep 14.07
Darlington	arr 16.41	Darlington	dep 14.58
Newcastle	arr 17.31	Harrogate	dep 15.49
Edinburgh	arr 20.12	Leeds	dep 16.30
Glasgow	arr 21.22	King's Cross	arr 20.10

The up Queen of Scots runs into Edinburgh Waverley soon after the train's re-establishment in 1948, hauled by the as yet un-renumbered Gresley 'Pacific' No 2574 *St Frusquin. Steamchest*

The journey time between London and Edinburgh in either direction was now about an hour longer than in 1939, with considerable slowings on the London-Leeds and Newcastle-Edinburgh sections; on the former the 55 mph average was barely exceeded, while on the latter, with a train lighter by two cars, the average speed was about 46 mph.

Over the next few years, as the condition of the track improved, timings improved with them, and by 1955 the schedule was as follows:

Northbound:		Southbound:	
King's Cross	dep 12.05	Glasgow	dep 10.50
Leeds	arr 15.19	Edinburgh	dep 12.00
Harrogate	arr 15.58	Newcastle	dep 14.17
Darlington	arr 16.49	Darlington	dep 15.01
Newcastle	arr 17.34	Harrogate	dep 15.50
Edinburgh	arr 19.47	Leeds	dep 16.35
Glasgow	arr 20.59	King's Cross	arr 19.48

The total time taken between the two capitals was now about the same as in 1939 - slightly more in the down direction, slightly less in the up. The most

The down Queen of Scots approaching Potters Bar in May 1951 headed by Peppercorn 'A1' 'Pacific' No 60114 W. P. Allen. ***Brian Morrison***

striking acceleration was that between Newcastle and Edinburgh, where the average speed was much better than anything ever previously scheduled. Advantage was now taken of the speed potentialities of this route, with its lengthy racing ground between Chathill and Beal. Here the attainment of 80 mph or more was not common in pre-war days, except with the lightweight Coronation, but frequent enough with the post-war Pullman. Moreover, the timings along this stretch were to become faster still, to culminate in 1963 with 125 minutes down and 122 minutes up - the latter exceeding the mile-a-minute average and being only 2 minutes short of the former Coronation schedule. With an eight-car train, loading some 30 tons or so more than the streamliner, this was as demanding a timing, particularly as the 'A1' 'Pacifics' did not have the slight advantage that their streamlined shapes gave to the 'A4s'.

1963 was the Queen of Scots' final year. In BR the 'mood at the top' was now a ruthless determination to prune services which did not appear to bring in more than was expended on them. As far as Harrogate the train was covering its costs of operation through fares charged; north of Harrogate it was a different story. The whole service was therefore terminated at Harrogate, and since the existing title was now irrelevant as the train no longer went across the Scottish Border, it was re-named the White Rose - the title being transferred from another non-Pullman train. In this guise it continued into the era of diesel operation, the splendid fleet of East Coast 'Pacifics' being withdrawn and going for scrap except for the few which have been preserved.

Towards the end of the train's career, in May 1961, 'A1' No 60148 *Aboyeur* picks up water at Langley troughs, south of Stevenage, on the up service. *Steamchest*

However, the writing was on the wall. Though the White Rose just made it into the 'Deltic' era and achieved a much faster timing as far as Leeds than any Pullman before it, it was taken off in 1967. Except on the London to Manchester service, where a short-lived Pullman era was just beginning, the all-Pullman train was now on the way out in Britain; within a few years they would all be gone.

* * *

The Yorkshire Pullman was also resuscitated in 1947, to run in much the same schedule slots as before, though, as with the Queen of Scots, to easier timings. The same towns were served as in 1939, a single rake of cars being sufficient. It left Leeds late in the morning and returned from King's Cross late in the afternoon, calling at Wakefield as before and picking up or setting down a portion for Hull at Doncaster. The times in 1947 were as follows:

Southbound:		Northbound:	
Harrogate	dep 10.20	King's Cross	dep 15.50
Leeds	dep 11.03	Doncaster	arr 18.44
Wakefield	dep 11.24	Hull	arr 20.05
Hull	dep 10.45	Wakefield	arr 19.12
Doncaster	dep 11.58	Leeds	arr 19.39
King's Cross	arr 14.50	Harrogate	arr 20.20

The 4½ hours taken from London to Harrogate in both directions contrasts with the 3¾ hours of 1939. However, as with the Queen of Scots, there was a gradual quickening. In 1949 the train left King's Cross 1 hour and 40 minutes later, and took even longer in either direction to complete its journey, but a gradual acceleration brought the 1955 timetable much nearer to the 1939 one. In that year it was as follows:

Southbound:		Northbound:	
Harrogate	dep 10.07	King's Cross	dep 17.30
Leeds	dep 10.45	Doncaster	arr 20.13
Wakefield	dep 11.05	Hull	arr 21.18
Hull	dep 10.30	Wakefield	arr 20.41
Doncaster	dep 11.40	Leeds	arr 21.02
King's Cross	arr 14.30	Harrogate	arr 21.42

Subsequently there was some deceleration.

The Yorkshire Pullman had a longer life than the Queen of Scots. It was a convenient train for West and East Riding businessmen returning home from London, many of whom in 1938-39 would have gone in the West Riding Limited streamlined train which, in those years, managed to reach Leeds in 2¾ hours from King's Cross. It was the last express train of the day to the regions it served. So it lasted up to 1978, into the era of the High Speed Trains. With

The Yorkshire Pullman heads south past Oakleigh Park in February 1953 in the charge of 'A1' No 60134 *Foxhunter*. *Brian Morrison*

diesel haulage it was speeded up again in its later years. In 1967 it shed its Hull portion, which became a separate train that, for five years, ran, diesel-hauled, to King's Cross and back again in a faster time than ever before. The former 45-minute timing of the two-car portion of the Yorkshire Pullman was not repeated between Doncaster and Hull, since over this section time had to be allowed for halts to pick up or set down London passengers at Brough-on-Humber and Goole, but beyond Doncaster the rate was much faster. The schedules were as follows:

Up:		Down:	
Hull	dep 10.35	King's Cross	dep 17.30
(stops at Brough and Goole)		Doncaster	arr 19.46
Doncaster	dep 11.30	(stops at Goole and Brough)	
King's Cross	arr 13.44	Hull	arr 20.45

The increased in speed over the main line south of Doncaster was an index of the greater power available in the 2,750 Class 47 Brush-Sulzer diesel locomotives in contrast with that of the steam ones formerly used. The train was a light one, six cars and a van, and in its later years displayed the new livery of light grey and blue.

In 1968 this train was given a stop at Retford in the up direction and slightly slowed in consequence. At the same time the Second Class cars were taken off and ordinary Second Class coaches took their places. Increased patronage led

A few miles further south and 20 years later, a Class 47-hauled up Yorkshire Pullman approaches King's Cross in March 1973; the locomotive is No 1519. ***Brian Morrison***

to greater locomotive power being needed, and 'Deltics' replaced the 2,750 hp machines. It continued to run until the eve of the advent of the High Speed Trains, and in its last year, 1977-78, came up from Hull in 3 hours 5 minutes, and returned (there being no Retford stop) in 2 hours 58 minutes; it had now outlasted all the other Pullman trains on the East Coast main line - though of course since 1968 it had been an 'all'-Pullman train only in regard to its First Class accommodation.

* * *

The Harrogate Sunday Pullman also returned in 1951, the cars on this service being a rake used in the Queen of Scots on weekdays, which otherwise would have been idle. The same towns and cities were served as before and the train ran in much the same time-slots. As with the Queen of Scots there was a gradual quickening until 1955, though not so markedly as on the weekday train.

Two cars were detached at Leeds to serve Bradford. Timings for 1951 and 1955 were as follows:

Down:		1951	1955
King's Cross	dep	09.45	09 .45
Leeds	arr	13.28	13.15
Bradford	arr	14.01	13.46
Harrogate	arr	14.06	13.53

Up:		1951	1955
Harrogate	dep	15.45	15.50
Bradford	dep	15.55	16.00
Leeds	dep	16.25	16.30
King's Cross	arr	20.15	20.05

Subsequently the train was decelerated and a Doncaster stop included in the northbound run. Its 1963 schedules were as follows:

'A1' No 60119 *Patrick Stirling* lifts the down Harrogate Sunday Pullman through the gloom near Potters Bar in September 1952. *Brian Morrison*

Down:		Up:	
King's Cross	dep 9.40	Harrogate	dep 15.23
Doncaster	arr 12.55	Bradford	dep 15.25
Leeds	arr 13.57	Leeds	dep 16.02
Bradford	arr 14.34	King's Cross	arr 20.00
Harrogate	arr 14.34		

The short turn-round at Harrogate will be noted; no doubt there were occasions when the late arrival of the cars from the south delayed the departure of the up train, but with such a generous schedule south of Leeds it should have been possible to make up lost time. Like the Yorkshire Pullman the train lasted until 1978.

21

New Pullman services from and to King's Cross

1948-75

The first newly-established all-Pullman train to be put into service by BR was in effect a replacement for the former Silver Jubilee streamlined train, which had run from 1935 to 1939. This had left Newcastle at 10.00 each weekday from Monday to Friday on a 4-hour run to King's Cross, stopping *en route* only at Darlington, and returning from King's Cross on a similar timing at 17.30. As explained in the previous chapter, so rapid a schedule was for the moment out of the question, but the need for a fast train at these times of the day had become evident, and the new train, christened the Tees-Type Pullman, was well patronised once it had begun to run, despite being much slower than its predecessor, and was destined in its later career to beat the latter in regard to speed, despite making more stops *en route*.

A pointer towards that happy outcome was the quickening of the schedule within a few months of its inauguration in September 1948. Twenty minutes were cut from it in May 1949 and a further 25 minutes the following September. This was a surprisingly large acceleration to happen in 12 months, and while it reflects a determination on the part of BR to expedite such an important service it was also partly made possible through a change in locomotive working. At first it had been necessary for operational reasons to introduce a stop at Grantham to change engine crews, but once agreement had been reached for the same crew to work the train throughout the stop could be abolished, several minutes being thus saved. The train's schedules over these first 12 months were as follows:

Up:		Sept-May 1948	May-Sept 1949	From Sept 1949
Newcastle	dep	09.00	09.15	09.15
Darlington	dep	09.51	10.00	10.00
King's Cross	arr	14.16	14.15	14.08
Down:				
King's Cross	dep	17.30	16.45	16.45
Darlington	arr	21.57	20.56	20.50
Newcastle	arr	22.50	21.40	21.37

The down Tees-Tyne Pullman at Brookmans Park in June 1949. The locomotive, 'A4' 'Pacific' No 60028 *Walter K. Whigham* was formerly named *Sea Eagle*. *LCGB, Ken Nunn Collection*

Subsequently there was a gradual paring of timings throughout the years, despite the imposition of an additional stop at York by the down train in 1954 to make a connection for Scarborough. By 1958 the King's Cross-Darlington time, York stop included, was down to 233 minutes for the 232.3 miles; in the opposite direction, a non-stop 235 minutes were allowed.

During its first decade locomotive provision had usually been an 'A4' 4-6-2, but soon afterwards powerful diesel-electric locomotives replaced steam and further accelerations became possible. The new 'Deltic' locomotives, of 3,300 hp, revolutionised the main-line timings out of King's Cross, being potentially half as powerful again as the 'Pacifics' they displaced. 'Deltic'-hauled, the Tees-Tyne Pullman first approached and eventually surpassed the schedule of the Silver Jubilee, acceleration continuing right up to its final year, after which the even faster High Speed Inter-City 125 trains replaced locomotive-hauled ones on the East Coast Main Line services and were far faster even than the 100-mph 'Deltics'. What was expected of the latter can be seen by examining the Tees-Tyne timings for 1974 and 1975 which were as follows:

Up:		1973/4	1974/5
Newcastle	dep	09.12	09.20
Durham	dep	09.28	09.35
Darlington	dep	09.49	09.55
York	dep	10.28	10.32
Doncaster	dep	10.59	11.02
King's Cross	arr	13.08	13.08

Down:

King's Cross	dep	17.00	16.30
Doncaster	arr	18.30	
York	arr	19.30	
Darlington	arr	20.10	19.35
Durham	arr	20.32	19.56
Newcastle	arr	20.51	20.15

Despite the fact that the train was some 150 tons heavier than the Silver Jubilee had been, and had three intermediate stops instead of only one, the down service in its penultimate year was 9 minutes faster than the streamliner, and in its final year 15 minutes faster. Between Darlington and York the timing came down to 35 minutes non-stop, an average speed of 75.6 mph, whereas the Jubilee had been allowed 41 minutes start-to-pass.[1]

Between King's Cross and Doncaster, northbound, the average speed required was 78 mph. In 1939 such a timing would have seemed incredible, yet

[1] The Silver Jubilee could have been given a faster timing, had it been possible to keep two signalling block sections clear ahead of it, as was done south of York, but the system of colour-light signalling recently installed north of York could not be thus operated.

Twenty-five years on, in June 1974, and only a year of so from withdrawal, the up Tees-Tyne Pullman pulls away from Darlington behind 'Deltic' No 50011 *The Royal Northumberland Fusiliers*. Note the new Pullman carriage livery. *Brian Morrison*

in comparison with what the High Speed Trains were about to achieve, it was to be rather small beer. And even the latter are now being outpaced by electric trains which can reach Edinburgh from King's Cross in the time the Jubilee took to reach Newcastle.

Not surprisingly the Tees-Tyne Pullman became *the* prestige train on the East Coast Main Line, with only the non-stop Elizabethan from King's Cross to Edinburgh and back vying with it. So far as performance was concerned, with picked engines work of more than Silver Jubilee quality was frequently seen in the later days of steam haulage. In his book *The Gresley Pacifics*, O. S. Nock cites a run on the up train in 1954, behind 'A4' No 60029 *Woodcock* and a 335-ton gross load, when signal delays had put it behind time and the driver set about recovering the lost minutes after Newark. With maxima of 72 on the level near Claypole and as much as 75 through Grantham, and with a minimum of 65½ at Stoke, *Woodcock* then raced away down the subsequent 1 in 178 and 1 in 200 descents to reach 103½ near Little Bytham, when the driver eased the locomotive as the train was now back on time again, so that subsequent running was more restrained.

Ronald I. Nelson, in *Locomotive Performance: a Footplate Survey*, describes a run with double-chimney No 60034 *Lord Faringdon*, also with a 335-ton load, soon after the York stop had been inserted in the schedule of the down train. Against the slightly rising tendency of the road, the 41-minute start-to-stop timing was beaten by over 3½ minutes, despite a signal check outside Darlington costing half a minute. By Tollerton speed had mounted beyond the 80s and remained there almost the whole way until steam was shut off, with only a slight easing to 75 over Wiske Moor troughs and a minimum of 78 at Eryholme summit. 90 mph was attained beyond Thirsk and 87 at Croft Spa. Such performances were beyond even what had been usual with the Silver Jubilee. With 'Deltic' haulage in later years 100 mph maxima even on level track became common - but behind so mighty a machine the excitement for recorders was not so great.

The Tees-Tyne Pullman was originally made up of eight cars, two of them being Pullman brakes. It was later found necessary to strengthen it with an extra car, and replace the brakes with full-length saloon vehicles, adding an ordinary bogie van for luggage and the guard. A further inducement for travellers was the Hadrian Bar in a rebuilt car, in emulation of the Trianon Bar of the Golden Arrow. In its later days it therefore loaded to a weight half as much again as the seven lightweight vehicles of the Silver Jubilee.

The end came inevitably when the new-style High Speed Train, with engines before and behind the eight Mark III coaches, took over the express passenger running on the East Coast route. With such trains running close behind one another, at maximum speeds of 125 mph, special locomotive-hauled Pullman trains could not be fitted in - and the engines to haul them at such speeds did not exist in any case. With First Class accommodation of the quality the HST could offer, at no extra charge, it is doubtful, even supposing a train of adequate speed could have been laid on, whether it could have retained its former patronage. So, made redundant at the height of its success, the Tees-Tyne Pullman was withdrawn in 1975.

* * *

The last all-Pullman train of the traditional type to take the rails was the Master Cutler, which began to run in September 1958. As in the case of the White Rose, an existing title was transferred from one train to another. Since 1925 Sheffield had had no Pullman service, and for a long while no complete train to London by the East Coast route, although that actually provided the shortest journey. During the later 'thirties there had been a through coach, leaving Sheffield at 8.20 am, which was attached to the 7.50 from Leeds at Retford and reached King's Cross at 11.20, and this had been much used by the business community in Sheffield, but it had not been reinstated after the war. Sheffield's main link with London was by the former Midland Railway route to St Pancras, with the former GCR route to Marylebone also connecting the two.

In the years before the First World War the latter route had had some very fast trains on the Sheffield service from Marylebone, including one that took less than 3 hours. After BR had taken over the LNER it also inherited a recently re-introduced Sheffield service, which ran up from Victoria station and reached Marylebone soon after 11 am, returning at Sheffield nearly 4 hours later; this train had been named the Master Cutler and was specially aimed at businessmen; however, it was very slow by pre-war standards and something brisker was needed. The former GCR route was also out of favour with the BR authorities; it had never paid its way since it had been built, and the decision was taken to run it down, providing only local services and reducing the number of trains.

If a service offering the facilities of the existing Master Cutler were to be established in place of it, there was a choice between the route to St Pancras and that to King's Cross. For a really fast service the former was scarcely suitable, since it ran through a colliery area at its northern end, in which permanent speed restrictions because of subsidences existed for many miles; it was also somewhat heavily graded in places. The route to King's Cross was similarly troubled with speed restrictions as far as Worksop, and there was the awkward curve on to the main line to be negotiated at Retford, but after that it was a high-speed line as far as the capital, with only one permanent speed restriction of any consequence, at Peterborough. So the new Pullman service used this route, and was timed faster than any train before it. No only so, but it made two double journeys each weekday between Monday and Friday, so that the single rake of cars covered almost 650 miles in revenue-earning service daily. The schedules from 1958 were as follows:

Up:			
Sheffield	dep	07.20	15.20
Retford	dep	07.55	15.55
Grantham	dep		16.29
Peterborough	dep		16.55
King's Cross	arr	10.05	18.15

Down:			
King's Cross	dep	11.20	19.20
Peterborough	arr	12.32	
Grantham	arr	13.05	
Retford	arr	13.38	21.26
Sheffield	arr	14.17	22.05

There were recovery allowances between Peterborough and King's Cross in the up direction and between Retford and Sheffield going down.

The regular formation of the train when it began its career was six Pullman cars, a Second Class brake at each end and four First Class cars between, so that, in accordance with its business status, it had more First Class seats than Third. However, photographic evidence shows that it soon needed to be strengthened, at first to seven cars, later to eight. During its career, too, the type of car used on it changed. Instead of the traditional vertical sides, the newer cars, largely constructed in the same way as Mark I ordinary coaches, had curved sides, which gave a little more room inside and enabled the fitting of 2 + 1 seating in the First Class cars without the seats having to be narrowed. This does not seem to have been disapproved of by their users, who no doubt often found it convenient to sit three or four at a table. As will be seen in a later chapter, the new 'Blue Pullmans' of 1960 onwards had similar First Class seating.

As regards patronage, one imagines that the First Class seats were pretty well filled in the first up and last down service of each day, but that the midday and afternoon services saw Second Class passenger usage preponderate. I travelled in the train once, between Retford and Sheffield, just to see what it was like, and that was what I observed. The new curved-sided cars had comfortable enough Second Class seats, and were quiet-riding at the moderate speeds necessary between Retford and Sheffield.

This train right from the beginning had diesel haulage. The usual locomotive was one of the recently introduced Class 40 1-Co-Co-1 2,000 hp diesel-electric engines, the first ones that BR had built in any numbers. They were limited to 90 mph but could keep time well on the Master Cutler when the load was 350 tons or less. In his book mentioned earlier, Ronald Nelson includes two very complete logs of journeys on the footplate of one of these engines, heading the mid-morning Pullman to Sheffield and the mid-afternoon return service; with seven cars it kept time in both directions, making up a loss of 1½ minutes through signal delays before Peterborough by hard running after Grantham in the down direction. Later in its career the train enjoyed Class 47 haulage by Brush-Sulzer 2,750 hp diesel locomotives. It would have been interesting to know how a 4-6-2 would have coped with it; it would have been within its powers, no doubt, but one could hardly imagine that the same steam locomotive could have made the double journey twice each way every day, as the diesels had to.

In 1971 the Master Cutler service was moved once more, this time to the

PULLMAN
AMBER

No smoking

The up Master Cutler approaching King's Cross in October 1958 with an unusually long train of eight cars. The locomotive, No D206, later Class 40, was one of those usually providing the motive power. ***Brian Morrison***

former MR route via Leicester, and ceased to be a Pullman train. There was much annoyance in Sheffield when this happened. The replacement, which went to and from St Pancras instead of King's Cross, though it took less time over the journey was nothing like so popular as the Pullman had been. Its further acceleration lessened criticism, and at the present moment (1991) a schedule of 2 hours 8 minutes, in a dedicated HST set, leaves the former service to King's Cross in the shade. Since it offers 'Pullman service' to its First Class passengers, such as still survive of its 1958 clientele have no doubt become resigned to the change.

Left **Exterior and interior views of First Class Pullman car** ***Amber,*** **one of many introduced on the main-line Pullman services to and from King's Cross, in the original umber and white livery. Built in 1960, the vehicle displays a much simplified lining scheme and, inside, a corresponding simplicity of style to suit contemporary taste.** ***both NRM, York***

22

The steam-hauled South Wales Pullman

1955-61

BR's decision to establish an all-Pullman service on the Western Region, on the Paddington to South Wales route, came as something of a surprise at the time. A quarter of a century earlier a similar train to Torquay and Paignton, admittedly introduced without much enthusiasm, had been discontinued after falling passenger numbers made it a money-loser. Since that time Pullman cars had been conspicuous by their absence as much at Paddington as at Euston or St Pancras. Furthermore, the experiment of serving Devon by an all-Pullman train from Waterloo had also been discontinued from lack of support.

However, these had been trains for holidaymakers, and experience had shown, both before and after the Second World War, that an extra-fare train, offering extra attention and convenience, would often be welcomed by the business community if it were timetabled to suit their needs. The Yorkshire Pullman and Tees-Tyne Pullman were showing this was so; each was developing a regular clientele. If one had to travel up to or down from the capital to keep a business engagement, which might mean that in a day's out-and-home journey one spent much more time travelling than doing business, the extra comfort of a specially appointed vehicle was more than worth the additional supplement - which could be reclaimed as a business expense in any case. There seemed no reason why a London businessman should not be offered the same facilities when he went to the cities of South Wales as when for an afternoon's engagement in Southampton, using the Bournemouth Belle.

In fact, South Wales appeared as obvious an objective as Tees-side and Tyneside or the West Riding of Yorkshire. All the larger centres of population in the Principality were grouped along the northern shore of the Bristol Channel. Not only coal-mining but steel manufacture were carried out in that area, and production in these industries had not yet begun to decline. A train based on the capital would permit Pullman employees, who resided mostly in the London area, conveniently to do their work on it and return home every night. Moreover, the Pullman Car Company had vehicles to spare, for the Devon Belle had just ceased to run. So a new South Wales Pullman service was organised, running from Monday to Friday. It was planned to begin operation on 13 June 1955, but a rail strike caused it to be postponed for two weeks, and the first journey was on Monday 27 June, when the engine in charge was No

The rake of cars used on the South Wales Pullman is seen standing at Swindon on 21 June 1955 after a special run organised for members of the Railway Correspondence and Travel Society. The locomotive is No 7004 *Eastnor Castle.* *Brian Morrison*

5016 *Montgomery Castle*. The timetable then and for the two subsequent years was as follows:

Down:		Up:	
Paddington	dep 09.55	Swansea	dep 16.35
Newport	arr 12.21	Port Talbot	dep 16.57
Cardiff	arr 12.41	Cardiff	dep 18.00
Port Talbot	arr 13.35	Newport	dep 18.19
Swansea	arr 14.00	Paddington	arr 20.45

Subsequently it was found that the morning times were too late for the convenience of passengers - $2^3/_4$ hours at Swansea was scarcely time enough in which to transact any business - and from 1957 the schedules were altered as follows:

Down:		Up:	
Paddington	dep 08.50	Swansea	dep 16.35
Newport	arr 11.21	Port Talbot	dep 17.00
Cardiff	arr 11.40	Cardiff	dep 18.00
Port Talbot	arr 12.28	Newport	dep 18.20
Swansea	arr 13.10	Paddington	arr 20.45

The extra 5 minutes required by the down service was probably because of pathing problems at this hour.

Compared with such a contemporary express as the Bristolian - also a businessman's train and, moreover, one which charged no extra supplement - the schedule cannot be called fast. In fact, trains to and from South Wales had always had comparatively leisurely schedules, though in 1939 one down express had managed to reach Newport from Paddington in 137 minutes. The difficulty was of course the need to use the Severn Tunnel. There was a general 60 mph limit through it, so that in neither direction could an express hurtle down the approaching gradient in order to get impetus to help the climb beyond.

Up trains were more generously timed than down ones because, whereas going westward the climb from the middle of the tunnel was only to a little over sea-level, going eastwards it was to a considerable height, to the point near Badminton where the line pierced the Cotswold limestone ridge through Sodbury tunnel. The long drag of 20 miles, 6½ of them at between 1 in 68 and 1 in 100, with most of the remainder being at 1 in 300, was one of the most difficult stretches of main line in England, and the South Wales expresses were for the most part not lightweights like the Bristolian, but 12- or 13-coach trains. Furthermore, the GWR's most powerful engines, the mighty 'Kings', which were still the last word in tractive effort on the Western Section of BR, were debarred from the South Wales route because they were too heavy. In the old days the two-cylinder 4-6-0 'Saints' had predominated on the Cardiff and Swansea expresses; later the 'Stars' and then the 'Castles' took their places. The latter were to be the regular type for working the South Wales Pullman, though occasionally a 'Britannia' had a look in.

The train itself was made up of three First Class cars and four Second Class, the latter including a bar vehicle, the Daffodil Bar. This was the third such vehicle to be included in an all-Pullman train after those on the Golden Arrow and the Tees-Tyne Pullman. No doubt a certain amount of business was done in them by company executives over drinks, standing up or perched on stools. An eight-car train of some 320 tons tare, on such a timing between Paddington and Newport, was of course a mere plaything for a 'Castle' in the westbound direction, if a little harder coming back. Perhaps this is why no logs appear to have been published of runs on this train in either direction during its short career; unless there was a late start from Newport, really high speeds could scarcely be looked for. The train never loaded above the eight-car level and was sometimes one car short of this.

The South Wales Pullman certainly established itself on the route to Cardiff and Swansea, and made it obvious that there was a market at last for a de luxe train out of Paddington. As will be related later, it was eventually replaced by an up-to-date multiple unit diesel-electric Pullman, which not only performed one double journey to South Wales and back on each working day of the week, but was later extended to make two - and even, for a while, three. By then the emphasis had shifted from serving the Londoner to catering for the Welsh business community. The new trains were well liked (except for the tendency to sway about) and since BR had to keep a train of older Pullman cars in reserve for when the diesel sets needed maintenance or repair, it was sometimes possi-

The last day of operation of the South Wales Pullman as a steam-hauled train was 8 September 1961. The last down service arrived at platform 4 of Swansea High Street station behind No 5048 *Earl of Devon* (*above*), and made the final return journey behind No 4090 *Dorchester Castle* (*below*). *Both Hugh Ballantyne*

ble even after 1960 to recapture the previous experience, and ride rather more smoothly, if less speedily, as in the old days, and not risk the possibility that the food on one's fork might find its way on to one's clothing or table napkin instead of into one's mouth.

The final journey of the steam-hauled South Wales Pullman was on 8 September 1961. The outward service was handled by No 5048 *Earl of Devon*, and the return by No 4090 *Dorchester Castle*, recently equipped with a double chimney and cleaned for the occasion at Landore shed so that its paintwork and brasswork shone like new. Green, gold, umber and white were now on the way out, to be replaced by blue and white and the new Pullman order of things - which itself was not to endure very long, as will be seen in later chapters.

23

The diesel-electric 'Blue Pullmans' of 1960: concept and construction

In the years which followed the end of the Second World War in Europe, as the Continental states settled down to peace again and their inter-connecting railway systems recovered their previous satisfactory standards of maintenance, the idea arose of the establishment of a group of special expresses with de luxe accommodation plying internationally between the larger European cities west of the Iron Curtain at times suitable for businessmen. Such trains, it was hoped, could be expected to compete successfully with air services since, although they could not match the speed of aircraft, they could operate between city centres from which short car or taxi journeys could whisk passengers to their destinations; airports, on the other hand, were generally on the outskirts of cities and when an air journey was made delays at either end were inevitable. A traveller's total journey time might well be no greater if the distance to be covered were not more than two or three hundred miles, while the ambience of a comfortable saloon coach would be more conducive to work, or to mutual discussion, than an aircraft interior.

As first envisaged, such a scheme was to have been organised by an international body separately responsible for the fleet of special trains and for their cross-frontier running, but national interests and prejudices prevented this, so that the system, when introduced, was hampered by multiple control and local restrictions. However, it worked effectively and was well patronised. It was an advantage that all the countries involved had a common gauge, the same as in Great Britain; west of the Iron Curtain only Spain, Portugal and the Republic of Ireland differed in this respect. Accordingly, in 1957 Trans-Europ-Express began operation, with First-Class-only trains that charged supplements and provided meals and refreshments at every seat, as Pullman cars did. They were distinctively liveried in vermilion and cream, and each service had its own distinctive title.

One feature of the first T-E-E trains was that they were not locomotive hauled, but were composed of diesel-powered end cars with trailer coaches between, each end being rounded off into a nose which gave the impression of streamlining - though in fact the trains never travelled fast enough to achieve significant economies in fuel use through being so shaped. There was good reason for this 'double-ending'. Many of the main railway stations that needed to be served had been built as termini, where through running was not possible and quick reversal had to take place. With a locomotive-hauled train a change of engines would have been necessary, while a train with a power car at either end simply required the driver to move from one to the other when necessary. So even at a terminus a short stay was possible.

An inevitable disadvantage of such a train formation, of course, was its inflexibility. One could not add or subtract coaches if traffic were heavy or light. On the T-E-E services, however, the amount of custom was reasonably foreseeable and the trains were usually well-filled. In 1965 I took the Edelweiss between Strasbourg and Luxembourg, booking at the last moment, and found I had the only spare seat in the coach. In later years the inflexibility was found to be more of a nuisance, and many of the T-E-E trains were given new stock which could be locomotive-hauled.

The T-E-E experiment was observed with interest by British Railways. It was not a system with which we could co-operate; the Straits of Dover made that impossible. It was all very well to have a train ferry service for sleeping cars to run between London and some Continental destinations, but with the Night Ferry speed did not matter. In a daytime service, on the other hand, on which one would hope to travel out and home again the same day, the obstacle posed by the Channel meant that several hours would be taken up in the crossing; it would require the completion of a Channel Tunnel to allow the Continental capitals to be reached from London at T-E-E speeds.

Nevertheless, within limits the idea might be adopted here; perhaps a Trans-England-Express system of a similar sort would be possible. One advantage was that Great Britain had a unified railway system; there would be no need for haggling or bargaining between companies. Here the need was not for links between all the cities - special cross-country business trains have never been a feature of British railway working, and it will have been noted that all the trains described in this book ran to or from the capital. But London was the business centre, and there was a handful of other large cities which could be brought within a 2- or 3-hour journey from it; the business communities in them might well value a special de luxe link, and the Pullman Company had the expertise in providing such travel. Over distances no greater than that between Manchester and London, air travel would not offer an attractive alternative.

So the 'Blue Pullman' scheme got under way in the late 'fifties. Something akin in appearance to the Brighton Belle units might perhaps have been expected, with round-nosed motorised end cars, the familiar Pullman umber and cream livery externally and typical Pullman furnishings internally. However, BR was determined to be thoroughly up-to-date and project an image of the 'sixties, not the 'thirties. In association with the Pullman Car Company it commissioned an independent design consultant, Mr Jack Howe, to advise on all details of interior equipment and external appearance, and he may fairly be termed the architect of the new train. The result was something very different indeed from the traditional style of Pullman train, and also in many respects different from the typical T-E-E train on the Continent.

The nose end of a 'Blue Pullman' set to be used on the Midland Pullman when the unit was being tested on the Bedford-Hitchin line shortly before introduction. The diesel motors and current generator were behind the louvres on the end car; the actual electric motors drove the wheels of that car's rear bogie and the bogie at the front of the adjacent coach. The 'blunt wedge' shape of the front end can clearly be seen, together with the draw-hook cover and warning horns below it, and the newly modified Pullman coat-of-arms. Note also the massive coil springs on the bogies which nevertheless did not prevent the uncomfortable swaying which bedevilled the ride of the cars after their first few years of use. *Colin J. Marsden Collection*

Power production and transmission were also different from those on many of the latter, in which diesel-hydraulic traction was common. Each 'Blue Pullman' motorised end vehicle included, in the end nearest to the nose, two main diesel engines, together capable of 1,000 hp, and having 12 cylinders arranged V-shaped, each directly coupled to a main and auxiliary current generator; the first supplied the traction motors, the second produced current for exciting the main generator, charging the main engine starter battery, working air compressors for the braking system, operating oil-priming pumps and energising the driving cab heaters. A second pair of diesel engines, of 190 hp each, were sited beneath the cars adjacent to the two motorised cars, each being coupled to an alternator that provided current for lighting the cars, working the air-conditioning system, effecting refrigeration and charging the stand-by lighting batteries.

Transmission of power to the wheels was through bogies with suspended electric motors. These were not beneath the motor vehicles at either end; one was under each of these at the end remote from the nose, while the other was beneath the outer end of the car next to it. The bogies were of the Metro-Schlieren type, which had proved themselves on the Continent on similar trains; they incorporated helical springing and hydraulic dampers. All the bogies, not merely the motored ones, were of this type, and it was confidently expected that they would furnish a smooth ride.

The train was fitted with air brakes of the Westinghouse type, with two additional safety features, a system of automatic slack adjustment, and a device which, when the train was moving at high speed, automatically increased the brake pressure to allow for the lessening of the co-efficient of friction which occurred then. These were the first trains in the country to have such two-stage braking. Also a 'first', so far as Great Britain was concerned, was the air-conditioning system, in which used air was cooled and dehumidified by a refrigeration system whose compressor and condenser units were attached to the underframes of the cars, while the evaporator units were installed in the ceilings. By means of thermostats a constant temperature appropriate to the time of year could be maintained. These thermostats were under the control of the cars' attendants; there was no need to open or shut ventilators, and in fact none were provided. Fans above the inner ceilings circulated a mixture of outside and inside air, drawing it over warming or cooling elements as might be appropriate before introducing it into the car's atmosphere.

The cars' interiors differed completely from what a frequenter of the Brighton Belle or Queen of Scots might have expected. The 'de luxe' atmosphere was not that of the domestic parlour but of the board room. Gone were the period-style moveable chairs, the polished brasswork, the pink-shaded table lamps and glass-topped tables, which made such pleasant surroundings for an intimate tête-à-tête between friends but were not particularly relevant to business discussion. Gone, too, in the First Class saloons, was the 1 + 1 seating; 2 + 1 took its place, so that people travelling alone or in a pair could still be private together, but larger groups could confer or discuss across a larger table. This in effect meant that half as many First Class passengers again as before could be accommodated in the same space, but this does not seem to have provoked any adverse comment. (On the Continent 2 + 1 seating was the rule in First Class accommodation - though admittedly the coaches there were wider.) First Class seats were still well apart from each other frontally, and had the advantage of being adjustable so that one could either sit or semi-recline.

Second Class passengers also enjoyed 2 + 1 seating, though they naturally had less room for their legs and their seats were fixed. Upholstery was of foam rubber. Table-tops were plastic covered, with anodised aluminium edges. Small lamps with pearl shades, oval in section, attached to the walls below the windows by swan-neck holders, shone downwards on to the tables. The windows were double-glazed with venetian blinds between the panes - another 'first' in British practice, though some Continental luxury trains were thus fitted.

Passengers enjoying afternoon tea in one of the Western Region 'Blue Pullman' units. ***Colin J. Marsden Collection***

Coach-length racks above the windows provided space for hand-luggage.

As to the appearance of the saloon interiors, one may quote from the description in *The Railway Magazine* of August 1960, which, with a slight discounting of advertiser's language, will allow the reader to imagine the total effect, and compare it with that of the inside of a present-day Mark II or Mark IV coach.

> The interior decor varies from vehicle to vehicle and has been chosen to give pleasing and colourful combinations, mainly of decorative rosewood and ebony veneers, grey plastic hide, plastic facings, and contrasting seat upholstery in red or blue striped fabric trimmed with black and grey plastic hide. The partitions forming the ends of each passenger saloon are strikingly decorated with wood veneers or abstract plastic inlays. The access door in each partition has glazed panels, incorporating glass with a vertical striped pattern which has the property of a mirror but allows unimpeded vision at close quarters.
>
> The body side walls of the vehicles are surfaced with plastic hide from floor

> level up to and including part of the continuous hand luggage rack running the length of each passenger saloon. Above the racks walls and ceiling surfaces are lined with plastic facings in pearl grey, with a fine black line pattern superimposed, which continues up to the end of the central lighting panel in the ceiling. The floors are carpeted in kingfisher blue or cardinal red, laid on plastic underlays. The exposed parts of the hand luggage racks, the table edges and the window-surrounds are all of anodised aluminium, satin finished in aluminium for the First Class cars and in pale gold for the Second Class. The heater grilles, mounted low on the bodyside alongside the seats, are of satin-finished stainless steel.
>
> Warm, white fluorescent lighting, concealed by opal diffuser panels, is the principal form of illumination, supplemented by individual table lamps...
>
> The entrance vestibules at the ends of the cars are wide and spacious, and the walls are faced in pearl-grey plastic, with plastic hide trimming around the entrances to the air-tight passenger access gangways between vehicles. These are of a new design and wider than usual. They are mounted on pivots at the ends of each vehicle and, when joined together, form semi-floating units between pairs of cars, providing a level platform free from the oscillation associated with normal gangways. Rubber seals cover the outsides of the gangways and prevent draughts and loss of efficiency in the air-conditioning of the train...
>
> The toilets are equipped to include such fixtures as towel dispensers and hygienic spray washing facilities which give an automatically-timed flow of water. The temperature of the washing water can be selected to suit individual needs and is automatically maintained until the timed flow ceases. The toilet floors are paved in coloured mosaic with easy-to-clean hygienic skirtings; the ceilings are painted matt white and the walls are faced with plastic surfaces in flame, clover pink and grey. Most of the metal fittings are finished in satin chromium plate.

Each of the two kitchens in each complete train was lined with easily-cleaned plastic material, while all utensils and working surfaces were of stainless steel. A constant supply of boiling water was available, and a refrigerator-cum-deep-freeze occupied one corner.

Here, then, was Pullman luxury of a new type, different from what other British all-Pullman trains offered but, it was hoped, a pointer to the future. It is worth making some comparison with the luxury non-Pullman trains, the Silver Jubilee, Coronation, West Riding and East Anglian, which the LNER had put into service a quarter of a century earlier. These, too, had been stylistically up-to-date in their day and offered a definite measure of extra comfort to those who paid extra to travel in them, as well as extra speed. They, too, had interior decorations which broke with tradition; they too made wide use of plastic materials. They also, like the new diesel Pullmans, sported striking external liveries and, when headed by the appropriate locomotive, had a streamlined appearance. But they lacked some of the refinements of the 'Blue Pullmans', such as the adjustable seat-backs, double-glazed windows and air-conditioning.

The Pullman livery in the new trains was distinctively different from the familiar umber and cream, though the Pullman coat-of-arms, prominently dis-

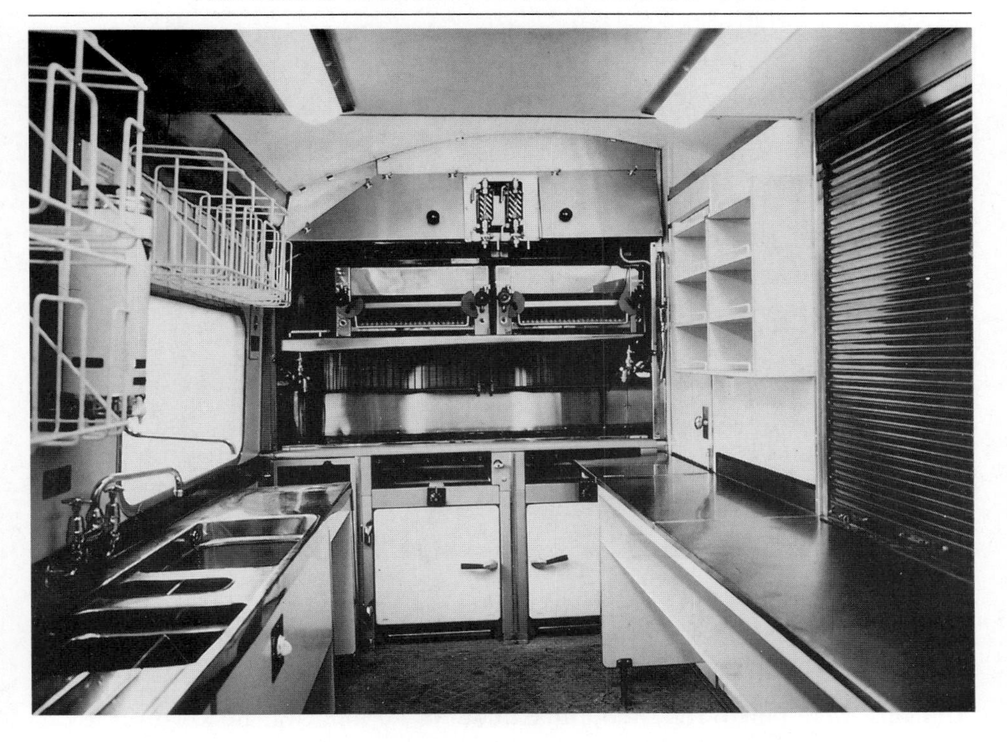

The interior of a Pullman kitchen in one of the WR 'Blue Pullmans'. ***Colin J. Marsden Collection***

played, proclaimed their association with that company. The predominant external colour was blue above and below a broad white band that extended the length and width of the windowed section along each side of the vehicle except where the motors were housed; here the colour was blue from cant-rail to lower edge. Each motorised car had a rounded nose which came to a blunt edge midway and above waist-level and broadened out to a flat sloping triangle below; here the Pullman coat of arms was prominently displayed. Below were three head-lamps arranged in a line above the buffers, between which a hinged door concealed the draw-hook; under the lower edge three chiming alarm-horns were visible. Windscreen wipers operated when necessary across the forward windows.

The total effect was pleasing and effective, but the suggestion of streamlining was more for the look of the thing than for effecting fuel economy. The train's front end was somewhat in advance of its time - a cross, one might say, between the forward end of the Brighton Belle and that of a present-day High Speed Train. It certainly looked more comely than the latter, no doubt in part because it was not painted yellow. As a high-speed train, one may say that it pulled its punches. The state of the track on British Railways generally was not conducive to the safe attainment of high speeds on the sections on which the 'Blue

Still under test, one of the two Midland Pullman units enters St Pancras early in 1960. Note the livery, predominantly blue with a broad white band running down the train at window level. ***Colin J. Marsden Collection***

Pullmans' were put to run, and a maximum of 90 mph was imposed on them. (Their speedometers were only calibrated to 100 mph.) They were definitely not greyhounds. The Eastern Region 'Deltics' and Bulleid 4-6-2s could beat them on downhill stretches any day, with more substantial loads, often attaining 100 mph or more. What the 'Blue Pullmans' did have, as will be seen later when their performance is considered, was a capacity to run to the top of their speed limit not only on level track but uphill.

The 'Blue Pullmans' were beautiful pieces of railway architecture, a joy to the eye both within and without, and one is sorry they have disappeared. But in one respect they were a mistake. There was no need to have them built as diesel multiple units, inflexibly coupled together. Their counterparts on the Continent needed to be in order to make quick turn-rounds at terminal stations, but no such reversals after brief stops were needed on any of the services on which they were employed in this country. A rake of such coaches, and some specially painted locomotives to haul them, much as Gresley had organised with his streamlined trains, would have served as well and been more flexible in operation; if demand had required a service to be strengthened one could then have added an extra coach or two in the usual way, much as can be done with HST trains now, despite their double-ended nature.

Another disadvantage was that so few trains were built. Only five sets were constructed - two all-First-Class with six cars and three First-and-Second Class with eight cars. If one of the latter had to be taken out of service, all that could be done was to substitute a rake of ordinary Pullman cars and provide a locomo-

The driver's controls of a Midland Pullman unit. *Colin J. Marsden Collection*

1	Brake controller (EP/ Westinghouse), shown in emergency position
2	Driver's side window wiper valve
3	Brake cylinder gauge
4	Main reservoir/brake pipe pressure gauge
5	Speedometer
6	Main generator ammeter
7	Cab heat switch
8	Engine stop indicator light
9	General fault alarm light
10	EP brake indicator light
11	Auxiliary heat switch
12	Control switch (button)
13	Engine start button
14	Engine stop button
15	Overload re-set button
16	Horn valve
17	Main power controller
18	Master switch (FOR/EO/OFF/REV)
19	Instrument light switch
20/1/2	Left/middle/right front marker light switch
23	Instrument light dimmer switch
24/5/6	Left/middle/right front marker light repeater
27	Loudaphone unit (driver-Guard)

tive to haul them. Possibly more would have been built if BR thinking had continued to be in the later 'sixties what it had been in the 'fifties. As it was, they were not replicated. It is much to be regretted that one set was not preserved - but in the 'seventies BR had begun to be economy-conscious, and since nobody offered to buy any of the discarded sets, all were scrapped.

24

'Blue Pullmans': The Midland Pullman

1960-66

As indicated in the previous chapter, BR's new diesel Pullman units, like their counterparts on the Continent in the T-E-E system, were angled towards the business traveller. However, unlike the T-E-E services, they formed, once established, not a network but radially directed routes with the capital being the hub, such as had characterised all previous all-Pullman trains in Britain.

Their internal furnishings were comfortable and convenient rather than being 'artistic'; a contemporary business executive wished to study what was in his briefcase rather than regard marquetry or fancy brasswork. Furthermore, he wished to be carried to his destination at a time which allowed him to spend as long as possible with those he was going to see. Hence the new fleet of trains, operating into and out of London termini where the traditional Pullman umber and white had seldom or never been seen, ran up from their provincial bases at a suitably early hour, to return in the evening. The long gap between the main inward and outward journeys could be conveniently filled in with extra out-and-back trips from the capital, not so much now for businessmen as for all and sundry; quite a moderate passenger complement would justify such intercalated services, which would not necessarily cover the whole of the early morning and late evening itinerary.

The first Pullman diesel sets to be put into daily service were the two First-Class-only six-car units, to run up to London from Manchester and back between Monday and Friday. (At weekends they were also occasionally given special assignments such as trips to race meetings.) One of the two units operated the main scheduled service while the other was on stand-by, and from time to time they changed over. The choice of Manchester as the starting point of Britain's first diesel train intended to take business executives out and back the same day, leaving adequate time for business in between, may at first glance seem a little surprising, remembering that in 1925 the extension of the Sheffield Pullman to that city had not generated much extra traffic, and that since then no Pullman train had come near it. But things had changed in 35 years; there was now more business travel than before, and what was now on offer was not a train taking over 4 hours but one that would do the journey in a little more than 3.

Manchester's usual and quickest link with London had always been, and was later to be again, the former LNWR route from London Road station to Euston,

The 'High-Speed Diesel De-Luxe Pullman' display at BRB Headquarters prior to the introduction of the Midland Pullman in 1960. *Colin J. Marsden Collection*

The Lord Mayor of London, Sir Edmund Stockdale, gives the 'right away' for the departure of the Midland Pullman on its first down journey from St Pancras at 18.10 on 4 July 1960, watched by the Lady Mayoress of the Borough of St Pancras, Mrs L. Arabin. *Colin J. Marsden Collection*

and immediately before the Second World War there had for a while been a morning up service timed in 3¼ hours, with a similarly scheduled down train in the evening. As will be seen later, this was the route to be taken later by the Midland Pullman's successor from 1967 onwards, with new Pullman stock and electric haulage. But in 1960 use of this route was precluded because of the massive electrification operations that were working southwards from Manchester and Liverpool to Birmingham and London. So the former Midland Railway route was selected, with Manchester Central (now closed) as the originating station, and the line through the Peak District was taken to the outskirts of Derby (whose station was bypassed by an avoiding line) and through Leicester and Kettering to St Pancras. Use of this route, with its heavy gradients, especially north of Ambergate, prevented a 3-hour schedule, but the new train was nevertheless slightly faster than the former 3¼-hour service to and from Euston by a few minutes in either direction.

Manchester was the fourth largest city in Great Britain, the Birmingham conurbation being a little greater and that of Glasgow greater still. Why then was it selected for such VIP treatment? In fact, Birmingham did at about the same time receive its own 'Blue Pullman' service, as recounted in the following chapter, though not an exclusively First Class one. As for Glasgow, it was too far away for the running of a special out-and-back business train; an arrival in London even as late as midday would have necessitated a start from the Scottish city before 6 am, and a return service would have had to arrive back there at about midnight. Glasgow businessmen going to London preferred either to use the sleeper service or to fly to Heathrow. BR research had targeted Manchester as the right place from which to dispatch a luxury business train to

The Midland Pullman on a test run heading north through Kettering early in 1960. ***Colin J. Marsden Collection***

London, and the researchers were entirely correct as the future showed.

The new Midland Pullman at first left Manchester at 8.50, called at Cheadle Heath to embark passengers who lived in the southern suburbs of the city, and then ran non-stop to St Pancras, arriving just after midday; it returned at 18.10 on a similar timing, making the same intermediate stop to set down. However, demand arose for an earlier start, so after a while the departure of the up train was advanced to 7.45, with a 10.55 arrival in London; the northbound timings remained the same. This pattern continued throughout the period of the train's existence. Between Cheadle Heath and London the 181.3 miles were booked in 177 minutes in both directions. This was the fastest start-to-stop timing over a distance exceeding 100 miles that the MR system had ever known; the nearest approach to it had been the express timing of the northbound Thames-Forth immediately before the war, which had covered the 123.4 miles from St Pancras to Nottingham in 123 minutes. The Midland Pullman's timing was over a route which for many miles, where it negotiated the Peak District, involved climbing gradients of 1 in 100 or steeper, and reaching an altitude of almost 1,000 feet above sea level. Because of their reserve of power the new Pullman units were able to tackle the steep banks in a way no steam locomotive could ever have done, so that very high downhill speeds were unnecessary.

After the train had been put into service it was given extra time-filling duties, at first with an out-and-back trip to Leicester, and then, in the summer of 1961, proceeding further to Nottingham with an intermediate stop at Loughborough. Timings for the whole sequence of daily journeys are tabulated below. The run between St Pancras and Leicester was the fastest that had ever been scheduled over this stretch, beating the former 99-minute expresses of the late 'thirties by almost a quarter of an hour and just reaching the 70 mph average; it was in fact the fastest booking in Great Britain at this time.

Schedules: The Midland Pullman, 1961-7

Up:		Down:	
Manchester Central	dep 07.45		
Cheadle Heath	dep 07.59		
St Pancras	arr 10.55		
		St Pancras	dep 11.20
		Leicester	arr 12.45
			dep 12.50
		Nottingham	arr 13.20
Nottingham	dep 15.45		
Leicester	arr 16.15		
	dep 16.20		
St Pancras	arr 17.45		
		St Pancras	dep 18.10
		Cheadle Heath	arr 21.07
		Manchester Central	arr 21.21

I once travelled on the outward midday service - though not over its record-breaking section - when returning from my home in Coventry to a college in Lincoln where I was doing a course for adult students in connection with my work. The two bumpy rides in ordinary diesel multiple unit trains from Coventry to Leicester and from Nottingham to Lincoln contrasted markedly with the much smoother passage of the 'Blue Pullman' between Leicester and Nottingham. (The riding qualities of the bodies had not yet begun to deteriorate as they did later.) We seemed to drift along in no particular hurry, yet kept time easily. It was not, of course, a very fast stretch, and half an hour's running time for the 27½ miles no doubt allowed for some time recovery if necessary. An impecunious schoolmaster, existing at that time on an exiguous allowance, in those days I felt slightly guilty about indulging in First Class travel when I could have done the journey almost as quickly in an ordinary service train, but I was curious to know what the Pullman felt like to travel in. So, if the occasional extravagance be a fault, I enjoyed, in the Scriptural phrase, the pleasures of sin for a season, luxuriating in the very comfortable seat at one of the single tables.

The Midland Pullman set some entirely new standards. With the great power at the driver's disposal, gradients that would have taxed the abilities of even the largest steam locomotive scarcely seemed to matter. In *The Railway Magazine* for November 1960 O. S. Nock described a journey he made in the cab of the up train soon after it had entered service, and his comments are worth citing:

> It is really difficult to convey one's impressions of travel at the head-end of this remarkable train - at any rate in the terms usually associated with the running of high-speed express passenger trains. For the most part we were travelling so smoothly and placidly that from time to time I had to make some quick mental calculations to make sure we were running to schedule. It is certainly true that we had a trip singularly free from incidental delays ... The one out-of-course check, for relaying at Bakewell, had an almost negligible effect, so that this run shows the minimum in the way of speed that is needed to keep the schedule ... The driver chose to even out his running, to lose a little time on the most sharply-timed sections and regain it over the stretches where there is a recovery margin. In this way, of course, the passengers are given a much more 'even' ride. There is ample power for time recovery if necessary, but it was not needed on my trip. My friends in the cab, Driver A. Bailey and Inspector Barber, told me that in the earlier weeks of the schedule two very heavy slacks were in force on the up road - one at Great Glen and the other at Radlett. Day after day they were going all-out up the long bank from Bedford to Leagrave, sustaining 90 mph for most of the way...
>
> Driving up this toilsome grind of an incline [the 1 in 90 up to Dove Holes tunnel] ... was something quite new in rail-roading. It was the same sort of feeling that one gets taking a powerful motor-car up some hill that is hallowed with memories of youthful struggles on a push-bike. Rain was driving across the high moors of Kinder Scout, but with the screen wipers in action we had a perfectly clear vision of the line ahead, and the gloomy aspect of the hills, the low cloud and the dive into the very mountain side at Dove Holes tunnel all seemed to

Two views of up Midland Pullmans in service in 1961 near Bedford. *Colin J. Marsden Collection*

emphasise the complete mastery of the railway over wild nature - at any rate, so far as this train is concerned ...

Finally came the high speed section from Leicester to St Pancras ... At Kibworth we went over the summit at nearly 80 mph. Desborough bank was climbed with speed rising to 66 mph at the summit, while up the continuous 1 in 120 from Irchester to Sharnbrook summit we accelerated from 67 to exactly 70 mph. From Sharnbrook station, passed at 88 mph, we coasted the whole way to Bedford, and as we were $2^1/_2$ minutes early at this point, with 4 minutes recovery time in prospect beyond St Albans, the driver used no more than notch 6 up to Ampthill tunnel and ... speed fell right away to the minimum of 60 mph. Use of notch 7 from Flitwick gave us a sustained 67 mph up the continuation of the 1 in 200 rise to the summit at milepost 34. The finish was made under relatively light power, and from ... the London side of Elstree tunnel we were coasting all the way in.

The journey was accomplished without any extreme speed. With a clear road such as we had it would have been quite possible to keep time without exceeding 80 mph anywhere, let alone the maximum of 90 to which these trains are limited. The designers have built in an ample reserve of power, which is used for rapid acceleration and high speeds uphill. This, from every point of view, is most desirable. The passenger looks for nothing more than a smooth ride, and if maximum speeds can be kept down, by running faster uphill, the wear and tear on permanent way and stock will be lessened. The Midland Pullman has been widely and justifiably acclaimed for the magnificence of the passenger accommodation; as an operating proposition it seems to have achieved an equally resounding success.

O. S. Nock's comments on the smooth riding appear ironic in retrospect, for it was in this regard that deterioration was soon to set in. Nevertheless, in regard to the maintenance of even speed up hill and down dale the Midland Pullman certainly led the way, foreshadowing the even faster running of the High Speed Train of the 'seventies. The steam-hauled streamliners of the LNER had gone some way in this respect, but never quite to the extent of regularly surmounting gradients of 1 in 200 at 90 mph. During the 'sixties such a speed could not be greatly exceeded over a road which had not received the kind of improvement later carried out on the East Coast and West of England main lines to allow 125 mph running.

The Midland Pullman was to have only a short life. As soon as electrification between Manchester and Euston had been completed, the former LNWR route again became the recognised racing ground, and a later chapter describes the all-Pullman service established on it after 1966. The six-coach Pullman units had then to find another sphere of operation on the Western Region; what happened to them there is recounted in the next chapter. At about this time, too, they suffered the indignity of having their nose-ends painted yellow in order to make them more visible to men working on the line - something that all BR's diesel engines and multiple unit trains received - but it seems insulting nevertheless for those magnificent front ends to have been thus treated, with the consequent obliteration of the elaborate Pullman coat-of-arms, making an aristocrat look like a clown.

25

'Blue Pullmans' on the Western Region

1960-72

The former Great Western Railway, since 1948 the Western Region of British Railways, served three large English cities and three large Welsh ones, Bristol, Birmingham, Plymouth, Newport, Cardiff and Swansea. With the exception of Plymouth (which was indeed later considered as a possible base for a special Pullman service, but rejected, as will be mentioned later) these were selected to be given 'Blue Pullman' services in 1960 - not, as was the case with Manchester, for First Class passengers only, but for both classes, though the needs of the business communities in these places were of course studied, as the timetabling of the new trains showed.

Since they were to convey both First and Second Class, the units used on the Western Region had two additional cars each; the motors in the end power cars were powerful enough to cope with the extra weight without difficulty, though of course they did not have as much in reserve as did the six-coach Midland Pullman. Each powered rake was allotted to a separate service; it was hoped that all needful maintenance could be done at weekends so that no unit would need to be out of service for more than 48 hours. This expectation turned out to be over-optimistic and it proved necessary to provide a stand-by rake of traditional Pullman cars, locomotive-hauled, which could be substituted at short notice for the designated units.

The Birmingham unit catered for the largest of the three populated areas and, like the Midland Pullman, filled in time between its morning up and evening down journeys with additional down and up services, so that each day some 470 miles were covered. The special purpose of the Birmingham Pullman was to meet a temporary need, to give a fast service for businessmen to and from London using the route to Paddington, at a time when the usual and more frequently used route by way of the former LNWR line through Coventry and Rugby to Euston was subject to so many changes and cancellations because of electrification works. Between 1960 and 1967 only three trains ran by the latter route each way, and made many stops and took the Northampton loop, so that their former journey times were extended by something like an hour. Formerly, when the LMS and GWR had competed for the London-Birmingham traffic, each had run trains that took 2 hours, stopping once in either direction. The former came to have rather the better of it once it had six-coupled engines available to head its trains, and was able to cut 5 minutes off the timings of many of them. So the usual business route until 1960 had been from Birmingham New Street to Euston. But from 1960 to 1967 it was the other way round. Paddington was the preferred London terminus; more fast trains were put on the former GWR route, and the Birmingham Pullman was the most prestigious one.

The timings of the new train, when it began to run in 1961, are given below. It will be noted that, so far as the main business service was concerned, the schedules showed no improvement on those of the existing expresses, still steam-hauled - indeed, between Leamington and London in either direction, rather the reverse. There were probably a number of contributory causes to this - pathing difficulties in the rush-hour, the heavier gradients on the Western Region's main line as compared with those on the London Midland Region, and possibly the weight of the train (Birmingham to Euston trains had always been fairly light ones, seldom exceeding 300 tons). However, it proved possible to speed the Pullman up slightly in its later years, and by 1965 it was some 5 minutes faster. The timings in 1961 and 1965 are shown in the following table.

Up:		1961	1965	Down:		1961	1965
Wolverhampton	dep	07.00	07.00	Paddington	dep	12.10	10.10
Birmingham Snow Hill	dep	07.30	07.30	High Wycombe	dep		10.38
Solihull	dep	07.40	07.39	Leamington Spa	arr	13.34	11.35
Leamington Spa	dep	08.00	08.00	Birmingham Snow Hill	arr	14.05	12.03
Paddington	arr	09.35	09.30				
				Paddington	dep	16.50	16.50
Birmingham Snow Hill	dep	14.30	13.00	Leamington Spa	arr	18.19	18.13
Solihull	dep		13.08	Solihull	arr	18.44	18.36
Leamington Spa	dep	14.55	13.28	Birmingham Snow Hill	arr	18.55	18.50
High Wycombe	arr		14.25	Wolverhampton	arr	19.20	19.13
Paddington	arr	16.25	15.00				

The rather faster timings between Paddington and Leamington in the midday and afternoon services no doubt reflect the fact that it was easier to provide paths for them than for the morning and evening ones. At a later point in the train's history the departure times were advanced to 10.10 from Paddington and 12.30 from Birmingham, possibly in the hope of better patronage of the restaurant facilities. The reason for the later acceleration of all four services was presumably that the unit had proved it could keep to a tighter schedule. Certainly nothing like a 2-hour timing from Birmingham to Paddington with three intermediate stops had ever happened before, and with steam haulage would probably have been out of the question.

The train proved popular with both classes of passenger. The simpler and sleeker style of interior decoration does not seem to have deterred anyone - it has to be remembered that there had never been Pullman services before on this particular route, so there was nothing with which to compare the new train. The only drawback, though it was a serious one, was the unsatisfactory quality of the ride, which deteriorated because of the unsuitable pattern of the bogies. I travelled from Leamington to London by the Birmingham Pullman on one occasion soon after it was introduced, and found the riding smooth enough then. We were using the morning service, and what was specially noticeable was the rapidity with which the banks were climbed, from Leamington to Fenny Compton, Aynho to Ardley and Haddenham to Saunderton, and the way in which, beyond the points where the gradient flattened out or began to go downhill, speed rose rapidly to the allowed 90 mph maximum, after which brake applications tended to be made. The 95-minute allowance was more than adequate, and after High Wycombe we took things very easily, to arrive in Paddington a minute or so early.

The Birmingham Pullman was taken out of service in March 1967 as soon as electrification operations on the neighbouring line were completed. On the latter very much faster timings were now achievable than were possible on the Western Region route. A special non-Pullman service now began to run from Birmingham New Street to Euston, which was nearly half an hour faster than the Pullman had been, and the route by way of Banbury and High Wycombe began to slip back to what it has now become - no longer a main traffic artery but a route for commuters into Buckinghamshire and North Oxfordshire, served by diesel multiple unit trains making many halts *en route*.

The 'Blue Pullman' unit which had operated along it was now diverted for service on the main London to Bristol line. There had been some talk of using it on the Golden Hind morning and evening services from Plymouth to Paddington and back, but this was ruled out since it was felt that its 2,000 hp engines were not forceful enough to manage the banks between Newton Abbot and Plymouth. A 2,200 hp 'Warship' or 2,700 hp 'Western' diesel-hydraulic locomotive could manage, and could if necessary be piloted - but there was a risk that the less powerful Pullman unit would stall going up, say, Dainton or Rattery Bank on the westbound run, or on Hemerdon incline on the eastbound run. One wonders whether a new Torquay Pullman, which would not have needed to climb these banks, might not have proved commercially successful if run at times suitable to the leisure traveller. But the Torbay area was not a generator of business traffic, and the 'Blue Pullmans' were conceived as businessmen's trains, which tapped not only individuals' pockets but also their expense accounts, both as to fares and catering, and the Bristol and South Wales routes seemed the most suitable ones where the cars could be deployed. In 1967, therefore, there was a shuffle of vehicles, in which the spare Midland Pullman and Birmingham Pullman units together formed new trains whose timetables and destinations appear a little further on in this chapter.

* * *

Bristol was the largest commercial centre on the former GWR system and had been one of the first provincial cities in England to be given a specially fast link with the capital for the convenience of businessmen. In 1935 a special train was established, named the Bristolian, which ran down from London in the morning and back in the evening, non-stop, in 105 minutes each way. Limited to seven coaches, it was well within the haulage ability of a 'Castle', and an even easier task for a 'King'; engines of the latter class were rostered for a while to work it, but their enormous potential power was wasted on so light a load, and eventually the 'Castles' replaced them. After the Second World War, once the state of the track allowed it, the train was re-instated in its former timetable slot, and eventually quickened to cover the distance in 100 minutes. No supplement was charged to users and no specially luxurious stock was assigned to it. Its speed was the main attraction.

When it became known that a 'Blue Pullman' set would come into service on the Bristol run, there were hopes that it might be given a schedule easier than the Bristolian's, but expectations were disappointed. As with the Birmingham Pullman, no chances were taken. A non-stop schedule of 110 minutes was initially laid down. It came up to Paddington early, left in the late afternoon and, in order for it not to remain idle in the middle of the day, it was, like its fellow on the Birmingham run, given an intermediate out-and-back trip to Bristol again, this time taking the route through Bath, though before and afterwards running by way of Badminton. The daily timings, excluding Saturdays, were as follows:

Up:		Down:	
Bristol	dep 07.45	Paddington	dep 10.05
Paddington	arr 09.35	Bath	arr 11.40
		Bristol	arr 12.00
Bristol	dep 12.30	Paddington	dep 16.55
Bath	dep 12.47	Bristol	arr 18.45
Paddington	arr 14.25		

However, demand arose in Bath for the up morning and down late afternoon services to call there as well, so they were soon re-routed; at the same time the evening down service was put back by 50 minutes and the morning up Bristol departure by half an hour. A stop at Chippenham in either direction was also made from 1962 onwards by the intermediate services. The timings now became:

Up:		Down:	
Bristol	dep 08.15	Paddington	dep 12.45
Bath	dep 08.32	Chippenham	arr 14.09
Paddington	arr 10.10	Bath	arr 14.25
		Bristol	arr 14.45
Bristol	dep 15.15	Paddington	dep 17.45
Bath	dep 15.32	Bath	arr 19.20
Chippenham	dep 15.50	Bristol	arr 19.40
Paddington	arr 17.15		

In 1964 it was decided to extend the intermediate services to serve Weston-

The Bristol Pullman mid-morning service from Paddington approaches Bath on 1 April 1969. This is one of the six-car sets used latterly after the Birmingham Pullman service had been discontinued and some rearrangement of vehicles became possible. The only alteration in the livery at this stage was the painting of the nose-ends yellow, with the consequent disappearance of the Pullman crest. Note also that the draw-hook is no longer kept behind a cover, since this train on its early morning up and evening down journeys was coupled to another similar set, making up a 12-coach train. *Hugh Ballantyne*

super-Mare, some 20 miles west of Bristol. This required the putting forward of the Paddington departure by an hour, to leave time for the turn-around at Weston. For one brief year the latter resort, which was indeed no Bournemouth or Torquay in status, though a favourite venue for Bristolians, enjoyed a Pullman service. However, it does not seem to have been sufficiently appreciated, for the experiment was not repeated the following year; the Paddington departure was instead brought forward by yet another hour, the Chippenham call was replaced by one at Reading, and the service speeded up so that it took no longer than the morning up and later afternoon down trains. Reading now received its fastest service ever in the down direction, though coming back the need to leave a recovery margin caused the Pullman to take a full 40 minutes. The 1965 timings were:

Up:		Down:	
Bristol	dep 08.15	Paddington	dep 10.45
Bath	dep 08.31	Reading	dep 11.17
Paddington	arr 10.05	Bath	arr 12.18
		Bristol	arr 12.40
Bristol	dep 13.15	Paddington	dep 17.45
Bath	dep 13.31	Bath	arr 19.20
Reading	arr 14.30	Bristol	arr 19.40
Paddington	arr 15.10		

In 1967 there was some re-organisation. The setting free of the Midland Pullman and Birmingham Pullman units enabled them to be utilised on the main line through Swindon; the result was a strengthening of the Bristol service and (as will be seen later) the introduction of a new service to South Wales. The unit used to Bristol became a double one which could separate into two and operate independently, and while both units, each of six vehicles, were used on the up morning and down late afternoon services, for a while only one was used on the intermediate ones, the other making a separate out-and-back excursion to Oxford. Certainly the latter was a prestigious enough destination, and the idea seems to have been that visitors from the USA would travel in style to one of England's most famous university cities and have 3 hours in which to inspect its architectural delights before returning in the same set of cars. However, the idea does not seem to have caught on and, again, after one season the experiment was abandoned. The 1967 timetable was as follows:

Up:			Down:		
Bristol	dep 08.15		Paddington	dep 10.45	12.15
Bath	dep 08.31		Reading	dep 11.17	
Paddington	arr 10.05		Oxford	arr	13.15
			Bath	arr 12.23	
			Bristol	arr 12.45	
Bristol	dep 13.15		Paddington	dep 17.45	
Bath	dep 13.31		Bath	arr 19.13	
Oxford	dep	16.15	Bristol	arr 19.35	
Reading	arr 14.40				
Paddington	arr 15.20	17.15			

It will be noted that, allowing for the time taken to stop and re-start at Bath, the up morning and down late afternoon trains were now almost as fast as the Bristolian. In its final year the claims of Chippenham were again recognised and a stop made there in each direction by this pair of trains, which now

The Bristol Pullman arriving at Bath in June 1969, composed of two six-car units. Apart from the yellow nose-ends the livery remains unaltered. *Hugh Ballantyne*

became much faster, achieving the Bristolian's 105-minute timing despite stopping twice *en route*; the Reading stop, however, was now eliminated. For the Bristol trains the timings were now (1972) as follows:

Up:		Down:	
Bristol	dep 8.15	Paddington	dep 16.45
Bath	dep 8.31	Chippenham	arr 17.58
Chippenham	dep 8.43	Bath	arr 18.14
Paddington	arr 10.00	Bristol	arr 18.30

Now at long last the schedule of the Bristolian had been reached in both directions, and with two stops *en route*. The down run from Paddington to Chippenham averaged 77¼ mph, the up run 73¼ - but the allowance here included a recovery margin. Since 1967 the 12-car train had 4,000 hp available, whereas before that eight cars had only had 2,000 hp. So even with the faster schedule there was still power in reserve, and no doubt a further speed-up would have been possible if the High Speed Train had not been waiting in the wings.

I have not been able to find records of the Bristol Pullman running in daily practice, apart from one cited by O. S. Nock in the columns of *The Railway*

Magazine for December 1960 when the Badminton route was being taken on the 110-minute non-stop timing. A leisurely start, with no fast uphill running, put the train $1^1/_4$ minutes behind time at Badminton; speed then rose to 90 mph and fluctuated around that figure until slowed to 60 at Wootton Bassett; it then rose to 91 at Shrivenham, fell to $86^1/_2$ at Wantage Road, and then to a prolonged 10 mph for a permanent way slack near Steventon. The 90 mark was again reached at Cholsey, but despite being $5^3/_4$ minutes late in passing Reading was eased through that station, and after another 90 at Maidenhead eased a second time so that speed fell to 64 at Ealing; nevertheless, the recovery allowance was so generous that Paddington was reached $1^1/_4$ minutes early. On a 110-minute schedule, time-keeping at this stage in the train's career was supremely easy; with the introduction of intermediate stops it became a little less easy but was always comfortably attainable.

* * *

Unlike Birmingham and Bristol, the three chief cities of South Wales had enjoyed the benefits of an all-Pullman service since 1955, as already related in a previous chapter. When a 'Blue Pullman' set replaced the umber and white one in 1961, however, the emphasis was reversed; the new train was primarily for the benefit of Welsh rather than London businessmen and was based at Swansea, running up to the capital in the morning and back in the evening. It was also much faster - more so, indeed, than its fellow on the Bristol run, which it followed to London - and was by degrees to become faster still, cutting the Newport-Paddington timing to a figure never before known. Whereas the steam-hauled Pullman had needed more than 4 hours each way between London and Swansea, the new diesel train which bore its name needed, after its first acceleration in 1963, only $3^1/_2$ hours, despite making more stops. The schedules for the main train in 1961, 1963 and 1965, as in the accompanying table, indicate the gradual increase in speed.

Up:		1961	1963	1965	Down:		1961	1963	1965
Swansea	dep	06.40	06.50	06.55	Paddington	dep	16.55	16.40	17.40
Neath	arr		07.05	07.10	Newport	arr	19.02	18.46	19.41
Port Talbot	dep	07.03	07.15	07.19	Cardiff	arr	19.20	19.02	19.55
Bridgend	dep	07.19	07.30	07.32	Bridgend	arr	19.49	19.30	20.21
Cardiff	dep	07.50	08.00	08.00	Port Talbot	arr	20.08	19.44	20.35
Newport	dep	08.08	08.15	08.15	Neath	arr		19.54	20.43
Paddington	arr	10.15	10.15	10.10	Swansea	arr	20.40	20.10	21.05

In 1965 the long wait which the train had so far made between its morning arrival at Paddington and evening departure therefrom was filled with a return trip to Cardiff, and this became a regular feature as long as the train continued to run. The unit's daily mileage was now lifted well above those of the other three 'Blue Pullmans', to over 680 miles. Timings on these down morning and up afternoon services resembled those of the main train, the down run to Newport being a shade quicker than that of the corresponding evening departure, at 113 minutes, an average of 70.8 mph. Schedules were as follows:

The 'Blue Pullman' used for the new South Wales Pullman after the withdrawal of the steam-hauled service. The set is seen at the end of a test run from Paddington to Cardiff on 8 September 1961. ***Hugh Ballantyne***

Down:		Up:	
Paddington	dep 11.00	Cardiff	dep 14.30
Newport	arr 12.53	Newport	dep 14.45
Cardiff	arr 13.10	Paddington	arr 16.40

In 1967 a third 'Blue Pullman' service was introduced on the South Wales route, the unit from the Birmingham Pullman, which had now ceased operating, becoming available. Newport and Cardiff now for a few years had an *embarras de richesse* of Pullman services from and to London; only the Brighton Belle offered as many as that. The timings, resembling those of the other trains, were as follows:

Down:		Up:	
Paddington	dep 09.00	Swansea	dep 15.55
Newport	arr 10.50	Neath	dep 16.10
Cardiff	arr 11.07	Port Talbot	dep 16.19
Bridgend	arr 11.34	Bridgend	dep 16.32
Port Talbot	arr 11.43	Cardiff	dep 17.00
Neath	arr 11.52	Newport	dep 17.15
Swansea	arr 12.10	Paddington	arr 19.10

Between Paddington and Newport this service provided an even faster timing than that of the 11.00 down in 1965, the average speed being 72.8 mph. Passengers to and from South Wales were now being given an even better service than those to and from Bristol.

The next five years saw little change in this pattern, but the 'Blue Pullman' service was doomed to an early demise. The new concept of the High Speed Train was in the offing, and the characteristic swaying ride of the 1960 vehicles, though to some extent mitigated by adjustments and alterations, was never properly cured. So all were withdrawn in 1973, as also from the Bristol route, and trains of non-Pullman stock were substituted as a stop-gap until the track had been brought into good enough fettle to receive the new HSTs. The last 'Blue Pullman' left Paddington on its regular run at 17.53 on 4 May 1973.

The following day a specially assembled set of eight First Class cars set out on a 'Farewell Tour', following an unusual route. From Paddington to Leamington the former GWR line taken by the Birmingham Pullman was used; there was then a divergence through Kenilworth and Coventry to Birmingham New Street. Thence to Bristol the former Midland route was taken as far as Yate Junction, whence to Bristol Temple Meads, where there was another divergence through Winterbourne and Stapleton Road. Reversing out of Bristol, the train then made for the Severn Tunnel and so on to Newport, Cardiff and Swansea. Many were the enthusiasts travelling on the train or watching from the lineside with cameras at the ready. So far as its appearance was concerned, they did not see the train as it was in former days, for the livery had now been changed; the relative positions of the lateral bands of colour along the car-sides had now been reversed and it was now a predominantly light grey train with blue only around the windows, similar to the new electric Manchester Pullman. Even more disfiguring were the yellow nose-ends which no longer bore the splendid Pullman Company's crest. But the train's performance, once it was on a stretch of track where it could show its paces, was fully up to the mark, and the return from Swansea was noteworthy - a swan-song from an ageing prima donna who could still reach her top notes - or in this case her top speeds. An article in *The Railway Magazine* by M. G. James includes a description of the event.

> Leaving Swansea on time, the train made an unscheduled stop at Neath, to 'deport' an elderly gentleman who claimed to have mistaken it at Swansea - but if the truth be known, probably wanted a ride on the last 'Blue Pullman'. Cardiff was then reached by 18.00, 8 minutes early. After a few minutes for crew change the special departed at 18.04 7 minutes ahead of the booked time ... From Newport the fireworks began to happen. With a completely clear road the train ran the 56 miles to Swindon in only 44 minutes, an average speed of 76.3 mph - this over a twisting road via the Severn Tunnel, Pilning, Patchway and Badminton. From Swindon the speed increased, and the 41 miles to Reading over the racing ground was completed in 28 minutes, an average of 87.8 mph. Reading was passed in the high 80s and the final 36 miles were also run in 28

The South Wales Pullman passing through the disused station at Badminton in March 1969 on its westward journey. Note the change in the livery, the colour now being mainly light grey with a blue band enclosing the windows. The nose-ends are yellow. *Hugh Ballantyne*

> minutes ... The 133 miles from Newport to Paddington had been covered in an incredible 99 minutes, an average speed of 80.6 mph. Paddington was reached at 20.02, in 2 hours 52 minutes from Swansea.

Mr James provided a log of the run, but only to the nearest minute. It is a pity that a more detailed one was not made. The unit was probably running well within its capacity, for from Swindon onwards it was no faster than the record set by the Cheltenham Flyer in 1932, and it was not to be long before HST trains over this route were running very much faster indeed.

Thus ended the story of the 'Blue Pullmans' on British Railways. As Mr Cecil J. Allen, with his partiality for Latin tags, might have said: 'Sic transit gloria mundi'.

26

The Manchester Pullman

1966-85

In the spring of 1966 the electrification of the West Coast Main Line between Manchester and Liverpool and London was completed. As in the case of other electrification schemes, this enabled a more frequent service to be instituted; it was also faster due to the haulage abilities of the new electric locomotives. For the first time a journey from London to Manchester or Liverpool in less than 3 hours was made possible, and it was no longer necessary to run a special Pullman train for business customers over the route to St Pancras; in addition, the Midland Pullman ceased to be the right kind of train to provide it, because it was limited to 90 mph, whereas the route to Euston allowed 100 mph travelling and the new electric locomotives were geared to such a speed. In preparation for the transference of the luxury service to the electrified route, British Railways had therefore built 29 new Pullman vehicles for the Euston-Manchester and Euston-Liverpool service at Derby Works, and these were ready to be incorporated in new Pullman trains.

Of the 29 vehicles, 16 were for the Manchester run and eight for the Liverpool run, with five held in reserve. Each car was basically built like the other Mark II express passenger coaches, with standard underframes, body-sides and roofs, but there were a number of modifications made to conform to special needs. The vestibule connections at the end of the coaches were wider than normal, which necessitated the placing of the vertical 'collision pillars' further apart. There was a removable panel in each roof to give access to the air-conditioning apparatus. Some re-adjustment was made to the body-sides to allow for the fitting of double-glazed windows, between whose panes venetian blinds could be operated. The ends of each side were altered to allow the fitting of flat doors which opened inwards.

Externally the cars were liveried in the new style adopted with Pullman vehicles, in standard BR light grey and blue, the light grey predominating, continuous above and below window edges; bands of blue included the windows, so were only prominent in the spaces between them. The word PULLMAN appeared in somewhat small blue capitals at waist level towards the left-hand end of each car side. This differed from the original Blue Pullman livery on the diesel trains, which were subsequently themselves repainted in the new style. Thus Pullman cars were again readily distinguishable from ordinary coaches, as

The electrically-hauled Manchester Pullman commences its northbound run from Euston on 6 June 1973, topping Camden Bank behind E3117. Note the new carriage livery, predominantly light grey with blue enclosing the windows. ***Brian Morrison***

had been the case when they had been liveried in umber and white.

Internally there was a general similarity to the interiors of the 'Blue Pullmans', together with some differences. The same 2 + 1 arrangement of seats was provided, the seats being similarly adjustable. Side panels and table-tops were in French grey, and the end walls were covered with rosewood veneer. The toilet interiors were finished in red, silver grey and blue 'Wareite' plastic. Seat upholstery was in rust-red, peacock blue and black and the floors had black carpeting. All the metal fittings were of anodised light alloy. In contrast to the traditional First Class Pullman car interiors, the effect was luxurious but restrained.

In two directions efforts were made to improve the internal environment. The first was in providing as thorough a sound insulation as was possible. The double-glazed windows excluded much outside noise, and foam fillings between exterior and interior walls served the same purpose. Most of the noise in a railway vehicle comes upwards from the wheels through the floor, however, and much care was taken to minimise this. Each car's internal flooring, of multi-ply wood 3/4 inch thick, rested on six equally-spaced longitudinally-arranged strips of cork bonded with Neoprene adhesive; in addition, both the underside of the floor and the longitudinally-corrugated steel base beneath it were covered with layers of Aquaplas coating, while below that was a sprayed-on thickness of asbestos. In addition, to minimise noise from the bogies, rubber packings were inserted between the underframe pedestals and the bogie pivot bearings. A further refinement was the obviating of metallic contact between underframe and bogie when brakes were applied; part of the brake pull-rod was made of rubber. Above the car floors a layer of 'sound barrier' felt matting was placed under the fitted carpet. Through these means it was hoped to quieten the interior of each car so that normal conversation would be easily possible.

The air-conditioning system was also elaborate and sophisticated. Air was introduced into the car interiors and electrically warmed through current from a transformer fixed to the underframe and itself fed by a supply from a generator in the locomotive. This mixed with the air inside the cars and was circulated by means of a fan working from the 24-volt lighting system. Thermostats sensing the interior temperature controlled the warming of the air, shutting off or restarting the heaters as might be necessary. Four levels of temperature were possible - that of the exterior air, 68°-70°F, 71°-73° or 74°-76°. All this system was contained in the car's roof. Floor heating was also provided, fixed behind grilles in the body-side beneath the windows. Such air as escaped to the exterior did so through exhaust grilles fitted within the toilet compartments. A very slight extra pressure of air was always maintained within the saloons themselves. A public address system was installed so that the attendant in each of the kitchen cars could contact passengers through a microphone in his own compartment and loudspeakers mounted in the saloon ceilings.

In each group of four cars one was a Kitchen car with 18 seats for passengers, one toilet compartment and one luggage alcove; two were Parlour cars with full-length saloons holding 36 seats, two toilet compartments and two luggage alcoves, and one was a brake vehicle with 30 seats, one toilet compartment and one luggage alcove. Half of each Kitchen car was taken up by the kitchen itself, an adjacent pantry, a staff compartment and a staff toilet, together with a small cupboard for linen. The kitchen contained a coffee-making machine as well as the usual cooking range, which latter was heated with propane gas stored in cylinders beneath the underframe; there was also a sink unit and steriliser. A refrigerator and deep-freeze opened both into the kitchen and the pantry, which latter also had a sizeable sink unit. Sinks and working surfaces were all of stainless steel.

These, the last Pullman cars to be built in Great Britain, provided the sort of luxury travel that the businessman of the mid-'sixties required and, indeed, appreciated during the 20-year life of the Manchester Pullman. While the four cars that were assigned to the business trains to and from Liverpool did not attract as much custom as was at first expected, it was otherwise with each eight-car Manchester train, which generated not merely traffic but a certain amount of customer loyalty; there was genuine regret when after 20 years the vehicles were taken out of service and, after being used for a while in special trains, sold to a private company for hiring out to customers willing to pay a stiff price for the privilege of using them. They were to be the last word in Pullman travel comfort, albeit not provided by the original Pullman Car

Company, which by 1966 had ceased to exist, BR having absorbed it completely. Not only were they the acme of comfort, but, on the Manchester to Euston run, faster than any train before them, and slightly faster than the ordinary services from 1966 onwards.

Two and a half hours each way between Manchester and London was a hitherto unheard-of timing, particularly as two stops were made *en route*. Moreover, right from the start it was not one but two return services that were provided - and for a short while there were even three, one eight-car unit doing the double journey twice daily. On Fridays, however, when business travel tended to be much less than on other working days, four of the cars were taken from both the trains and replaced with Second Class ordinary coaches.

During the first year of the Manchester Pullman's operation the 2½-hour timing was exceeded by a few minutes on each of the four daily runs, but from March 1967 the schedules were pared to bring all the London-Manchester and Manchester-London times down to 150 minutes for the 188¼ miles. Timings during that year were as follows:

Up:			Down:		
Manchester	07.35	17.00	Euston	07.50	18.00
Stockport	07.44		Watford	08.06	
Wilmslow	07.52	17.17	Wilmslow		20.07
Watford		19.14	Stockport	10.11	20.17
Euston	10.05	19.30	Manchester	10.20	20.30

During the short period when a third return service was provided, between April 1967 and May 1968, the schedule was slower and more stops were made. The down train, leaving Euston at 10.50 (three-quarters of an hour after it had come up from Manchester) called at Stafford, Stoke-on-Trent, Macclesfield and Stockport and reached Manchester at 13.40; after scarcely half an hour in which to turn round it left again at 14.15, made the same calls in the reverse order and was back at Euston at 17.05.

In 1983 there was a change in the train's livery. It was repainted to match the Advanced Passenger Train (an enterprise that was soon, alas, to be discarded) and the centre of each waist-high coloured band bore a name, being that of a person associated with the history of Manchester. This revived, for a short period, the practice of naming First Class Pullman cars, which had been given up when the 'Blue Pullmans' were introduced.

With the end of the Manchester Pullman's 20th year in service the cars were withdrawn. Several of them were for some time used on specially chartered services, but were eventually sold to a private company entitled Travelling College Limited. They then had to undergo very expensive alteration, since the asbestos originally applied to the underfloor parts of the cars as part of the sound-deadening system had to be removed, for it was now known that this material posed a health risk. The new owners then found that there was little demand for hiring the train and were forced to sell it and go out of business.

Left **Another change of livery for the Manchester Pullman, seen entering Euston on 13 October 1983 behind No 86231. The colour scheme is now in imitation of the ill-fated Advanced Passenger Train, and the cars bear individual names.** ***Hugh Ballantyne***

Below left **The last down evening Manchester Pullman passes into history near Norton Bridge, Staffs, on 10 May 1985; locomotive No 86231 again, re-liveried to match the stock.** ***Hugh Ballantyne***

Another newly-formed company bought them, the Manchester Executive Railway Company, and it has recently (late 1991) announced that as from September 1992 they will be available for hire after being refurbished at the BREL workshops in Derby. They are to receive a new livery, of claret below the waist and gold above, separated by a red band - rather a gaudy ensemble, one feels - and new curtains and table lamps will be fitted. Each car will also be given a new name. The train so assembled now comprises seven 36-seat saloons, a 30-seater brake and two Kitchen cars, from which the seating has been removed in the parts that were formerly passenger saloons in order to allow extra storage space. It remains to be seen whether these transmogrified vehicles can be profitable in their old age.

27

The new Pullman concept

1985 onwards

In one of his 'Alice' books Lewis Carroll features a Cheshire Cat which after several sphinx-like utterances eventually fades away. Eyes, ears, fur and whiskers disappear, but the last part to vanish is its grin, which persists for a while. Something like this has happened to the all-Pullman train. One by one its separate manifestations disappeared from the timetable until only the Manchester Pullman was left; then that went as well. But the name, like the grin, remained to be used in a variety of circumstances, to betoken real or alleged extra comfort.

I recall once spending the night on board a Greek ship between Brindisi and Corfu during the 'seventies. One had the choice of resting on a reclining seat or else, for a consideration, occupying a 'Pullman' bunk - mattress, pillow, one blanket. George Mortimer Pullman gave his name first to a coach, then to a train, and finally to a notion, that of relative comfort in contrast to relative austerity, Sybaris instead of Sparta.

In Great Britain, whatever might have been the case elsewhere, the name eventually became the property of British Railways, which had taken over the Pullman Car Company in 1963 after having been for some years its principal shareholder and, in this country, sole customer. BR, had they pleased, could have built further Pullman cars, but for reasons discussed in the following chapter they chose not to do so. Alternatively they could use the name, to which there clung in people's minds the associations of superior comfort and service. So far as comfort is concerned, an Inter-City First Class carriage of the latest Mark III or Mark IV type cannot well be bettered.

What delighted the eyes of our grandfathers and grandmothers, and reminded them of their chintzed, cosy parlours at home, no longer appeals to their grandchildren. For them the reality of travelling comfort is a roomy and adjustable seat, ergonomically designed so that it fits the anatomy, a table wide enough to spread things on, whether they be documents or food and thermos flasks, a double-glazed window and sufficient sound insulation to reduce interior noise so that one may talk to one's neighbour, at the right temperature introduced without draughts being caused, and a ride smooth enough to allow writing. All these things can be had without any supplementary fee in a modern Inter-City First Class coach, or in the admirable First Class accommodation in

The Merseyside Pullman on its morning run from Liverpool Lime Street to Euston near the site of Standon Bridge station, Staffs, on 13 May 1985. As with the other trains illustrated in this chapter, the only 'Pullman' element is in the service provided in the First Class carriages. The locomotive is No 87008. ***Hugh Ballantyne***

one of the latest Network Express trains between London and Weymouth. Even meals at one's seat can be had if one waits for the travelling trolley. What more could a Pullman car of contemporary design provide?

BR decided that to such existing First Class accommodation it could add an enhanced degree of personal service. To certain designated trains, in which such accommodation was always in the vicinity of the kitchen and buffet sections, specially trained attendants would be attached, to offer passengers that little extra attention. Without behaving like obsequious flunkeys they could still approach the former Pullman attendant's standard of service in regard to the little things that make a First Class traveller's life sweet - the morning paper, gratuitously, in case he wished to see how the market was doing, his cup of tea or coffee as he liked it, and a well-served meal at his seat - including, of course, for the early customer, the Great British Breakfast. For all this there would be no supplementary charge. In part this was because not every traveller wanted the extra attention, though of course he did not object to having it if it came free. Were a supplement imposed he might conceivably shrug his shoulders and transfer himself to Standard Class accommodation on his next journey. In part, too, there was the expectation that the extra consideration shown might generate additional revenue from the sales of meals and refreshments, all of which would go into BR's coffers, not those of a separate Pullman Car Company.

In May 1985, therefore, the month of the demise of the Manchester Pullman as the last all-Pullman train, Inter-City launched the Pullman marque as an up-market brand name for business travel. It was made available in selected trains (including of course those that now ran in the paths of the former Manchester Pullman services) which ran to and from London at times suitable for the business executive; the whole of the First Class accommodation in these trains became an 'all-Pullman' train in the new sense of the word. The object of this new venture was to retain the existing business custom on trains which businessmen used to and from London (or would be likely to use as new similar trains were introduced) having regard to possible competition from the private car and from aircraft.

In regard to the latter, up to a certain distance air travel, while no dearer or not much dearer than First Class rail travel, is also no quicker or not much quicker when the time taken to and from the airports used is added to the time one is actually in flight. With the higher average speeds now possible on some Inter-City services, the former critical distance of about 200 miles could perhaps be doubled. Edinburgh is now within 4 hours of King's Cross, and unless one lives almost next door to Turnhouse airport one cannot get to the City of London by air much more rapidly than that. As regards actual comfort while travelling, at certain key stations BR has now installed 'Pullman Lounges' so that travellers having to wait for a connection to or from a Pullman service can do so in relaxed comfort, enjoying complimentary cups of tea or coffee while reposing in a soft chair in quiet surroundings. In some lounges photocopying services are also available. Possession of a First Class ticket admits one to such premises.

Special training has been provided to produce the right kind of attendant for the new Pullman service. Mature experienced catering staff are being supplemented by school-leavers who have volunteered for the work as a career and have been trained as stewards and stewardesses. Such training is not only for the newcomers; there is in-service training as well. For example, chief stewards have one-day courses in wine-appreciation.

What may the customer expect in the way of food-provision? To quote from an article in *Modern Railways* of June 1987, by Brian Perren:

> The Great Pullman Breakfast ... now includes Copella English apple juice, black pudding has been added to the grill and two pork chipolatas have replaced the traditional single sausage. To provide some variation for frequent passengers who may tire of the grill tray, a Continental Breakfast Platter of cold smoked ham, Dutch cheese garnished with tomato and hard-boiled egg is offered as an alternative. Hot chocolate is also served. Light breakfast ... is unchanged. Regrettably the traditional 1 lb pots of Frank Cooper's Coarse Cut Oxford Marmalade are no longer placed on restaurant car tables and have been replaced by a range of Cooper's 1 oz individual jars of various preserves. As coarse-cut marmalade cannot packed in a small jar, this long-standing BR feature has been replaced by the less dense 'Country Cut' marmalade ...

> Depending on what you choose, a three-course Pullman lunch or dinner plus aperitif, wine and coffee costs something between £16 and £23 [1987 prices - more now!] but you can spend more if you wish. Lunch and dinner menus, which are changed weekly, offer a selection of six starters, three main courses of which one is fish and one cold, three sweets, cheese board and savoury. Vegetables include two styles of potatoes plus two other items ... As well as Inter-City's house wines, Pullmans carry a range of seven *Appelation Controlée* wines and seven brands of beers, as well as a range of spirits.
>
> The needs of passengers not requiring full meal service are met by the Pullman Parlour Car menu, which has recently been expanded ... The Parlour Car menu is particularly useful for passengers returning in mid-afternoon who may have taken lunch and only require a light snack, but you can keep hunger at bay with the sandwich selection (three half-rounds of prawn, egg and cress and roast chicken with stuffing) and half a bottle of good wine ...
>
> Given the technical opportunities offered by the modular 'Cook-Chill' technique, Inter-City Catering Services plan to introduce more adventurous dishes as Cuisine 2000 cars take over Pullman services. For example, a fruit compote - poached pear, pineapple, prunes and apricot - may be offered as a breakfast starter, together with a choice of three different teas - Earl Grey, Darjeeling and Super-Ceylon. Also under consideration is the introduction of a carving trolley, where the chef will pass through the train carving meat to customers' individual requirements. This has been a feature in the first class cabin of Boeing 747 jumbo jets.

One imagines that the reader's gustatory juices have already begun to show their presence, reading such an account. One pays of course for what one gets, and happy is he who can charge it to his expense account.

The morning northbound King's Cross-Leeds Yorkshire Pullman restarts from Wakefield Westgate, electrically hauled by Class 91 No 91008. ***Brian Morrison***

Above On the left of the photograph Class 87 No 87022 *Cock o'the North* brings the Birmingham Pullman into Euston on 10 July 1989. *Brian Morrison*
Below The Paddington-Penzance Golden Hind Pullman running alongside the Exe Estuary near Starcross on 20 June 1990. The Class 43 HST power car is No 43159.

Since the new concept of Pullman service was introduced in 1985 the number of trains on which it is offered has gradually increased. At the time of writing (late 1991) it stands at 50, operating into and out of four London terminal stations, King's Cross, St Pancras, Euston and Paddington, and serving 62 separate stations at which 236 stops are made daily between Monday and Friday - some being to pick up or set down only. It is interesting to note that the former Southern Railway lines, on which so many all-Pullman trains ran in previous days, are now right out of the picture, this being because it does not now run trains on which there is a full meal service. North of the Thames and westwards from Paddington, East Anglia excepted, most of the principal centres of population are served - and many smaller places also at which it is convenient for the trains to stop to pick up non-business passengers. Most of the up services are early morning ones; most of the down services are in the evening.

One might give a comprehensive list, with names of places and times of calling set out in detail, but it would take up too much space and be out of date as soon as this book is published. In the accompanying table, however, is a short list of the principal services with their names and those of the places each served, as in the 1991/2 timetable. Those marked with an asterisk ran only in the up direction and many of the stops made by particular trains were in one direction only. The greater part of the down services ran during the evening hours and those in the opposite direction were mostly morning trains arriving in London at or before 10.00. All ran to fast schedules - some of the latter, on parts of the East Coast Main Line, averaged over 100 mph.

Name of service	No of trains daily	Places served by one or other down or up train, from or to London
The Scottish Pullman	5	York, Darlington, Newcastle, Edinburgh, Motherwell, Glasgow, from and to King's Cross
The Tees-Tyne Pullman	2	Grantham, Doncaster, York, Northallerton, Darlington, Durham, Newcastle
The Newcastle Pullman	1	Durham, Newcastle
The White Rose	1	York, Stevenage
The Yorkshire Pullman	9	Stevenage, Peterborough, Grantham, Newark, Doncaster, Wakefield, Leeds, Harrogate
The Bradford Pullman	2	Stevenage, Doncaster, Wakefield, Leeds, Shipley, Bradford
The Hull Pullman	2	Stevenage, Peterborough, Grantham, Doncaster, Brough-on-Humber, Hull
The Master Cutler	2	Leicester, Derby, Chesterfield, Sheffield
The Robin Hood	2	Leicester, Loughborough, Nottingham
The Lancashire Pullman	3	Watford, Crewe, Warrington, Wigan, Preston, Kirkham (Lancs), Poulton-le-Fylde, Blackpool

Name of service	No of trains daily	Places served by one or other down or up train, from or to London
The Manchester Pullman	11	Watford, Milton Keynes, Stafford, Crewe, Stoke-on-Trent, Macclesfield, Wilmslow, Stockport, Manchester
The Merseyside Pullman	4	Watford, Stafford, Crewe, Runcorn, Liverpool
The Birmingham Pullman	1	Birmingham, Birmingham International
The Red Dragon Pullman	1	Swansea, Neath, Port Talbot, Bridgend, Cardiff, Newport, Bristol Parkway
The St David Pullman	2	Reading, Swindon, Bristol Parkway, Newport, Cardiff, Bridgend, Port Talbot, Neath, Swansea
The Golden Hind Pullman	2	Reading, Taunton, Exeter, Newton Abbot, Plymouth, Liskeard, Bodmin Parkway, St Austell, Truro, Redruth, Penzance

This, then, is the new Pullman concept of on-train service as it stands at the moment. BR intends to up-grade all Inter-City First Class accommodation eventually to the same level. When that happens the Pullman appellation will no doubt become redundant, and finally disappear like the Cheshire Cat's grin.

Epilogue

A single century saw the all-Pullman luxury train rise, flourish, decline and vanish in this country. During this period one can distinguish four main phases in its life-history which reflect contemporary society and the use it made of the railways.

The first was the period before the First World War, when the luxury train was the travel equivalent of gracious living enjoyed by the upper ranks of society. Journeys of any length were not often undertaken by those in its lower strata. Weekly wages did not run to that sort of thing. Seaside holidays, if taken, were spent at nearby resorts, such as Blackpool and Morecambe for the Lancashire towns, Brighton or Southend-on-Sea for the London area. The more leisured upper middle classes, whose life-styles are reflected in Pinero's plays and Galsworthy's novels, did travel. At recognised vacation times they might spend periods in Devon, Cornwall, North Wales, the Lake District, or even the Scottish Highlands, where some of the more affluent had shooting lodges where they killed time by killing birds and animals. The train took them and brought them back, travelling First Class and accompanied by enormous piles of baggage. For more frequent and shorter excursions the luxury train came into being; leaving their own well-furnished parlours, they occupied the Parlour cars of the Pullman Company, extending familiar domestic surroundings almost to the sea-front. During the Edwardian period the practice increased, so that the Southern Belle of 1908 had twice as much room for passengers, all First Class, as had the earlier Pullman train it replaced.

The First World War followed, when, in Sir Edward Grey's memorable phrase, 'the lights went out all over Europe'. The Edwardian *dolce vita* came to a sudden end for those who had previously savoured it, and for a short while luxury travel also came to an end. But even before the war had ended the Pullman train was again in evidence, now with the addition of Third Class accommodation which indicated that one result of the conflict was that the classes were coming together, and that for those who survived the slaughter wages and salaries were rising.

Other all-Pullman trains were established, still catering mainly for the holidaymaker but also reaching out in the direction of the business executive. The newly-formed LNER, inheriting from the former GER Pullman cars which had been intended to duplicate, along the East Anglian coast, the provision the SR was making for visitors to the coasts of Kent and Sussex, chose to deploy them in a more enterprising way over greater distances, believing that the larger cities on its system would supply customers. Sheffield, Nottingham and Manchester failed to do this, but Leeds and other West Riding towns, Newcastle, Edinburgh and Glasgow provided enough patronage to justify long-distance Pullman services and, as the second decade of the inter-war period arrived, further attempts were made to serve distant seaside resorts; one failed, the other was decidedly successful. Continental travellers were similarly offered luxury travel in the Golden Arrow. After an intermission East Anglia also profited again from the running of the incredibly inexpensive Eastern Belle.

A second European War ensued, which eventually became global. Less bloody than the earlier conflict, so far as Britain was concerned, it nevertheless interfered more with daily life, and leisure travel was actively discouraged, both by petrol rationing and injunctions to people to stay put unless their journeys were really necessary. Pullman cars everywhere disappeared from public use and were stored. Once the fighting was over they were brought out and used again in the areas where they had previously run, and new all-Pullman services were begun which, south of the Thames, continued (with one exception) successfully until electrification caused most of them to disappear. The Golden Arrow likewise returned, more splendid than before, to run for a quarter of a century until patronage fell away and caused it too to disappear.

North of the Thames the East Coast Main Line Pullmans had others added to their number, and their speeds increased. The businessmen of Sheffield eventually succumbed to their blandishments. Hull saw its own six-car train in place of the pre-war pair of coaches. Finally even Paddington accepted a Pullman train for South Wales. In 1955 it might well have seemed to the onlooker that the all-Pullman train was going to be a permanent feature on the railway landscape.

But BR was already in the process of taking over the Pullman Car Company, and developing its own ideas, the first of which was the multiple-unit diesel-electric Pullman service for the business community. A reversal of tradition took place; the new 'Blue Pullmans' ran into and out of London termini which had previously rejected Pullman cars, and served the business communities in the larger provincial cities and towns. The new style of luxury train reflected the needs of their users, and as further cars were built for use on other locomotive-hauled services their interiors became sleek rather than luscious. These businessman-angled services now began to preponderate as electrification displaced the all-Pullman trains from the lines to the Kentish, Sussex and Hampshire coasts. Most successful of all, the Manchester Pullman began its 20-year career. Its eventual disappearance marked the end of the fourth phase, and of Pullman travel as it had been known. By 1985 the wheel had come full circle again, and only First Class Pullman travel was available.

So to the present situation, when the word denotes no longer a vehicle but a quality of passenger service within it. As with human life, memories are retained of the dead, which themselves gradually fade. Probably the 'new Pullman concept' will fade out as First Class Inter-City accommodation is brought up to the same standard everywhere, and the name will pass out of experience into history. But in its day it betokened something.

Pullman lives! The interior of the renovated VSOE First Class Pullman car *Vera*, formerly part of the five-car Brighton Belle set, guarantees the survival of that special Pullman aura. *Brian Morrison*

Index

Note '1st PC' denotes a First Class Pullman Car

Pullman trains to which a chapter is devoted in the book are not listed